D0500890

BURT WOLF'S MENU COOKBOOK

My table at the Hotel Certosa di Maggiano in
Siena, Italy. It's the spot where I wrote my
scripts. The intersection of high-tech and high-
touch.

by the same author

Burt Wolf's Table
Eating Well
What's Cooking

BURT WOLF'S
MENU COOKBOOK

BURT WOLF

DOUBLEDAY
New York London Toronto Sydney Auckland

PUBLISHED BY DOUBLEDAY
a division of Bantam Doubleday Dell Publishing Group, Inc.
1540 Broadway, New York, New York 10036

DOUBLEDAY and the portrayal of an anchor with a dolphin are
trademarks of Doubleday, a division of Bantam Doubleday Dell
Publishing Group, Inc.

The recipes for Chocolate Cheesecake and Chocolate Layer Cake
with Coconut Pecan Frosting are copyright © 1994 by Kraft General
Foods, Inc., and are reprinted with permission.

BOOK DESIGN BY CAROL MALCOLM RUSSO/SIGNET M DESIGN, INC.

Library of Congress Cataloging-in-Publication Data
Wolf, Burton.
  [Menu cookbook]
  Burt Wolf's menu cookbook / Burt Wolf. — 1st ed.
    p.   cm.
  Includes index.
  1. Cookery, International.   I. Title.
  TX725.A1W5832   1995
  641.59—dc20   95-13791
                                  CIP

ISBN 0-385-47273-0
Copyright © 1995 by Burt Wolf
ALL RIGHTS RESERVED
PRINTED IN THE UNITED STATES OF AMERICA
AUGUST 1995
FIRST EDITION
10 9 8 7 6 5 4 3 2 1

THIS BOOK IS DEDICATED TO RAYMOND W. MERRITT

It was the winter of 1969 and I was living just outside Geneva, in Switzerland. A large multinational public company, headquartered in the city, was restructuring its top management and had come up with the idea of creating an Office of the President, which was to consist of a creative type with an understanding of law, and a lawyer with an understanding of creativity. The board of directors appeared to have made their selection of the two individuals, held preliminary talks with one (the lawyer), and decided that he should contact the other person to see if they would be an effective team.

Raymond W. Merritt was the lawyer, I was the other. Ray called me. We met. We talked. We were flattered by the offer but we declined. We also discovered that we enjoyed one another's company.

For twenty-five years we have been meeting, talking, and still enjoying one another's company. With the support of his partners and associates at Willkie Farr and Gallagher, he has guided me through the complexities of our legal system and given me an extraordinary understanding of the value of a good and honest attorney. I truly respect and enjoy my relationship with his firm, and these days there are few people who feel that way about their lawyers.

He has his own recipe for our relationship, approaching my problems and opportunities with a substantial helping of brilliance, blending in his own unique creativity, adding the necessary level of common sense, and enrobing the entire thing with unwavering loyalty. Not an easy technique, but the results have been outstanding.

We have celebrated together when celebration was appropriate. We have consoled each other at the points where consolation was appropriate. We watched our children get older, as we got younger. We came to realize that we would not live forever and shared our feelings on the subject. We have each benefited from the complexities of a friendship that has gone on for a quarter of a century and that has plans for at least a quarter of a century more. He is the only person I know who can write me a very personal and moving letter and add an additional thought, marking it "See Rider A."

In dedicating this book to Ray, I am simply making a public statement of appreciation for his friendship, as well as that of his wife Carol and his children Ray Jr. and Kim. They have made it possible for me to do the work I love, including this book and the companion television series.

ACKNOWLEDGMENTS

All of the television shows used as the basis for this book were videotaped on location in Europe, South America, the United States, Canada, and Asia. Hundreds of people were involved in the development, production, and distribution of the series: researchers, press officers, government representatives, airline staff, hotel and restaurant personnel, chefs, manufacturers, television teams, book designers, and talented specialists in dozens of other crafts, who helped me get the job done. I thank each of them and I hope they realize how much I appreciate their efforts on my behalf.

There are, however, some individuals whom I would like to mention by name, because their contributions run throughout the entire undertaking.

The Television Team
Emily Aronson, Executive Producer
Caroline McCool, Senior Producer
David Dean, Senior Editor
Steve Hoppe, On-Line Editor
Katherine Alford, Hillary Davis,
    Jenna Holst, Recipe Testing and
    Development
Vanessa Stark, Production Assistant

Cable News Network
Tom Johnson
Burt Reinhart
Jay Suber
Ted Turner

Public Television
Mike LaBonia
Gene Nichols

The Travel Channel
Dalton Delan
Patricia Newi
Roger Williams

Grey Advertising
John Fox
Ken Levy
Tony Pugliese
Hy Rosen

Crate & Barrel
Gordon Segal

In Addition

Gretchen Achilles

William G. Barry

Honora Horan

Natalia Ilyin

Kenneth Jackier

Stephen Jacoby

Judith Kern

Joel Kleiman

Jonathan Korn

Jenifer Harvey Lang

May Mendez

Anita Michael

Larry Ossias

Janet Pappas

Steven J. Ross

Tanya Sparer

Judy Turner

Susan Van Velson

CONTENTS

INTRODUCTION

This book contains the history, folklore, and recipes that we gathered during the production of twenty half-hour television shows being broadcast under the title "Burt Wolf's Menu." The shows were videotaped on location in Europe, North and South America, and Asia. In addition to the recipes that we taped in each of the countries we visited, there are recipes that we developed when we got back home. The added recipes were included in order to round out a menu for a full meal. There are over fifty meal menus in the book.

Caroline McCool, senior producer.

We selected the particular locations because we felt they would provide interesting stories and good recipes. **Caroline McCool** is the senior producer for the series. She makes all the arrangements for the trips, and is responsible for every detail in the plan. Flights, passports, government regulations, hotels, locations for videotaping, meals, authorities to be interviewed—all sit on Caroline's plate.

Emily Aronson, executive producer, directing the action while viewing a monitor. The script book is in front of her.

Once a city has been chosen, I read two or three books on its history. I also try to relate the general story of the place to its food, which is usually not very difficult. I travel to the city and spend about two weeks researching the locations and writing the scripts. For better or worse, I do all my own research and writing. At that point the executive producer, **Emily Aronson**, arrives with the video crew. The executive producer of a program is "the real boss." Emily is responsible for making sure that my script is interesting and entertaining. She directs and produces the actual shooting, and must bring it in on time and on budget. When we are shooting the recipe segments, she usually sits with a television monitor so she can control the action. In front of the monitor is the script book.

Jeff Daly comes in for a close-up in the bowl.

Bernard holds his camera just above the ground and moves along with the dancers in order to give you a close-up of the action (Santiago, Chile).

Our crew usually consists of a cameraman, a sound specialist, and a lighting grip. There were two teams for this series, **Bernard Couture** (camera) and **Guy Francoeur** (sound), both of whom come from Montreal, Canada; and **Jeff Daly** (camera) and **Gary**

The crew, our guide, and Bernard's son Nicolas on the glacier in Alberta, Canada.

My son Andrew, who took vacation days from his work as a cameraman at Cable News Network (CNN) to shoot for dear old Dad.

Scharlach (sound), who live near San Francisco, California. Much of the material on chocolate was shot by my son **Andrew Wolf** while he was on a week's vacation from his regular job as a cameraman for Cable News Network (CNN).

The slice of cake in the lower left-hand corner of this photo is about to be placed onto the plate. The camera will be taking a close-up shot and will need to be in perfect focus. Guy holds his hand in place so Bernard can focus his camera on the exact spot where the cake will arrive.

Jeff Daly, Gary Scharlach, and my son James Wolf. James designs motorcycles in Tokyo, but he spent some of his vacation working as a grip on our shoot in California. You might think that everyone in this photo is very busy studying the script plan for the next segment. Not quite. They are checking out the restaurant's menu so they can order lunch. There are clear priorities in life, and it is important to keep them in their proper order.

Our lighting grip, second-unit camera, and production guide during our shoots in South America is always Igor Jadue-Lillo. Here he is watching the dancers in Santiago, Chile.

I am in Siena, Italy, talking about the painting behind me, which describes "The Effects of Good
and Bad Government." Giovanni Andreini, our
grip and production guide during our shoots in
Italy, is holding a reflector in order to diffuse
the light coming in through the windows. Part of
producing a television show requires making the
most unnatural conditions look natural.

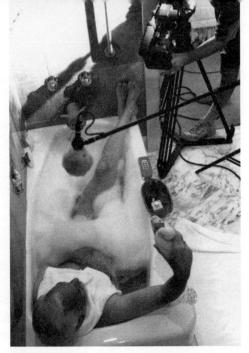

This is what it really looked like in the
room when we were doing a "bathtub"
shot. Just as we start to shoot, I use all
my powers of concentration to make
believe that I am all alone talking to one
person who is sitting in the camera lens.

The majority of the recipes shot on location were tested by Jenna
Holst, who also developed most of the additional recipes that
rounded out the menus.

The scene as we started to shoot a recipe segment outdoors. The beautiful sunlight in your picture comes not from Mother Nature's sky but from the lamp in the upper right-hand corner. The real sunlight is controlled by the screen above our heads. Normal sunlight would change as the hours went by; the camera requires uniform light during the entire segment.

Emily applies a little powder so I won't "shine."

When we have finished all of the location shooting, the tapes come back to New York to be edited. The individual shots must be put together to make a full show. The music needs to be put in. My bad jokes need to be taken out. David Dean does that under the inspiring direction of his son Joshua.

When the show has been "cut," it goes to a production house where "dissolves" are put in, type goes on, the introduction and closing effects are added, as well as the other elements that complete the show. Steve Hoppe is the on-line editor.

Soups

Avocado Soup

CHILE

MAKES 4 SERVINGS

1 tablespoon olive oil
1 small red onion, chopped
1 clove garlic, chopped
2 teaspoons chopped fresh
   ginger
1 large ripe avocado, or 2
   small avocados, peeled,
   pit removed
1 tablespoon fresh lemon
   juice
1 cucumber, peeled,
   seeded, and diced
2 tablespoons chopped
   fresh chives
1½ cups chicken broth,
   chilled
⅓ cup nonfat sour cream
½ teaspoon salt
1 tomato, seeded and
   chopped, as a garnish

1. In a sauté pan over medium heat, heat the olive oil. Add the onion, and cook for 2 minutes. Add the garlic and ginger and cook, stirring, for another minute. Remove from the heat and set aside.

2. Chop the avocado and place the meat in a bowl and toss with the lemon juice. In a food processor, puree the avocado and cucumber until smooth. Add the sautéed onion mixture and the chives and process again.

3. Transfer the avocado mixture to a large bowl. Stir in the chicken broth and sour cream until smooth. Season with salt. Chill the soup thoroughly in the refrigerator.

4. Serve, garnished with the chopped tomatoes.

The morning fruit and vegetable market, which has been at the same location in Valdivia, Chile, for 1,000 years.

Carrot and Walnut Soup

SINGAPORE

1. In a large saucepan, melt the butter over moderate heat. Add the carrots and onion and sauté for 2 minutes. Stir in the walnuts and sauté for 1 minute.

2. Add 2 cups of the chicken stock and bring to a boil. Add a pinch of salt, pepper, and nutmeg; reduce the heat, and simmer for 45 minutes, until the carrots are very tender.

3. Puree the soup until smooth in a processor or blender.

4. Return the soup to the pan and stir in the remaining 1½ cups of chicken stock and the heavy cream or buttermilk. Cook, stirring, until heated through. Season with salt and pepper to taste.

5. Garnish with chopped walnuts.

MAKES 6 SERVINGS

2 tablespoons unsalted butter
1 pound carrots, peeled and cut into ½-inch lengths
¼ cup chopped onion
½ cup chopped walnuts, plus extra as garnish
3½ cups chicken stock
Salt and freshly ground black pepper
Pinch of ground nutmeg
1 cup heavy cream or buttermilk

Chilean Beef Soup

SANTIAGO PARK PLAZA HOTEL, CHILE

MAKES 6 SERVINGS

2 tablespoons olive oil
1 pound lean beef, cut into
   bite-sized strips
2 cloves garlic, minced
1 hot chili pepper, chopped
2 teaspoons dried oregano
Salt and freshly ground
   black pepper
1 cup sliced onion
1 cup potato (suitable for
   boiling), cut into bite-
   sized pieces
1/2 cup white wine
6 cups beef stock
4 egg whites
1 teaspoon dried parsley

Santiago is divided into very distinct neighborhoods, each with its very own character. Providencia is a neighborhood which is associated with excellent residential areas, both in beautiful private homes and apartment buildings. In addition, it's famous for its great shopping. Providencia is also known as the home of Santiago's most elegant hotel, the Park Plaza. The hotel only has about a hundred rooms, which makes it small enough for the staff to give excellent service to the guests.

1. In a sauté pan over medium heat, heat the oil. Add the beef, garlic, and chili pepper, and sauté for 5 minutes. Add 1 teaspoon of the oregano, salt and pepper and onion, and sauté for 5 minutes more. Add the potato and the wine, and simmer until all the moisture has evaporated. Transfer the ingredients to a saucepan.

2. Add the beef stock and simmer for 20 minutes. While the soup is still simmering, whisk in the egg whites.

3. Divide the soup into the serving bowls and sprinkle a little of the remaining oregano and the parsley on each.

Chilean Seafood Soup (Paila Marina)

SANTIAGO PARK PLAZA HOTEL, CHILE

Chef Joel Solorza at the Park Plaza Hotel has a home near Viña del Mar, and has mastered many of the local seafood recipes. This fish soup is a perfect example.

1. In a large saucepan over medium heat, heat the oil. Mince 2 of the garlic cloves and add them to the oil. Add the dried chili and mix. Add the onion and sauté for 3 minutes. Add the tomato and sauté for 3 minutes more.

2. Slice the third clove of garlic and add it to the pot. Add the paprika, oregano, and 2 tablespoons of the chives. Add the remaining ingredients (except tablespoon of chives). Simmer for 10 minutes and serve with a sprinkling of the remaining chives on top.

Fishing boats tied up at the dock in Valdivia, Chile.

MAKES 4 SERVINGS

2 tablespoons vegetable oil
3 cloves garlic
1 dried red chili, seeded and chopped
1 cup sliced onion
1 large tomato, sliced into bite-sized pieces
1/2 tablespoon paprika
1/2 tablespoon dried oregano
3 tablespoons minced fresh chives
1 cup white-fleshed fish, cut into bite-sized pieces
1 cup shrimp, shelled and cleaned, cut into bite-sized pieces
1/2 cup oysters (about 10)
1 cup white wine
Salt and freshly ground black pepper
3 cups fish stock, or 1 cup clam juice and 2 cups water

FLY-FISHING IN CHILE

When you fly-fish you don't actually cast the lure, what you really cast is the line itself with a fly tied to the end of it. The length and weight of your rod, the type of line you use and, of course, the fly are all major considerations. But in the beginning these things are left up to the guide. You can go after everything from a trout to a salmon. The line itself is made from an inner core of Dacron coated with a smooth vinyl plastic. When fly-fishers talk about the weight of a line, what they are describing is the weight in grams of the first thirty feet of line. You are casting the line, and how it is shaped and what it weighs are critical to the experience. Some lines are designed to float on or near the surface of the water. They are for fish who like to take supper at the top. Some lines sink to the bottom. Others hang out in the middle. When the line is cast it takes the shape of a rolling loop. As the line moves out, the energy of your arm is transferred through the rod into the line and the loop rolls forward. It's quite an art, and since you may end up doing this a few thousand times during a day of fly-fishing it can also be a muscle-building experience.

You need to put enough energy into the cast to sustain the loop until the line is fully unrolled. One way of doing this is to reduce the weight of the line as it gets near the fly at the tip. That's called a tapered line. There are also lines that are heavy up front and others that are heavy behind. Each will give you a different cast. Then there's the tapered leader, that holds the fly to the line, a very important element. It's the part that the fish is most likely to see, and if it doesn't like what it sees it doesn't go for the fly.

Which rod, which line, which leader, and which fly you go out with is a function of the eating habits of the fish you are going after. The really skilled angler knows a lot about what his fish likes to eat, also when and how. He or she also knows a lot about what supper should look like and how it should act in order to bring the fish to the table. This is a lot like setting up a menu for a restaurant. You had better know a lot about your potential customers and how to properly prepare the dishes they like.

LEMON RICE SOUP

SONOMA MISSION INN, BOYES HOT SPRINGS, CALIFORNIA

1. In a large saucepot, heat the olive oil. Add the onion and cook over low heat until the onion is softened. Stir in the rice and turmeric or saffron. Add the lemon juice, lemon zest, wine, and chicken broth and cook for 30 minutes, uncovered.

2. In small batches, puree the soup in a blender or food processor, filling the container one quarter full of liquid before processing. Return the pureed soup to the stove to reheat, if necessary. Serve garnished with chopped dill.

NOTE: Different blenders and processors have a different "safe" capacity for hot liquids. Be careful not to overload your machine.

MAKES 4 SERVINGS

1 tablespoon olive oil
1 small onion, chopped
1/2 cup white rice
1 teaspoon ground
    turmeric, or 3 strands
    saffron
2 tablespoons lemon juice
1 tablespoon lemon zest
1/4 cup dry white wine
6 cups chicken broth
Chopped fresh dill
    for garnish

ABOUT RICE

The cultivation of rice in the United States began in the early 1700s. A ship sailing off the coast of South Carolina was damaged in a storm and headed into Charleston for repairs. The ship had been carrying some Golde Seede Rice as part of its cargo and the captain used some of that seed as part payment for his visit and the repair work. A local planter put the seeds into the area's fertile soil, and by 1726 the port of Carolina was exporting some 4,500 metric tons of rice—rice which soon became the world standard for quality.

In 1849, gold was discovered in California and hundreds of thousands of people rushed in, including forty thousand Chinese. Some were prospectors, some worked in supporting crafts, but all of them held on to their traditional Asian diet. Rice was the major element in the meals of the Chinese, and soon California farmers were growing rice to meet the new demand. The heavy clay soil near Sacramento was not ideal for most crops, but it was perfect for rice. Today, the United States is probably the world's most advanced and innovative producer of rice.

RIBOLLITA (TUSCAN VEGETABLE SOUP)

VILLA MONSANTO, CHIANTI, ITALY

MAKES 4 TO 6 SERVINGS

FOR THE BEANS:
1 cup Great Northern or
    cannellini beans
1 carrot, peeled and cut in
    half
1 stalk celery
1/2 red onion, halved and
    studded with 1 clove
1 bay leaf
1/2 teaspoon dried thyme
1 teaspoon kosher salt

FOR THE SOUP:
1/2 medium red onion,
    minced
1 leek, white and light
    green parts, rinsed and
    diced
1/4 cup olive oil, plus extra
    for drizzling on top
1 medium carrot, diced
2 stalks celery, diced
1 cup chopped savoy cabbage
1 cup firmly packed
    chopped Swiss chard
1 cup diced zucchini
1 baking potato, peeled
    and cubed
1 teaspoon kosher salt

The Villa Monsanto in the Tuscany region of Italy is the home of Juliana Bianchi. Juliana is one of the great family cooks of Italy. The following recipe is for a traditional Tuscan soup called *ribollita*, which means "reboiled." It is usually prepared the day before it is served.

1. To make the beans: Cover the beans with cold water and soak overnight. Alternatively, use the quick-soak method: Place the beans in a pot of water to cover and bring to a boil for 5 minutes. Remove from the heat and set aside for 1 hour.

2. Drain the beans and place them in a saucepan with the remaining ingredients and cover with water by at least 3 inches. Bring to a boil, and reduce the heat to a simmer. With a slotted spoon or ladle, skim off any foam that rises to the surface. Continue cooking until the beans are tender, 1 to 1½ hours. If not using the beans right away, let them cool in their liquid.

3. To make the soup: In a medium stockpot, combine the onion, leek, and olive oil. Cook over a medium flame for 3 to 4 minutes. Add the carrot, celery, cabbage, Swiss chard, zucchini, and potato. Add the salt and pepper. Cook for an additional 5 minutes, stirring occasionally.

4. Add the tomatoes to the pot. Puree the beans with 1 cup of their cooking liquid in a food processor, blender, or food mill. Add to the soup. Add the water. Simmer, covered, over a low flame for 3 hours.

5. To serve the ribollita, place slices of bread in the bottom of a soup bowl and ladle the soup on top. Garnish the soup with a drizzle of olive oil on top.

⅛ teaspoon freshly ground
   black pepper
2 cups canned Italian plum
   tomatoes, pureed
3 cups water
6 to 8 slices crusty Tuscan-
   style bread

✳

ABOUT MONSANTO

Fabrizio Bianchi is the president of a famous textile company, but he has always believed the same skills that are used to blend together various colors and textures in fabrics would lend themselves to making great wine. So, in 1962 he purchased an estate in Tuscany, just north of Siena, and decided to try and prove his point.

It is quite a place. The main building is a villa from the 1700s. There are almost two hundred acres of vineyards, a road built two thousand years ago by the ancient Romans, stands of cypress, and an orchard of olive trees. The property was known as Monsanto after the district that it occupied. Today, Monsanto is known as the name of one of the most respected wines to come out of the region.

But in addition to the story of wine, there is also an unusual story of love. Just after she graduated from the University of Milano law school, Fabrizio's daughter Laura realized that she preferred fermentation to litigation. So she came down to work in the family winery. She also fell in love with the son of another winemaker in the neighborhood. When they began to talk about getting married they decided that the real test of their relationship would be to try and produce a wine together, a wine that they both liked. When they finally finished making their wine, Laura felt that the wine would be perfect for drinking at a wedding, and yet it would have the capacity to age well for a long time. That was enough for her to say "yes."

Trout Soup with Spring Vegetables

BANFF SPRINGS HOTEL, ALBERTA, CANADA

MAKES 4 SERVINGS

1 tablespoon vegetable oil
1 medium onion, chopped
½ cup thinly sliced fennel or celery
½ cup julienne of leek
2½ cups chicken broth or water
½ cup dry white wine
6 strands of saffron (optional)
1 cup sliced zucchini
1 cup sliced carrots
1 cup chopped tomatoes
6 scallions, cut into 2-inch pieces
8 trout fillets, or several larger fillets cut into 8 pieces (about 1½ pounds total), skinned
½ teaspoon salt
¼ teaspoon freshly ground black pepper
Chopped fresh chives for garnish (optional)

Martin Luthi is a classically trained Swiss chef who prepared this recipe for a dish which is between a soup and a stew. It's easy and quite delicious.

1. In a large, deep sauté pan, heat the oil, then add the onions and cook for 2 minutes. Add the fennel or celery and leek and cook for 2 minutes longer. Pour in the chicken broth or water, wine, and saffron, if desired, and bring to a simmer. Add the vegetables.

2. Season the trout fillets with the salt and pepper. Add them to the broth and vegetables. Cover the pan and simmer for 3 to 4 minutes.

3. Serve in soup plates. Ladle some of the broth and vegetables into each soup plate then place 2 fillets in each. Garnish with the chopped chives.

Me and Executive Chef Martin Luthi, Banff Springs Hotel.

BANFF, CANADA

In 1883, Banff was designated as Canada's first national park, and with good reason. It has one of the most beautiful landscapes in the entire world. The views are almost shocking—jagged mountains that shoot thousands of feet into powder-blue skies, ancient glaciers feeding lakes with mirrored surfaces that reflect the pine forests, waterfalls, and alpine meadows. This is what happens when nature works with an unlimited budget and no deadline.

There is archaeological evidence that native tribes have been hunting in this area for at least eleven thousand years. The first men of European ancestry in the neighborhood appear to have been two trappers who came up from the United States in 1875. But the real development of Banff started in the early 1880s, when the Canadian Pacific Railroad selected this area as part of their transcontinental route.

On November 8, 1883, three railroad workers decided to spend their day off wandering around the mountains looking for mineral deposits. At one point they stumbled onto a hole with a hot spring below, and immediately realized that they had come upon something of great value.

First of all, hot water was hard to come by in a frontier environment and people would gladly pay for a warm bath. The men might also have been aware that bathing in this type of hot spring was considered as a way of curing a number of illnesses, and that people of great wealth would pay big bucks to use it. But the railroad workers were not the only ones to appreciate the hot springs.

William Cornelius Van Horn ran the railroad and clearly understood that the site was worth a fortune. He convinced the federal government to designate the area as Canada's first national park and to give the railroad the rights to develop the area. A bathhouse was built and the bathers showed up for "the cure." The railroad also started the construction of a series of magnificent resorts as part of its program to attract tourists. The Banff Springs Château was the first of these structures.

In the summer of 1887, Van Horn showed up to see how the work on his Château was coming along. Much to his surprise, someone had misoriented the construction drawings and the building was facing the wrong way. The guest rooms fronted onto a rock wall, the kitchens looked out on the great view. Now, personally, I think giving the kitchens the great view was the right idea, but Van Horn flipped things around, and when the hotel opened the following year the guest rooms faced the valley. There is a statue of Van Horn in front of the hotel and he is pointing to the valley, just to make sure there are no more directional problems.

When the hotel opened, it was the largest hotel in the world, with room rates starting at an astronomical $3.50 per day. The building was, and still is, a work of art.

STEWS, CASSEROLES, AND CHILI

Beef Stew

CHILE

MAKES 4 SERVINGS

3 tablespoons vegetable oil
1½ pounds beef chuck, cut
    into 1-inch cubes
2 cloves garlic, chopped
1 green bell pepper, cored,
    seeded, and cut into thin
    strips
1 red bell pepper, cored,
    seeded, and cut into
    thin strips
1 carrot, peeled and cut
    into thin strips
1 medium onion, sliced
Eight 1-inch-thick rounds
    of frozen corn on
    the cob, or 1 cup corn
    kernels
1 cup quartered string
    beans
½ teaspoon salt
6 cups beef or chicken
    broth or a combination
    of the two
4 new potatoes, cut in half
¾ cup rice
Chopped fresh parsley or
    cilantro as a garnish

1. In a large casserole over medium heat, heat the oil. Add the beef and brown on all sides. Add the garlic and cook for 1 minute. Stir in the bell peppers, carrot, and onion and cook for 5 minutes.

2. Add the corn, string beans, salt, and broth. Cover the pot and simmer for 30 minutes. Add the potatoes and rice. Cover the pot and continue to simmer for another 30 minutes, or until the meat is tender.

3. Place the solid ingredients in a soup plate and spoon on some of the broth. Garnish with the chopped parsley or cilantro.

SUGGESTED MENU:

Cheese Empanadas (page 225)
Beef Stew
Garden Salad with Pistachios (page 202)
Crumb Cake (page 274)

CHILEAN FISH STEW

CHILE

1. In a large Dutch oven or saucepan over medium heat, heat the oil. Add the garlic, bell peppers, carrot, and onion. Cook for 2 minutes. Then stir in the tomatoes and cook for another minute.

2. Add the fish to the vegetables along with the bay leaf, cumin, and parsley. Pour in the wine and water or broth and season with salt. Stir the ingredients together, cover the pan, and bring the liquid to a boil. Add the potatoes, cover the pan again, and cook for 15 minutes, or until the potatoes and fish are cooked thoroughly. Remove the bay leaf and discard.

3. Spoon the solid ingredients into serving bowls, then top with a little of the liquid.

SUGGESTED MENU:

Chilean Fish Stew
Stuffed Avocados (page 196)
Chocolate Sacher Cake (page 268)

Seafood offered for sale along the dock in Valdivia, Chile.

MAKES 4 SERVINGS

2 tablespoons vegetable oil
1 clove garlic, chopped
1 red bell pepper, seeded, cored, and sliced into thin strips
1 green bell pepper, seeded, cored, and sliced into thin strips
1 small carrot, grated
1 medium onion, sliced
2 cups cubed tomatoes
1½ pounds monkfish or Chilean sea bass fillets
1 bay leaf
1 teaspoon ground cumin
2 tablespoons chopped fresh parsley
½ cup white wine
1 cup water or vegetable, fish, or chicken broth
1 teaspoon salt
2 potatoes, peeled and sliced 1 inch thick

JAMBALAYA

SAMBA JAVA RESTAURANT, HEALDSBURG, CALIFORNIA

MAKES 10 TO 12 SERVINGS

1¾ quarts chicken broth,
    or four 13¾-ounce cans
1½ pounds medium shrimp,
    peeled, shells reserved
1 tablespoon vegetable oil
1 pound andouille, Cajun,
    or other spicy sausage
1 cup chopped celery
2 cups chopped green bell
    peppers
2 cups chopped onions
1 serrano or 2 jalapeño
    peppers, chopped
4 cloves garlic, minced
½ cup diced tomatoes
½ cup tomato juice
½ cup tomato paste
2 bay leaves
½ teaspoon crushed red
    chili flakes
¼ teaspoon salt (optional)
¼ teaspoon freshly ground
    black pepper
1½ cups long-grain rice
1 tablespoon chopped
    fresh basil, or 1 tea-
    spoon dried
Chopped scallions or
    onions for garnish

1. In a large stockpot, bring the chicken broth and reserved shrimp shells to a simmer. Let simmer for 10 minutes. Then strain and set the broth aside until ready to use in step 3.

2. In a second large stockpot, heat the vegetable oil, then slice the sausage into ¼-inch rounds, and cook it until lightly browned. Add the celery, bell peppers, and onions. Cook for about 10 minutes. Add the chilies and garlic and sauté for 5 minutes more. Stir in the diced tomatoes, tomato juice, tomato paste, and bay leaves.

3. Add the strained shellfish-flavored chicken broth and the crushed red chili flakes. Season the mixture with a little salt and pepper. Add the long-grain rice, cover the pot, and simmer for 15 to 18 minutes.

4. Finally, stir in the basil and add the shrimp. Cook for 5 minutes longer with the cover off. Be sure that the rice is almost cooked before you add the shrimp, so the shrimp won't overcook.

5. Serve in bowls and garnish with scallions or onions.

SUGGESTED MENU:

Jambalaya
Marinated Cucumber and Carrot Salad (page 200)
Honey Nut Tart (page 298)

Lentil Stew

CHILE

1. In a large pot, bring the water to a boil, then add the lentils and the salt. Lower the heat, cover, and simmer for 15 minutes.

2. In a sauté pan over medium heat, heat the oil. Add the onion and cook for 2 minutes. Stir in the garlic, oregano, pepper, and carrot and cook for 2 minutes more. Stir in the paprika and cook for 1 minute.

3. Transfer the vegetables to the pot with the lentils. Add the butternut squash or pumpkin, the sausage, and rice. Cover the pan and simmer for 20 to 25 minutes. After 10 minutes of cooking, check to see if you need any more water.

4. Garnish with the grated Parmesan cheese and chopped chives.

SUGGESTED MENU:

Beef Empanadas (page 222)
Chilean Salsa (Pebre) (page 215)
Lentil Stew
Apple Cake (page 271)

MAKES 10 SERVINGS

7 cups water
1 cup lentils
1 teaspoon salt
2 tablespoons vegetable oil
1 medium onion, chopped
1 clove garlic, minced
$\frac{1}{2}$ teaspoon dried oregano
$\frac{1}{2}$ teaspoon freshly ground black pepper
1 carrot, peeled and chopped
1 teaspoon paprika
2 cups cubed butternut squash or pumpkin
1 cup sliced sausage
1 cup rice
Freshly grated Parmesan cheese as a garnish
Chopped fresh chives as a garnish

GAUCHOS

During the 1700s, horses, bulls, and cows that had escaped from the large estates of South America roamed freely over the great Pampas. They were unhindered by most predators and bred into enormous herds. Eventually, a group of men came together to hunt these animals for the traders. They were called gauchos. They were usually mestizos, a mixture of European and native Indian ancestry, and they hunted with lassos, knives, and a piece of equipment called a bola. The bola is made up of a series of leather strips with three iron balls on the ends. The gaucho throws the bola at the animal he is chasing. The balls twist around the animal's legs and bring it to a halt.

For a time, the gaucho had also been the backbone of the armies that fought for independence against the Spanish Crown. By the end of the 1800s, however, most of the Pampas had been fenced off to make large ranches and farms. The wild herds were taken in, and sophisticated breeding techniques controlled their development. The old frontier life died away, and the gauchos ended up being hired as handlers.

They are still around and still wearing their traditional clothing: a chiripa around the waist; a woolen poncho; heavy leather boots; and their most distinctive piece of clothing, their baggy pants called bombachas. Bombachas are actually copies of the pants worn by a regiment of the French army during the Crimean War. The original shipment of the pants came to South America after the war as used clothing, and they have been copied ever since. I assume that this is just another example of army surplus chic.

Just after the best days of the gaucho had come to an end, a wave of nostalgia splashed over a group of South American writers and they suddenly began presenting the gaucho as a mythic character in the history of the Pampas. I think this might have been the same wave that inundated authors in North America, because at just about the same time, the same thing was done to the North American cowboy. It's so frustrating to become a folk hero after the good times are over. Most of us would like to be appreciated while we are still around.

Voyageur Stew

JASPER PARK LODGE, ALBERTA, CANADA

The first Europeans into the Alberta area were French fur traders known as *voyageurs*. They exchanged various manufactured goods with the local tribes, taking back furs which they transported to the east coast of Canada for shipment to Europe. One of the most common items in the trade were metal pots and pans, which had an enormous effect on the way the local tribes prepared their food.

Originally the natives cooked their meat by holding it directly over a fire or by boiling it with other ingredients. Moose, elk, or bear meat and water were placed into a sack made of animal hide. Because the hide could not go directly over fire, the food was heated by dropping hot stones into the sack. With the arrival of the *voyageurs* the natives were introduced to pan frying and recipes like the following.

1. In a sauté pan or Dutch oven large enough to hold all of the ingredients, heat the oil and cook the beef until the cubes are brown on all sides, about 5 minutes.

2. Add the onions and continue cooking for 3 minutes. Add the maple syrup and cook and stir for 1 minute. Add the potatoes, turnips, and scallions, and cook, stirring, for 3 minutes. Add the beef stock, salt, and pepper and simmer for 1½ hours, until the meat is tender.

SUGGESTED MENU:

Voyageur Stew
Corn Bread with Chives (page 220)
Spinach and Boston Lettuce with Grapefruit and Maple-Walnut Vinaigrette (page 207)
Peach Berry Crumble (page 236)

MAKES 8 SERVINGS

3 tablespoons vegetable oil
3 pounds lean beef, cut into 1-inch cubes
2 cups chopped onions
¾ cup maple syrup
3 cups potatoes, skin on, cut into 1-inch cubes
2 cups turnips, peeled, cut into 1-inch cubes
1 cup scallions, cut into small rounds
4 cups beef stock
Salt and freshly ground black pepper

THE BEGINNINGS OF THE TOWN OF JASPER

The fur trade in North America was based on the European fashion for beaver hats, and the major organization supplying those very valuable beaver skins from Canada was the Hudson Bay Company. One of the company's agents in western Canada was named Jasper. He operated a trading post and sold supplies to the trappers.

The building in which he conducted his business was known as Jasper House, and eventually the entire area was called Jasper. The first actual settler in Jasper was a man named Lewis Swift. He came up from the United States in 1893, built a cabin, traded with the natives, and raised cattle.

When the fashion for beaver hats came to an end in Europe, so did much of the fur trade in Canada. Jasper settled back to the mountain wilderness that it had been for thousands of years. But just south of Jasper, in a location called Banff, the joint was jumping. The Canadian Pacific Railway had gotten the government to declare the area a national park. A hotel had been built and Banff was becoming a major attraction for international tourists, producing income for both the railroad and the national government.

When a second transcontinental railroad was built on a more northerly route, it crossed through the Jasper area. The government soon realized that it had another opportunity to establish a national park and make a few bucks, which was only fair, since the government had spent a fortune to help the railroads get started.

In 1907, it set up the Jasper Forest Park. The original town was just a division point on the railroad, called Fitzhugh, with a row of tents that offered a place to "eat and sleep." An early example of honest advertising.

In the town of Jasper, in Alberta, Canada, there are canoe guides like Art Jackson of Rocky Mountain Voyageurs. They will take you down the river giving you a historical tour of the area as it was during the time of the original European trappers.

CHILEAN CASSEROLE OF BEEF AND CHICKEN (PASTEL DE CHOCLO)

TERMAS DE CAUQUENES, CHILE

Pastel de Choclo is basically a casserole of beef and chicken with a top crust of pureed corn kernels. It's one of the world's great one-pot recipes.

1. Preheat the oven to 400° F.

2. In a saucepan over medium heat, heat the oil. Add the onions and sauté for 1 minute. Add the beef and sauté for 2 minutes. Add the paprika, salt, and black pepper.

3. Divide the cooked beef and onion into four 2-cup heat-proof bowls. Place 3 olives into each bowl. Place one half of each half chicken breast into each bowl. Divide the raisins and the hard-boiled eggs among the bowls.

4. In a sauté pan over medium heat, melt the butter. Add the pureed corn, and 1 teaspoon of the sugar. Pour the pureed corn on top of the contents of the bowls to make a top crust.

5. Paint the egg wash onto the corn. Sprinkle 1/2 teaspoon of the sugar on top of each bowl, and bake for 30 minutes, or until the corn forms a lightly browned crust.

SUGGESTED MENU:

Chilean Casserole of Beef and Chicken (Pastel de Choclo)
Baked Sweet Potato Chips (page 151)

MAKES 4 SERVINGS

2 tablespoons vegetable oil
1 cup chopped onion
2 cups lean beef, cut into
  1-inch cubes
1/2 teaspoon paprika
1/2 teaspoon salt
1/2 teaspoon freshly ground
  black pepper
12 stuffed olives
2 boneless, skinless
  chicken breasts, halved,
  and cooked by steaming
  or sautéing
1/4 cup raisins
2 eggs, hard-boiled, each
  sliced into 4 pieces
1 tablespoon butter
2 cups canned corn
  kernels, pureed
3 teaspoons sugar
1 egg mixed with 2
  tablespoons water for
  egg wash

TERMAS DE CAUQUENES, CHILE

About seventy-five miles south of Santiago, resting against the side of a mountain pass, and looking down a river that races out of the Andes, is the Termas De Cauquenes. For over four hundred years there has been an inn on this spot, an inn where people come and rejuvenate themselves in the hot mineral baths that come up from deep inside the earth.

The idea of sitting in mineral baths goes back for thousands of years. The Roman soldiers, on their way home from the wars in northern Europe, would stop into a little town in Belgium and rest in the mineral pools. One of the reasons they felt better was that all of the salts in the warm water made them float. The floating feeling gave them a sense of well-being. The name of the town in Belgium, by the way, was Spa.

The Termas never had any Roman soldiers stop in, but most of the great military leaders in Chile's history spent a few nights, including the great leader of Chile's army of independence, Bernardo O'Higgins. The scientific community was represented when Charles Darwin popped in and rested his evolving bones.

Today the Termas is also an excellent resort under the direction of a Swiss hotelier and his family. René Acklin is his name and he has been living in Chile since 1973. Over the years he has become one of the country's most respected chefs. René is also an exporter of fish and quite an authority on the subject.

René Acklin moved to Chile from Switzerland in the early '70s and became one of the nation's most respected food authorities (Termas de Cauquenes, Chile).

LAMB CURRY

CHILE

---

1. In a large sauté pan over medium heat, heat the vegetable oil. Add the lamb and brown the meat on all sides. Stir in the curry powder and pepper. Add the onion and garlic and cook for 3 minutes. Then add the cucumber and salt and cook, stirring, for 2 minutes more.

2. Stir in the flour. Cook over medium heat for 1 minute. Pour in the wine or broth and add the potatoes. Lower the heat and simmer uncovered for 20 minutes. Add a little more wine or water, if necessary.

3. Serve with the cooked rice and garnish with chopped cilantro.

SUGGESTED MENU:

Avocado Soup (page 2)
Lamb Curry
Lemon Cheesecake (page 261)

MAKES 4 SERVINGS

3 tablespoons vegetable oil
1½ pounds lean lamb, cut
into 1-inch cubes
1 tablespoon curry powder
½ teaspoon freshly ground
black pepper
1 medium onion, chopped
1 clove garlic, chopped
1 medium cucumber,
peeled and diced
½ teaspoon salt
1 tablespoon all-purpose
flour
⅔ cup red wine or beef
broth
1 large potato, peeled and
cut into 1-inch cubes
4 servings white rice,
cooked according to
package directions
Chopped fresh cilantro

PATAGONIA

Chile's Patagonian pampas is a form of desert, a desert not made of drifting sand but a desert of low vegetation. The English scientist Charles Darwin found the dry plains of Patagonia to be one of the most haunting and impressive regions on earth.

The first Europeans to settle in this part of Chile were the employees of British-owned sheep companies. In 1877, a Mr. Henry Reynard brought in a flock of sheep from the Falkland Islands to test the business. And what a business it turned out to be. The land produced lots of healthy sheep, and the sheep produced lots of excellent wool. Gigantic farms called *estancias* were set up with their administration placed in the hands of executives from England and Scotland. Within a few years Patagonia looked like a part of the British Empire. But it didn't sound that way, because everyone spoke Spanish.

Patagonia's major southern city, Punta Arenas, became wealthy as a port, and the inland *estancias* made great fortunes for their owners. But when the Panama Canal opened, Punta got passed; it was much easier to go from the Pacific to the Atlantic or vice versa through the Panama Canal than around the tip of South America. And when the sheep farmers of Australia and New Zealand began to compete, the local wool and lamb market took a dive. Then in 1945, things began to turn up again. Oil and natural gas deposits were discovered in the area, and an important fishing center developed. In the 1950s, an impressive national park was set up. Today this region of Chile has one of the highest per capita incomes in the country.

One of the roads through the Torres del Paine National Park in southern Chile. A place where you are truly close to nature and free from the commercial aspects of tourism.

Ground Spicy Lamb Curry with White Rice

SINGAPORE AIRLINES, SINGAPORE

1. In a large sauté pan over medium heat, heat the oil. Add the cinnamon stick, fennel seeds, bay leaf, and cloves. Cook for 2 minutes. Add the onions, ginger, garlic, and coriander and cook for 1 minute more.

2. Stir in the cayenne pepper and tomatoes and cook for 2 minutes. Add the ground lamb or beef and simmer for 25 minutes. Season with the salt. Finally add the peas and the chopped cilantro. Cook for 3 minutes, or until the peas are heated through.

3. Serve with a garnish of chopped cucumber on the side and a portion of white rice.

SUGGESTED MENU:

Ground Spicy Lamb Curry with White Rice
Turmeric Potatoes with Green Bell Peppers (page 143)
Mango and Orange Salad (page 205)

MAKES 6 SERVINGS

3 tablespoons vegetable oil
1 stick cinnamon, about 2 inches long
1 tablespoon fennel seeds
1 bay leaf
6 whole cloves
2 medium onions, chopped
1 tablespoon minced fresh ginger
3 cloves garlic, minced
1 tablespoon ground coriander
$1/4$ teaspoon cayenne pepper
1 cup chopped tomatoes
2 pounds ground lamb or beef
1 teaspoon salt
1 cup frozen peas
$2/3$ cup chopped fresh cilantro
Chopped cucumber for garnish
Cooked white rice for serving

THE INDIAN COMMUNITY OF SINGAPORE AND THEIR COOKING

For well over 2,500 years, Indian trading ships have come across the Bay of Bengal to do business on the Malay Peninsula. At some point, the merchants began to set up permanent operations in the region.

The original Indian settlers in the area appear to have come for the precious metals and valuable stones. Twenty-five centuries before home shopping and there was already a thriving business in gold and emerald jewelry. The traders sent the jewels back to India and brought Indian culture to the peninsula. There are Hindu temples along the coast north of Singapore that date back over a thousand years. And the name Singapore itself comes from Sanskrit, which was the language of ancient India.

In 1816, Singapore became a center for British commercial interests and many Indian laborers arrived as indentured workers. They staffed the rubber plantations and the coffee growing estates. Some of the Indians who came, however, did not come of their own free will. For a number of decades the English used Singapore as a place to store Indian convicts. They did the same thing in the American colonies and in Australia, so Singapore was in excellent company.

Indian convict labor actually built some of the more important historical buildings in Singapore, including St. Andrew's Cathedral and the Istana, which is the official residence of Singapore's President. When the convicts finished their terms, they were allowed to remain there as free men, and many of them did so. Today, the Indian community represents about 15 percent of the Singaporean population and they make a vital contribution to the community. To be reminded of what a great and long-standing reputation Indian cooks have had for their ability to use spices, just recall why native Americans were originally called Indians. The first explorers to arrive in the New World were looking for *spices*. When they finally came to land they thought they were near India, so everyone they met got called an Indian.

With well over two thousand years of interaction between the indigenous people of the Malay Peninsula and the provinces of India, it's no surprise that Singapore has some of the best Indian cooking outside of India.

At the heart of Indian food is the use of spices. And, because of the extraordinary array of spices that are available to the traditional Indian cook, they are put to very elaborate use. *(cont. on following page)*

The regional cooking of India is as different as the regional cooking of China. But in general, the most important distinction is between northern Indian food and southern Indian food. The south has always been home to hotter seasonings, fiery curries, and rice as the basic starch to cool things down. It is also the part of India that developed some of the most famous vegetarian recipes.

The classic eating style is to set a banana leaf on a flat surface, place the food on top, and eat with your hands. To the untutored eye it may look like the food is just being picked up and eaten. But there is actually a very subtle bit of gastronomic skill involved. The spicier food is being kneaded together with milder food so the diner gets the precise level of heat that he or she wants at any point in the meal. Fingers are the ideal tool for this task.

The south coast of India is also home to the cooking of the Indian Muslim community, which uses seafood, poultry, lamb, and the hottest spicing of all. Thousands of years ago people learned that certain spices would bring moisture to the surface of their skin. As that moisture evaporated, their bodies became cooler. It is a natural system of air conditioning that is used in hot climates throughout the world.

The northern cooking of India has more meat and less fish than the south, and the starch is often wheat instead of rice. The traditional cooking method is the tandoor oven. Part open grill, part oven, the tandoor is used to prepare almost any recipe that is part of the cooking of northern India.

A goddess on a Hindu temple in Singapore. When I was preparing to make an offering, the priest asked me whether I would like to present a banana or a coconut. It appears the banana is used for everyday requests; major prayers require coconuts. I went with the coconuts.

Chuck Wagon Chili

RAFTER SIX RANCH RESORT, SEEBE, ALBERTA, CANADA

MAKES 6 SERVINGS

2 tablespoons vegetable oil
2 pounds lean round beef,
    cut into 1-inch cubes
2 cloves garlic, minced
2 cups chopped onions
2 cups beef broth
1 cup water
2 cups canned tomatoes
    and their juices
2 tablespoons chili powder
1 teaspoon dried oregano
1 teaspoon ground cumin
1/2 teaspoon cayenne
    pepper
Salt and freshly ground
    black pepper
4 cups cooked pinto beans
2 tablespoons finely
    ground cornmeal

The Rafter Six Ranch Resort is just to the west of Calgary. The name Rafter Six is a reference to the brand that was originally used on this ranch—a half diamond that looks like a rafter on the top and a number 6 underneath. The ranch was founded by Colonel James Walker of the Northwest Mounted Police.

The next person to take over the ranch was a hunter and a real character, Soapy Smith. I couldn't find out why he was called Soapy, but clearly it wasn't because he was 99 and 44/100 percent pure. When he was in his mid-seventies he married a young lady in her mid-teens and together they started a tour guide business at the ranch. After Soapy's widely anticipated demise, his widow remarried and turned the ranch into a guesthouse.

During the 1940s, the ranch became a location for the making of Hollywood films. One of Marilyn Monroe's early movies, *River of No Return*, was filmed there, as was *The Life and Times of Grizzly Adams* and *The Adventures of the Wilderness Family*. In 1976, the ranch was purchased by Stan Cowley and his wife Gloria.

Chili and beans were very common meals for chuck wagon cooks, and at Rafter Six Ranch they are combined in one recipe.

1. In a large deep-sided skillet or sauté pan over medium heat, heat the oil. When the oil is hot, add the beef and cook, stirring until the cubes are brown on all sides, about 5 minutes.

2. Add in the garlic and cook, stirring occasionally for 3 minutes. Add in the onions and cook, stirring, for another 3 minutes. Add the broth, water, tomatoes and their juices, and the seasonings. Mix well and simmer for 1 1/2 hours.

Add additional water if the chili begins to become dry during the cooking time.

3. Add the beans and the cornmeal and simmer for 30 minutes more.

SUGGESTED MENU:

Chuck Wagon Chili
Dutch Oven Brown Bread (page 221)
Tricolor Slaw with Buttermilk Poppy-Seed Dressing
   (page 206)
Apple Cobbler (page 235)

A traditional chuck wagon that is still in use at the Rafter Six Ranch in Alberta, Canada.

CHUCK WAGONS

The great cattle drives from the ranches of Texas to the railheads in Kansas took place from the middle of the 1860s to the middle of the 1880s. The whole business only lasted twenty years, but it produced enough cowboy folklore to become one of the mythic images of North America.

During the 1870s, big herds of cattle started coming into Canada by crossing from Montana. The chuck wagon headed the procession. Next came the lead steer, followed by fifty thousand steaks and chops spread out among two thousand head of cattle.

The chuck wagon was designed by one of the great cattle kings, Charles Goodnight, and he had a clear idea of what his crews needed for the cattle drive. Each wagon was divided into a series of drawers and boxes that would hold everything the cook needed for ten men, during thirty days. There was a large door at the back to protect the contents of the wagon. When it was time to start cooking, the door hinged down and became a worktable. The cook carried a supply of salt pork and bacon; there was a sourdough starter for making bread, flour, cornmeal, dried apples, coffee, and beans. Beans were served so often that meal times were often referred to as "bean time."

Real cowboys at the Rafter Six Ranch near the city of Calgary in Alberta, Canada.

Taking a coffee break on
the trail at the Rafter Six
Ranch in Alberta, Canada.

"Shorty" LeGoffe.

Vegetable Chili

SAMBA JAVA RESTAURANT, HEALDSBURG, CALIFORNIA

MAKES 10 SERVINGS

2 tablespoons vegetable oil
1 medium onion, chopped
2 stalks celery, chopped
1 green bell pepper,
    chopped
1 red bell pepper, chopped
2 serrano or jalapeño
    peppers, seeded and
    minced
4 cloves garlic, minced
2 teaspoons chili powder
1 teaspoon ground cumin
6 cups cooked beans, such
    as garbanzo, pinto, or
    navy
4 cups vegetable or
    chicken broth
1 tablespoon chopped
    fresh oregano, or
    1 teaspoon dried
1 tablespoon chopped
    fresh thyme, or
    1 teaspoon dried
1 tablespoon chopped
    fresh parsley
$3/4$ teaspoon salt

Colleen McGlynn started her cooking career when she took a job cooking in a Berlin restaurant. Actually it was more like a job *learning* to cook in a restaurant. Eventually she came back to the United States and opened a place where she practices her specialty, which is cooking with local California ingredients.

1. In a large, deep cast-iron pot or Dutch oven, heat the oil. Add the onion and celery and cook for 2 minutes. Stir in the green and red bell peppers and cook for 5 minutes more.

2. Stir in the chopped chili peppers, garlic, chili powder, and cumin. Then add the beans, broth, herbs, and salt. Simmer for 15 minutes. Thicken the chili with the masa harina or cornstarch. Stir in the cooked corn and zucchini and heat thoroughly.

3. Serve each bowl garnished with the Monterey Jack or Cheddar cheese and tortilla chips.

SUGGESTED MENU:

Vegetable Chili
Whole Wheat Onion Biscuits (page 218)
Banana Cake with Fudge Frosting (page 277)

Chef Colleen McGlynn, Samba Java Restaurant.

¼ cup masa harina (available in Latin American or Mexican grocery stores), or 3 tablespoons cornstarch mixed with 3 tablespoons water
2 cups cooked corn
2 medium zucchini, cooked and sliced
¾ cup grated Monterey Jack or Cheddar cheese
Tortilla chips

THE RUSSIAN RIVER AND HEALDSBURG, CALIFORNIA

For thirty years, starting in 1812, the Russian government maintained its most distant outpost in North America at Fort Ross. During that period, it conducted a series of detailed explorations of the local area. The explorations began along a river that ran inland from the region near the fort. The river eventually became known as the Russian River because the Russians were always on it.

Today, California's Russian River is one of the most picturesque spots in the country, with a stretch of water that offers some of the nation's best canoeing—canoeing that takes you past acre after acre of famous vineyards. This is prime California wine country. The main town along the river is called Healdsburg.

Harmon Heald had come to California from Ohio during the gold rush years. He hoped to strike it rich, but Harmon found no gold, so he took his next best shot and founded a town. In 1852, he built a home and a general store and laid out the town to which he gave his name.

The center of Healdsburg is the beautifully restored plaza, the perfect spot to spend a restful afternoon. Across the street is the Healdsburg Museum, housed in a 1910 Andrew Carnegie Library, and packed with historical collections, much of which has been donated by local families. Healdsburg is also the home of the well-respected Samba Java Restaurant, and its talented chef, Colleen McGlynn.

FISH AND SEAFOOD

Sautéed Cod with Roasted Red Pepper and Garlic

ITALY

MAKES 4 SERVINGS

FOR THE PEPPER
RELISH:
2 red bell peppers
1 head garlic
2 tablespoons olive oil
1 teaspoon dried oregano
1/4 cup white wine
1/2 cup clam juice or fish
   broth
Salt and freshly ground
   black pepper

FOR THE FISH:
4 cod fillets (6 ounces each)
Flour for dusting (optional)
2 tablespoons vegetable oil
2 tablespoons minced fresh
   parsley

1. To make the relish: Heat the broiler. Cut the peppers in half and remove their seeds. Put the peppers on a pan and position them in the oven so the peppers are close to the broiler. Roast the peppers until their skins blister and turn black. Place the charred peppers in a paper bag or in a bowl covered by a plate and let cool. When the peppers are cool enough to handle, rub off the skins with a paper towel. Cut the peppers into thin strips. Turn the oven to 350° F. Break up the head of garlic into individual cloves, toss with 1 tablespoon of the olive oil, place in a pan, and roast until tender, 20 to 25 minutes. Cool and peel. In a saucepan, heat the remaining tablespoon of olive oil, add the peppers and oregano. Cook for 1 minute, add the white wine, and cook over high heat until reduced by half. Add the clam juice or broth and cook until slightly thickened, 2 to 3 minutes. Season to taste with salt and pepper. Set aside while you cook the fish. This dish can be prepared up to this point 2 hours ahead of time.

2. To prepare the fish: When ready to serve, lightly dredge the cod fillets in the flour. Heat a sauté pan and add the oil. Place the fillets in the pan and cook until golden brown, 3 to 5 minutes per side.

3. Remove the fish from the pan and serve with the pepper relish. Sprinkle with the minced parsley.

SUGGESTED MENU:

Tagliatelle with Chicken Sauce (page 137)
Sautéed Cod with Roasted Red Pepper and Garlic
Panna Cotta with Caramel Oranges (page 246)

QUAIL LODGE

The land that makes up the Quail Lodge property was once a dairy farm owned by the brother-in-law of the famous aviator, Charles Lindbergh. During the 1930s, a local insurance salesman joined his son on a class outing to visit the dairy farm and saw how milk and ice cream were produced. The salesman's name was Ed Haber and he fell in love with the property. As he left the farm he told the owner, Dwight Morrow, that if Mr. Morrow ever wanted to sell the farm he would be interested in buying it. Haber definitely had an interest in buying it, but paying for it would have been a different story.

Ten years passed without Haber and Morrow running into each other, and then one day Morrow walked into Haber's office and announced that the property was available. Haber, in what might be described as an act of God rather than a business plan, was able to raise the money and buy the land.

Today, the Quail Lodge Resort and Golf Club is an 850-acre property and home to the Quail Lodge Golf Club. Quail Lodge is also the home of the Covey Restaurant, which is considered to be one of the best restaurants in the San Francisco area. It has a great location overlooking a quiet pond. The executive chef, Bob Williamson, is a native of England who has cooked in top restaurants throughout Europe, Canada, and the United States. His recipe for Mustard-Crusted Halibut is on page 38.

Mustard-Crusted Halibut with Watercress Sauce

QUAIL LODGE, CARMEL, CALIFORNIA

MAKES 4 SERVINGS

FOR THE WATERCRESS
SAUCE:
2 bunches watercress, large
stems removed
3 tablespoons chopped
fresh dill
4 scallions, green part only,
chopped
½ cup olive oil
2 tablespoons sherry wine,
red wine, or raspberry
vinegar
2 tablespoons water
1 tablespoon fresh lemon
juice
2 teaspoons sugar
½ teaspoon salt
¼ teaspoon freshly ground
pepper

FOR THE FISH:
4 halibut fillets (about
1 pound total)
½ teaspoon salt
¼ teaspoon freshly ground
pepper

1. Preheat the oven to 350° F.

2. **To make the sauce:** In a food processor, combine all the ingredients. Process until smooth, and set aside to serve at room temperature.

3. **To make the fish:** Season the halibut with the salt and pepper. Brush one side of each fillet with 1 tablespoon of the Dijon mustard. Then dip the mustard-coated side of the fish in the pan ko or bread crumbs. In a large sauté pan with an ovenproof handle, heat the oil. Place the fish, coated side down, in the pan and cook until lightly browned, about 2 minutes. Flip the fish over and cook it for 2 minutes more. Place the pan with the fish into the preheated oven for 4 to 5 minutes, or until the fish is cooked thoroughly.

4. **For the vegetables:** While the fish is baking, in a large skillet, reheat the vegetables in the water or broth. Drain completely.

5. **To serve:** Place the fish, crusted side up in the center of each plate. Ladle a little sauce next to the fish. Arrange the vegetables on each plate and serve with extra sauce on the side.

Artichokes Stuffed with Ratatouille (page 174)
Mustard-Crusted Halibut with Watercress Sauce
Noodles in Butter Sauce (page 140)
Poached Fruit with Caramel Sauce (page 233)

¹/₄ cup Dijon-style mustard, or more to taste
¹/₃ cup Japanese pan ko, bread crumbs, or cracker meal
2 tablespoons vegetable oil

FOR THE VEGETABLES:
10 baby beets or canned whole beets, cooked, cut in half
¹/₂ pound sugar snap peas or snow peas, cooked
¹/₂ cup water or chicken both

※

Keri-Keri Fish Hash with Creole Sauce

COSTA LINDA BEACH RESORT, ARUBA

**MAKES 4 MAIN
COURSE SERVINGS
OR 12 APPETIZERS**

FOR THE FISH:
1 pound white fish fillets,
    such as flounder, sea
    bass, or monkfish
1 tablespoon vegetable oil
1/3 cup chopped onion
1/3 cup chopped green bell
    pepper
1/3 cup chopped celery
2 to 3 tablespoons
    chopped hot chili,
    jalapeño, or serrano
    peppers
2/3 cup chopped tomatoes
2 tablespoons capers
1 tablespoon paprika
1/4 cup ketchup
12 large lettuce leaves

Most of the islands of the Caribbean have a similar geological history. They got started as volcanoes. Many also share a similar history of habitation by tribes of Arawaks and Caribes. And, they all passed centuries as European colonies.

As a result, you will often see a dish with local adaptations island by island. An example is a recipe that is basically a hashed fish fillet, which is often called keri-keri. Here's how it's prepared by Chef Scott Scheuerman at the Costa Linda Beach Resort on the island of Aruba.

1. Preheat the oven to 350° F.

2. Arrange the fish fillets on a baking sheet and bake for about 10 minutes, or until the fish is thoroughly cooked. Allow the fish to cool, then break the fish into small pieces.

3. While the fish is baking prepare the Creole sauce: In a medium sauté pan, heat the oil. Add the onion and bell pepper. Cook for 2 minutes. Add the garlic and cook for 1 minute longer. Add the tomatoes, salt, and red or cayenne pepper. Cook for 5 minutes, then simmer over low heat until ready to serve.

4. **For the fish:** In a large sauté pan, heat the oil, then add the onion, bell pepper, celery, and hot chili pepper. Sauté for about 2 minutes, then add the tomatoes. Cook for 2 minutes longer. Add the cooked fish, capers, paprika, and ketchup. Heat briefly, then hold the mixture in the pan, but off the stove.

5. Make a V-shaped cut in the lettuce leaves to remove any tough stems. In a large pot fitted with a vegetable steamer, steam half the lettuce leaves for 2 to 3 minutes, until just wilted, then steam the remaining lettuce. You can also wilt the lettuce by holding the leaf with a pair of tongs over a stove burner on medium heat for about 30 seconds.

6. Fill each steamed lettuce leaf with ¼ cup of the fish hash, then roll the leaf to form a packet. To serve, place a little of the Creole sauce on a dinner plate, top with 3 fish packets for a main course or just 1 for an appetizer, then put a little more sauce on the lettuce-rolled fish.

NOTE: I've also seen the fish hash served like a hamburger on a bun with some Dijon mustard and lettuce. To do this, add 1 egg white that's been whisked to the basic fish hash mixture after the fish, capers, paprika, and ketchup have been stirred in. Form into patties and sauté in 1 tablespoon vegetable oil for 2 to 3 minutes per side.

SUGGESTED MENU:

Keri-Keri Fish Hash with Creole Sauce
Island Confetti Rice and Beans (page 162)
Tropical Fruit Pie with Coconut Streusel (page 296)

FOR THE CREOLE SAUCE:
1 tablespoon vegetable oil
½ cup chopped onion
½ cup chopped green bell pepper
3 cloves garlic, chopped
1½ cups canned crushed tomatoes
½ teaspoon salt
⅛ teaspoon ground red or cayenne pepper

ABOUT THE CARIBBEAN

The islands of the Caribbean form a chain that runs from the tip of Florida to the coast of Venezuela. The larger islands in the north, like Cuba, Jamaica, Hispaniola, and Puerto Rico are known as the Greater Antilles. The smaller islands stretching for over a thousand miles from the U.S. Virgin Islands down to Aruba are known as the Lesser Antilles.

The business of greater and lesser is based purely on size. There are lots of things about the Lesser Antilles that are greater than the Greater Antilles. But size does have its impact on things. Starting with Columbus in 1492, the Spanish conquistadors bounced around the Caribbean yelling "finders keepers" over every piece of land they could put a boot on. On the larger pieces of land they also put sizable fortresses in an effort to stress the "keepers" part of their claim.

About twenty minutes after word of the New World got back to Europe, Spain's great rivals, the English, French, Danish, and Dutch, attacked the Spanish claims concentrating most of their attacks on the smaller, less fortified islands. They carried on this military madness for almost three hundred years.

As a result, the Lesser Antilles saw more action than the Greater Antilles, which was great for the Greater Antilles and less great for the Lesser Antilles. But while the European nations were busy raising Cain, they were also busy raising sugar. Almost every island in the Caribbean set up a plantation economy and started supplying sugar for Europe's enormous sweet tooth at equally enormous profits.

But there were a number of Caribbean islands that managed to escape this scenario and one of them was Aruba. Aruba is a small island just off the coast of Venezuela. The Arawaks of South America were the first people to inhabit Aruba, and they appear to have come over about five thousand years ago. They were followed by the Spanish in 1500, and in the next century by the Dutch. Those three groups are the major ethnic influences on Aruba, and they have produced a society of truly friendly and charming people.

Bacon-Wrapped Monkfish with Grapes in Lime Herb Sauce

THE CLIFT, SAN FRANCISCO, CALIFORNIA

1. Preheat the oven to 350° F.

2. Combine the herbs in a shallow bowl. Dip the fish in the herbs, coating both sides. Season the fish with the salt and pepper. Wrap the fillets in several slices of bacon.

3. Heat 1 tablespoon of the oil and 1 tablespoon of the butter in a large sauté or frying pan with an ovenproof handle. Add the monkfish to the pan and brown the fish on all sides for about a minute. Place the pan with the monkfish into the preheated oven for 12 to 14 minutes.

4. While the fish is baking, heat the remaining oil and butter in a second sauté pan. Cook together the sliced beans or snow peas and the red peppers for 3 minutes. Divide the sautéed vegetables among 4 dinner plates.

5. Remove the fish from the oven. Slice each fillet into cylinders and arrange them on the dinner plates. Garnish each plate with 5 grapes. Top with the Lime Herb Sauce, if desired.

SUGGESTED MENU:

Bacon-Wrapped Monkfish with Grapes in Lime Herb
  Sauce
Layered Potatoes and Onions with Basil (page 146)
Frozen Chocolate Soufflés (page 245)

MAKES 4 SERVINGS

1/4 cup chopped fresh
  parsley
3 tablespoons chopped
  fresh chives
1 tablespoon chopped
  fresh chervil or tarragon,
  or 1 teaspoon dried
4 medium-sized monkfish
  fillets (3 to 4 ounces
  each)
1/2 teaspoon salt
1/4 teaspoon freshly ground
  black pepper
1/2 pound bacon, sliced
2 tablespoons olive oil
2 tablespoons unsalted
  butter
3/4 pound green beans or
  snow peas, thinly sliced
  lengthwise
1/4 cup diced red bell
  pepper
20 seedless green grapes
1 recipe Lime Herb Sauce
  (optional, recipe
  follows)

Lime Herb Sauce

MAKES 4 SERVINGS

1 tablespoon fresh lime
 juice
2 tablespoons water
4 tablespoons unsalted
 butter, chilled and cut
 into ½-inch cubes
1 teaspoon chopped fresh
 chervil, parsley, or other
 herb, or ½ teaspoon
 dried

1. In a small saucepan over high heat, boil the lime juice and water until about 2 teaspoons of liquid remain (1 to 2 minutes). Turn off the heat.

2. Quickly whisk in the cold butter, a few cubes at a time, until it is frothy and creamy, keeping the remaining cubes cold until needed. Finally, whisk in the chopped herbs.

3. Pour the sauce into a small, heatproof bowl and set it in a larger bowl filled with barely lukewarm water. Do not heat the sauce or it will separate. If it does separate, it will still taste good, but it will not be as creamy. Hold the sauce at room temperature until ready to use.

The Clift hotel as it looked in the 1920s.

ABOUT GRAPES

Grapes have been cultivated for at least six thousand years. We have scientific evidence to support that fact from Bronze Age settlements that are being excavated in Switzerland. The ancient Greeks were big-deal grape growers, and so were the farmers of the ancient Roman Empire.

Grapes are commercially grown for three uses: to make raisins, to make wine, and to be eaten fresh as table grapes. California produces 97 percent of the table grapes eaten in the United States, and they are grown on vines that are actually direct descendants of the vines that were grown during the Bronze Age. It's nice to have a family history.

Since 1972, grape consumption has increased faster than that of any other fresh fruit. They are a good source of vitamins A, B complex, and C. They are also low in sodium and low in calories. A cup of grapes only contains about 100 calories.

GRILLED SALMON STEAKS WITH MUSTARD AND DILL SAUCE

JASPER PARK LODGE, ALBERTA, CANADA

MAKES 4 SERVINGS

4 salmon steaks, about
   1 inch thick
½ cup sugar
½ cup salt
½ cup minced fresh dill
Freshly ground black
   pepper

FOR THE SAUCE:
1 cup Dijon-style mustard
½ cup honey
2 tablespoons minced fresh
   dill
1 teaspoon vegetable oil

A traditional method of preparing salmon in Scandinavia is to make gravlax. The fish marinates for a few days in a mixture of salt, sugar, and dill, at which point it is thinly sliced and served with a mustard and dill sauce. Jeff O'Neill at the Jasper Park Lodge starts this recipe by marinating the salmon, but instead of stopping at the gravlax stage, he continues by grilling the fish, and ending up with double the flavor.

1. Place the salmon steaks into a glass or ceramic dish that will hold all of them, close together, in one layer. Put a tablespoon of sugar, salt, and dill on top of each of the salmon steaks and press the mixture into the salmon meat. Grind a little fresh pepper onto each steak. Then turn the steaks over and repeat the sugaring, salting, dilling, and peppering process. Cover the dish with plastic wrap and place it into the refrigerator for 24 hours.

2. To make the sauce: Whisk all of the ingredients together in a bowl. The sauce can also be made 24 hours ahead and held in a covered container in the refrigerator.

3. Ready your outdoor or indoor grill for cooking, or preheat your oven broiler. Remove the salmon steaks from the marinade and grill them for 4 or 5 minutes on each side, or until they reach the degree of doneness that you like.

4. Serve with the mustard and dill sauce.

SUGGESTED MENU:

Grilled Salmon Steaks with Mustard and Dill Sauce
Red Cabbage with Apples and Caraway (page 179)
Yellow Squash with Tarragon (page 192)
Chocolate Crème Brûlée (page 249)

✳

JASPER PARK LODGE

In 1922, Jasper offered a place to "eat and sleep," but things were getting a bit elegant. The Jasper Park Lodge had been built. For three dollars a day you could sleep in a log cabin and eat in the main lodge. You could dance in the ballroom or sit out on the verandah. Or you just might end up playing golf alongside superstars like Bing Crosby and Smokey the Bear. Today, the Jasper Park Lodge is a great resort that sits on over a thousand acres of majestic wilderness. The cabins look as rustic as ever on the outside, but the insides have the most up-to-date facilities.

The golf course was designed by Stanley Thompson, who had the fascinating idea of lining up the holes with the local mountain peaks. The natural, if somewhat unique, hazards on the course include elk, geese, and deer, and from time to time, a bear who appears to collect golf balls. There are facilities for canoeing; tennis; horseback riding; biking; and in the winter, ice-skating, downhill and cross-country skiing, snowshoeing, and riding around town in a horse-drawn sleigh.

SALMON POACHED IN RED WINE SAUCE

THE CLIFT, SAN FRANCISCO, CALIFORNIA

MAKES 4 SERVINGS

$^{1}/_{2}$ cup fresh or frozen corn
    kernels
1 cup fresh or frozen baby
    lima beans
1 bottle Cabernet
    Sauvignon or other red
    wine
4 salmon fillets (about 3
    ounces each)
3 tablespoons butter
1 cup sliced mushrooms
1 cup sliced scallion greens
    in 1-inch pieces
$^{1}/_{2}$ teaspoon salt

The farmlands of California produce some of the finest food products in the world, which is one of the reasons that the restaurant chefs of California have become famous for the high quality of their cooking.

One of my favorite good cooks in California is Chef Martin Frost. I first met Martin when he was working at the Four Seasons in Toronto. These days he is the executive chef at the San Francisco Clift. The following is his recipe, which combines a number of local ingredients—salmon, red wine, and baby lima beans.

1. Cook the corn and the lima beans and set aside.

2. In a large, deep sauté pan, heat the wine to a simmer. Add the fish to the simmering wine and cook for 12 minutes.

3. While the fish is cooking, in a large sauté pan, heat 1 tablespoon of the butter. Add the mushrooms, cooked corn kernels, and baby lima beans. Add the scallions and the salt. Heat thoroughly.

4. Remove $^{1}/_{3}$ cup of the wine from the pan where the fish is poaching and place it in another saucepan, over medium heat. Whisk in the remaining 2 tablespoons of butter.

5. Divide the vegetables among 4 dinner plates. Slice the salmon fillets in half and arrange them on top of the vegetables. Spoon some of the sauce onto each plate.

SUGGESTED MENU:

Salmon Poached in Red Wine Sauce
Herbed Wild Rice (page 159)
Angel Food Cake with Mixed Berry Compote (page 270)

✳

SALMON FARMING IN CHILE

One of the key points in the history of food was the shift from hunting and gathering to agriculture and the domestication and breeding of animals. It appears to have taken place between seven and ten thousand years ago and set the stage for the worldwide population increase that has taken place since then. One of the most obvious advantages of breeding animals is that your food supply is a lot more dependable.

When it comes to meat and poultry, we are all very much aware of the farming techniques—but the idea of a fish farm strikes many people as a new innovation, and that is not the case. The Chinese have had fish farms for over four thousand years, and there are paintings in the ancient tombs of Egypt that show fish farms in action over two thousand years ago.

The southern part of Chile has a coastline with the Pacific Ocean that is made up of Antarctic water coming from the bottom of the planet and glacial runoff from the ice in the Andes mountains, all of which is crisp, cold, and free from the pollution of industrialized shores. It is the perfect environment for raising salmon. So perfect, that Chile has become the second most important salmon exporting nation in the world. They produce coho and king and salmon trout. A little over half the export harvest goes to Japan. A third goes to North America, and the rest to Europe.

Chilean Sea Bass with Black Beans

TERMAS DE CAUQUENES, CHILE

MAKES 4 SERVINGS

2 tablespoons vegetable oil
2 pounds skinless, boneless
 sea bass fillets, cut into 4
 equal servings
Salt and freshly ground
 black pepper
1 cup flour, spread out on a
 plate
Juice of 1 lime
1 tablespoon butter
1 cup small cubes zucchini
1/2 each yellow, green, and
 red bell pepper, cored
 and sliced into thin
 strips
1 cup chopped tomatoes
 with their juices
2 cups cooked black beans
2 ounces fresh lemon juice
3 drops Tabasco sauce

1. Preheat the oven to 375° F.

2. In an ovenproof sauté pan over medium heat, heat the oil. Season the fish with salt and pepper. Dip one side of the fish fillets into the flour to give that side a light coating. Place the fish into the hot oil, floured side down. Pour the lime juice on the fish. Cook the fish for 2 minutes. Place the pan into the oven and cook for 5 minutes.

3. In a sauté pan over medium heat, melt the butter. Add the vegetables and simmer for 10 minutes.

4. Pour the beans into a blender or food processor. Add the lemon juice and the Tabasco and process to a puree. Pour the pureed beans into a saucepan and heat.

5. Divide the pureed beans onto 4 serving plates, covering the surface of the plate. Cut each portion of the fish in half and place the 2 halves next to each other on the plate. Allow a little of the bean sauce to show between the 2 pieces. Place the vegetables at the base of the fillets with some of the mixture running between the fillets.

SUGGESTED MENU:

Chilean Sea Bass with Black Beans
Tomato Rice Salad with Avocado and Corn (page 210)
Orange-Glazed Pumpkin Cake (page 282)

SNAPPER WITH LIME AND CILANTRO

COSTA LINDA BEACH RESORT, ARUBA

1. Place the bacon into a frying pan that has a cover and cook until done.

2. While the bacon is cooking, salt and pepper the snapper fillets. Pour the lime juice onto both sides of the fish and then dip the fish into the cornmeal, giving both sides a light coating.

3. When the bacon is cooked, remove it from the pan and break the strips up into small pieces. Place the fish fillets into the pan, skin side up, and cook them in the drippings from the bacon, 3 minutes on each side. Make sure that the skin is cooked until very crispy. Then remove the fish from the pan and hold it aside.

4. Into the same pan, add the garlic and vegetables and sauté for 3 minutes. Then add in the olives, capers, and cilantro and cook for 2 minutes more. Return the bacon to the pan. Add the white wine and cook for 1 minute. Place the fish on top of the vegetables. Cover the pan and cook for 2 minutes.

5. Place the vegetables and sauce onto a serving plate. Put the fish fillets on top, skin side down, and garnish with the lemon slices and sprigs of cilantro.

SUGGESTED MENU:

Snapper with Lime and Cilantro
Warm Lentil Salad (page 203)
Curried Potatoes and Vegetables (page 147)
Flan (page 252)

MAKES 4 SERVINGS

2 ounces bacon (about 3 strips)
4 red snapper fillets with skin on one side
Salt and freshly ground black pepper
Juice of 1 lime
1 cup cornmeal
2 cloves garlic, minced
1 large onion, chopped
1 green bell pepper, chopped
1 red bell pepper, chopped
1 scallion, sliced into $\frac{1}{2}$-inch strips
1 green (or red) tomato, chopped
$\frac{1}{2}$ cup chopped stuffed olives
2 tablespoons capers
2 tablespoons chopped fresh cilantro
$\frac{1}{2}$ cup white wine
Sliced lemon and fresh cilantro sprigs for garnish

CHARLIE'S BAR, ARUBA

In 1938, Charles Brouns moved to Aruba from his native Holland and took up the trade of tending bar. After a few years, he was able to open his own place. Being a straightforward and direct fellow, he called the establishment Charlie's Bar. It gets directly to the point, doesn't it? No confusion. It's not like trying to figure out what you're doing in Friday's if it's Monday. Or if Bennigan's is selling fries or ferns. When you're there, you are in a bar, and it's Charlie's. And because of its unusual history, Charlie's Bar has become somewhat of a national treasure.

Charlie's is at the gate of what was one of the most important oil refineries during the Second World War. German subs would attack the area and at the end of each attack everyone would go to Charlie's to make sure that everyone else was still alive and to celebrate the point with a few drinks. Those meetings made Charlie a regular part of the support and morale-building efforts that were directed to Allied seamen, and his activities actually earned him a Knighthood which was awarded by the Royal House of Holland.

Charlie's Bar has become a landmark on the island of Aruba and appears to be an essential spot to visit for all tourists.

SWORDFISH WITH FENNEL AND SAFFRON

ITALY

1. In a small nonreactive bowl, combine the garlic, citrus juices, saffron, fennel seeds, and salt and pepper. Whisk in the olive oil to make an emulsified sauce. Add the scallions.

2. Cut four 12-inch-square pieces of foil. Lay the foil out on a work space and divide the fennel evenly on the foil pieces. Dip each swordfish steak into the marinade to coat thoroughly, and place the steaks on top of the fennel. Wrap each swordfish steak individually into a package. Refrigerate for 1 or 2 hours to marinate.

3. To cook, set up a steamer so the packages lay flat on 1 or 2 shelves. Bring the water to a boil. Lay the swordfish packages in the steamer and steam, covered, for 10 to 12 minutes. Unwrap the swordfish and serve with the collected juices.

SUGGESTED MENU:

Spaghetti with Olives and Capers (page 134)
Swordfish with Fennel and Saffron
Ricotta Cheesecake (page 260)

MAKES 4 SERVINGS

3 cloves garlic, minced
1/4 cup fresh orange juice
1/4 cup lemon juice
1 generous pinch of
    saffron, crumbled
1 teaspoon fennel seeds,
    cracked
3/4 teaspoon salt
1/4 teaspoon freshly ground
    black pepper
1/3 cup olive oil
1 scallion, white and green
    parts, thinly sliced
1 fennel bulb, sliced into
    thin pieces
4 swordfish steaks
    (6 ounces each)

Trout with Pancetta and Rosemary

ITALY

MAKES 4 SERVINGS

4 whole trout
   (³/₄ to 1 pound each)
1¹/₂ tablespoons minced
   fresh rosemary, or
   ¹/₂ teaspoon dried
³/₄ teaspoon salt
³/₄ teaspoon freshly ground
   black pepper
¹/₄ pound pancetta
1 to 2 teaspoons olive oil
1 cup minced onion
1 clove garlic, minced
¹/₃ cup balsamic vinegar
1¹/₃ cups low-sodium
   chicken broth

1. Place the trout on a work space and open up the cavity of the fish, sprinkle in half the rosemary, season with ¹/₂ teaspoon of salt, and half the pepper. Then with the round pieces of pancetta, wrap each trout. Use 2 to 3 pieces along the top of the fish and 1 piece to seal the belly. Gently press the pancetta onto the fish. The fish should only be partially covered by the pancetta. Do not be concerned if the pancetta doesn't cover the whole fish, it will secure itself to the fish as it cooks.

2. Heat a large skillet that will accommodate all the fish in one layer or use 2 skillets. Add the olive oil to the pan. Place the fish in the pan and cook over moderate heat for 4 to 6 minutes per side, until the pancetta is crisp and brown and the fish is cooked. Remove from the pan and hold on a warm platter while you make the sauce.

3. Add the onion, garlic, and remaining rosemary to the pan and cook for 1 minute. Add the vinegar to the pan and scrape up any browned bits off the bottom of the pan with a wooden spoon. Cook over high heat and reduce the vinegar to a glaze. Add the chicken broth and reduce to thicken slightly. Season to taste with the remaining salt and pepper. Spoon the sauce over the fish and serve.

SUGGESTED MENU:

Spinach Rolls (page 190)
Trout with Pancetta and Rosemary
Tiramisu (page 247)

FISH SAMBAL WITH RICE

MARINA MANDARIN HOTEL, SINGAPORE

1. To prepare the sauce: In a sauté pan over medium heat, heat the oil. Add the shallots and cook for 2 minutes. Add the garlic and cook for 1 minute longer. Stir in the chili paste or sambal and ketchup and cook for another minute. Add the sugar, salt, and water and continue cooking for 1 minute. Remove from the heat and set aside.

2. To prepare the chutney: In a bowl, combine the mango, apple, and chili peppers. Stir in the sugar, salt, lime juice, vinegar, and chives and set aside.

3. To prepare the fish: Place each fillet on a piece of aluminum. The foil should be large enough to form a sealed packet around the fish. Spread the sauce on the top side of the fillet. Fold the aluminum foil over the fish and crimp the edges to seal. In a sauté pan (you may need more than one pan) over medium heat, heat the oil. Place the aluminum foil packet, sauce side up, in the pan. Cook the fish in the packet for 3 to 5 minutes per side, depending on the thickness of the fish.

4. To serve: Unwrap the packets and transfer the fillets to dinner plates. Top each fillet with a little chutney and garnish with the chives. Serve with white rice.

SUGGESTED MENU:

Fish Sambal with Rice
Curried Carrots in Yogurt (page 197)

MAKES 4 SERVINGS

FOR THE SAUCE:
3 tablespoons vegetable oil
2 shallots, minced
2 cloves garlic, minced
2 teaspoons chili paste or sambal oelek
6 tablespoons ketchup
2 tablespoons sugar
$1/2$ teaspoon salt
2 tablespoons water

FOR THE CHUTNEY:
1 ripe mango, peeled and cubed
1 small apple, peeled and cubed
2 bird's eye or serrano chilis, seeded and chopped
2 tablespoons sugar
$1/4$ teaspoon salt
1 tablespoon fresh lime juice
1 teaspoon balsamic or wine vinegar
1 tablespoon chopped fresh chives

FOR THE FISH:
$1 1/2$ pounds red snapper or other white fish fillets
2 tablespoons peanut oil
8 whole chives as a garnish
Cooked white rice

TOMATO-CRUSTED FISH WITH MANGO SAUCE

ROYAL VIKING SUN

MAKES 4 SERVINGS

6 tablespoons vegetable oil

1 cup roughly chopped onion

4 tomatoes, roughly chopped

1 cup sliced mushrooms

1/4 cup chopped fresh parsley

6 tablespoons unsalted butter, at room temperature

1/4 cup fine, dried bread crumbs

1/3 cup grated Gruyère cheese

1 tablespoon chopped fresh thyme leaves

2 tablespoons chopped fresh chives

4 firm white fish fillets, such as scrod (about 6 ounces each)

1 tablespoon chopped fresh basil leaves

1 recipe Mango Sauce (recipe follows)

1. Preheat the oven to 375° F. Generously butter a medium-sized baking dish or casserole.

2. In a medium skillet over medium-high heat, heat 2 tablespoons of the vegetable oil. Add half of the onions and sauté until translucent, 4 to 6 minutes.

3. Add half of the chopped tomatoes, all of the mushrooms, and half of the chopped parsley to the onions. Cook, stirring frequently, for 5 minutes. Set aside.

4. In a bowl, cream together the butter, bread crumbs, Gruyère, thyme, and chives. Spoon the mixture into a pastry bag fitted with a plain, wide tip and set aside.

5. In a large skillet over medium-high heat, heat 2 tablespoons of the vegetable oil. Add the fish fillets and sauté for 2 minutes on each side. Arrange the fish fillets over the bottom of the prepared baking dish. Top each fillet with a quarter of the tomato/onion/mushroom sauce. Pipe the butter/bread crumb mixture evenly over the sauce. Bake the fish for 15 to 20 minutes, or until the topping has a light crust.

6. Meanwhile, in a large skillet over medium-high heat, heat the remaining 2 tablespoons of vegetable oil. Sauté together the remaining onions and tomatoes with the basil and the remaining chopped parsley. Cook until the onions are translucent, 5 to 7 minutes.

7. Remove the fish fillets from the oven and transfer to a serving dish. Top with the tomato basil sauce and serve with the mango sauce.

SUGGESTED MENU:

Chick-Pea and Sesame Dip (page 214)
Tomato-Crusted Fish with Mango Sauce
Praline Sauce for Ice Cream (page 254)

Mango Sauce

MAKES 4 SERVINGS

$^1/_2$ cup chopped mango
$^1/_2$ cup chopped tomato
$^1/_2$ cup minced scallions
Salt and freshly ground
    black pepper
2 tablespoons olive oil
2 tablespoons rice wine
    vinegar

In a bowl, combine the mango, tomato, scallions, salt, and pepper. Stir in the olive oil and vinegar.

ABOUT RICE WINE VINEGAR

Rice wine vinegar is as tangy as regular vinegar, only it is made from rice wine rather than apple cider or grape wine. Rice wine, also known as sake in Japan, is a popular drink in Asian countries where rice is the main grain.

Rice wine vinegar is preferred in Asian dishes because of its unique flavor. Substitute a light cider vinegar if absolutely necessary, but avoid wine vinegars for recipes that call for rice wine vinegar.

THE STORY OF THE OCEAN LINER

The great ocean liner is the largest moving object on our planet. The old *Queen Mary* was almost as long as the Empire State Building is tall. Ocean liners are an amazing display of artistic and technological skills.

The first ship that could really be called an ocean liner was named *The City of New York,* and it was launched in 1893. The hull was made of steel instead of wood, and complex steam engines provided the power instead of sails. These turn-of-the-century ships had many of the comforts that we now associate with modern ocean liners: large public rooms for entertaining, electric power, elevators, and excellent food.

In 1907, the *Mauritania* came on line and set a new standard of luxury. The objective of the companies that built these ships was to create an environment of great opulence, to make the passenger feel that he or she was in the most elegant surroundings. They also did everything possible to keep their guests from remembering that they were on a ship.

One of the most important technical achievements was the oil-burning turbine engine. As coal was used up under the old system, the ship got lighter and lighter as it steamed along. By the time it reached port it was bouncing around like a cork. The oil-powered ships, however, would take in water to replace the burned oil. Taking on the sea water to replace the oil had the effect of weighing the ship down and that gave the passengers a much smoother ride.

By the early twenties, exercise had become an important part of the ships' services. There was a Promenade Deck for long walks, a swimming pool, a fully equipped gym. Some ships had squash courts, steam baths, and saunas. One vessel actually had tennis courts, and the game of miniature golf was invented for ocean liners.

During the 1930s, the Italian Line introduced the Lido Deck, an outdoor sports area with a swimming pool. The Italian ships used the southern route to cross the Atlantic and could take advantage of the warm weather.

But of all the comforts offered to the passengers of the ocean liner, the most important were those that dealt with eating and drinking. Food has always had the ability to be more than just physical nourishment. Food can be a symbol for wealth, a source of emotional comfort, a vehicle for reducing fear, and a distraction and an entertainment. The ocean liners used food and drink for all of the above.

The first liners had dining rooms with long tables and swivel chairs that were bolted to the floor. By the early 1920s, there were sumptuous dining saloons with free-standing chairs and extraordinary staircases that gave guests the opportunity to make a grand entrance. *(cont. over)*

The Hamburg-American Line even went so far as to reproduce London's chic Ritz-Carlton Hotel restaurant right on board one of their ships. Cunard introduced the Verandah Cafe, designed to look like the front porch of a great hotel. It was located at the rear of the ship and had potted palms and wicker furniture. And, almost anything that a guest might want to eat or drink was stocked onboard.

By the 1950s, however, airlines were taking over the passenger traffic and it looked like the great liners were going to become extinct—man-made dinosaurs of the sea. But once again love conquered all. In this case the love came in the form of a television show called "The Love Boat," which gave hundreds of millions of people a picture of how nice life could be aboard a cruise. Along with "The Love Boat" came a change in the way people wanted to spend their leisure time. There was an ever-growing number of folks who had the time and the money to spend a few weeks at a more relaxed pace. The ocean liner was transformed into the floating resort.

Walking through the mountains in Torres del Paine National Park in southern Chile.

CRAB CAKES WITH RED PEPPER SAUCE

CHILE

1. Preheat the oven to 375° F.

2. **To prepare the sauce:** Place the pepper on a baking sheet and bake for 25 minutes, turning every 5 minutes until the skin is browned. Remove the pepper from the oven and put it immediately into a paper or plastic bag, closing it tightly. When the pepper is cool enough to touch, take it out of the bag and peel off the skin. Discard the stem and the seeds. Cut the pepper into large chunks and place them into a blender or food processor. Add 2 tablespoons of the oil and puree until smooth. Add the remaining oil, vinegar, garlic, shallots, and salt to the blender. Process until well blended. Set the dressing aside.

3. **To prepare the crab cakes:** In a bowl, combine the crabmeat and cracker crumbs. Stir in the egg, mayonnaise, salt, parsley, and cayenne pepper. Form the mixture into 6 cakes, about 3 inches in diameter and about 1 inch thick.

4. In a large nonstick sauté pan over medium heat, heat the oil. Add the crab cakes and cook for 5 minutes per side, or until lightly browned.

5. Place a little of the sauce on a dinner plate and top with the crab cakes. Serve any extra sauce on the side.

SUGGESTED MENU:

Chilean Beef Soup (page 4)
Crab Cakes with Red Pepper Sauce
Corn Cheese Biscuits (page 219)
Broiled Pineapple with Rum Sauce (page 231)

MAKES 6 SERVINGS

FOR THE SAUCE:
1 large red bell pepper
1/2 cup olive oil
2 tablespoons red wine
   vinegar
1 clove garlic, minced
1 shallot, minced
1/4 teaspoon salt

FOR THE CRAB CAKES:
1 pound lump crabmeat,
   cleaned
1/4 cup cracker crumbs
1 egg, lightly beaten
2 tablespoons low-fat
   mayonnaise
1/2 teaspoon salt
1 tablespoon chopped
   fresh parsley
1/2 teaspoon cayenne
   pepper
2 tablespoons vegetable oil

ABOUT VALDIVIA

Valdivia is a classic example of the southern towns of Chile. It was founded by the Spanish explorer Pedro de Valdivia. Valdivia was an extraordinary man. He came to Chile from the north, passing through a desert on horseback—a desert that is difficult to cross today even with the most advanced technology. On one side of his horse he carried a wooden statue of the Blessed Virgin, on the other his beautiful mistress Inez de Suarez. Like so many of us, he was trying to balance his love of the pleasures offered in this world, with his hope for salvation in the next.

Valdivia arrived during the summer of 1552, which is only fitting since the town has become a well-known summer resort. The main reason, however, that he was interested in the area was the same reason that the native tribes had been interested in the area for thousands of years before Valdivia showed up.

The spot is at the crossroads of nine different rivers, sheltered from the open sea, and only a few miles upriver from the ocean. It is a perfect port town. The same kind of ideal situation in relation to the sea that worked for London and New York.

A BRIEF HISTORY OF ARUBA

The first people to settle down in Aruba were members of the Arawak tribes, who came over from the north coast of South America. It wasn't a very big trip. It's only about fifteen miles from the shores of Venezuela to the shores of Aruba. As a matter of fact, a few years ago a couple of Arubans made the point by swimming up and back between the two countries. The Arawaks, however, came here about five thousand years ago and they came because the fishing was good. It still is.

The Spanish stopped by in 1500, but they didn't see any gold, so they just moved on. Then about twenty-five years later they moved back and turned Aruba into one big ranch for raising cattle and breeding horses. You know, when you're out conquistadoring there are two things you really enjoy: a good horse and a steak. The Spanish maps of the time show Aruba as if it had a road sign that read "ENTERING THE NEW WORLD. EAT HERE, BUY GAS."

In 1636, the Dutch popped in with just the right number of soldiers to convince the local population that it was time to go Dutch. And since then Aruba has been part of the Kingdom of The Netherlands.

CURRIED SHRIMP

PAPIAMENTO RESTAURANT, ARUBA

1. In a large sauté pan over medium heat, heat the oil. Add the onion, red pepper, and green pepper and sauté for 2 minutes.

2. Add the ginger and sauté for 2 minutes. Add the shrimp and cook for 3 to 5 minutes, constantly stirring and turning the shrimp. Add the celery leaves and the curry powder, and cook, stirring, for 2 minutes. Add the salt and pepper to taste. Add the cream and cook for 2 minutes, or until the cream is thick enough to coat the back of a spoon.

SUGGESTED MENU:

Curried Shrimp
Snow Peas and Carrots with Mint (page 188)
Island White Rice with Lime (page 161)
Rum Cake (page 283)

MAKES 4 SERVINGS

2 tablespoons olive oil
1 cup chopped onion
1½ cups red bell pepper,
  cut into bite-sized pieces
1½ cups green bell
  pepper, cut into
  bite-sized pieces
¼ cup sliced fresh ginger
16 jumbo shrimp, cleaned
  and shelled
¼ cup celery leaves
3 tablespoons curry
  powder
Salt and freshly ground
  black pepper
1 cup cream

Oranjestad town square.

STIR-FRIED SHRIMP WITH WALNUTS

MARINA MANDARIN HOTEL, SINGAPORE

MAKES 4 SERVINGS

1½ teaspoons cornstarch
1 teaspoon water
1 egg white
1 pound shelled and
    deveined medium shrimp
3 tablespoons peanut oil
1 green bell pepper, cored,
    seeded, and diced
1 stalk celery, diced
⅔ cup chicken broth
1 tablespoon sherry
1 tablespoon soy sauce
1 teaspoon sesame oil
1 cup sliced straw or other
    mushrooms
1 cup whole walnuts

1. In a bowl, combine the cornstarch and water. Stir in the egg white. Add the shrimp, tossing to coat. Let the shrimp sit in the mixture for about 30 minutes.

2. Drain the shrimp from the egg white mixture. In a wok or sauté pan over high heat, heat the oil. Add the bell pepper and celery and stir-fry for 2 minutes. Then add the chicken broth. Add the shrimp and stir-fry until the shrimp are pink, about 2 minutes. Add the remaining ingredients. Stir-fry for 1 minute more.

SUGGESTED MENU:

Stir-fried Shrimp with Walnuts
Bacon Fried Rice (page 163)

Dried chilies in Singapore's
Indian Market.

SINGAPORE TODAY

Singapore is a major Asian city. Its downtown business district is as modern and up to date as any city in the world. Almost the entire population of Singapore lives on one island, which has a limiting effect on expansion, but only in the horizontal plane. Vertically the sky's the limit. For thousands of years the major economic activity of Singapore has been trade. Giant buildings house the corporate offices of the major companies that manage much of the world's oil business. Because Singapore is in the middle of the most important shipping routes of Asia, it has become one of the busiest ports in the world. Each year more than one hundred thousand ships pass through the facilities at the Singapore yards.

Singapore is also an outstanding financial center. Its banks handle hundreds of billions of dollars in international transactions. But if you are not interested in making money, that's okay; Singapore will help you spend it. Orchard Road has an impressive shopping area: mile after mile of stores, representing designers and manufacturers from all over Europe, Asia, and the Americas.

Clearly business is important, and so is shopping, but neither may be *the* single great compulsion for a Singaporean. The consuming passion in this town is the consuming of good food. No matter who you are talking to, within a few minutes the subject will come around to food. Singapore has some twenty-five thousand places to eat and a population that is slightly over 2½ million. Lots of competition and lots of great food.

One of the many palm trees of Singapore.

Shrimp Sambal with Rice

VIOLET OON, SINGAPORE

MAKES 4 SERVINGS

FOR THE CHILI SAUCE:
3 tablespoons vegetable oil
2 shallots, sliced
1 clove garlic, sliced
¼ cup macadamia nuts
1 tablespoon chili paste or
    sambal oelek
4 tablespoons ketchup

2 tablespoons peanut oil
1 pound shelled and
    deveined medium
    shrimp
1 tablespoon tamarind
    juice or rice wine
    vinegar
¼ cup water
¼ cup sugar
½ teaspoon salt
2 tablespoons fresh
    lime juice
4 servings white rice,
    cooked according to
    package directions

1. To make the chili sauce: In a food processor, combine the vegetable oil, shallots, garlic, and macadamia nuts and process until smooth. Add the chili paste or sambal and ketchup and process until blended.

2. In a wok or sauté pan over high heat, heat the peanut oil. Add the chili sauce and cook until the aroma of the paste is very strong, about 2 minutes. Add the shrimp and stir-fry briefly, just until pink. Add the tamarind juice, water, sugar, and salt and continue stir-frying for 1 minute. Remove from the heat and squeeze the lime juice on top.

3. Serve with the rice.

SUGGESTED MENU:

Chicken Satay (page 82)
Shrimp Sambal with Rice

SINGAPORE

The nation of Singapore sits on a group of islands at the tip of the Malay Peninsula. Just north of it is Malaysia and just above that is Thailand. Below it is the Strait of Singapore, and it is the key to the country's history.

About five thousand years ago, a commercial trading business began to develop between India and China. The Malay Peninsula was at the perfect midpoint of the trade route. Ships from southern India came into the area to deal in pepper, cinnamon, and ginger. The Chinese sailed down the coast to do a few deals and eventually the Arabs joined in. The area became a center of commerce. Actually, "center of commerce" is not a truly descriptive phrase. "Point for piracy" is more accurate. The Strait of Singapore is very narrow, and as the trading ships passed through, the local pirates came out to do what pirates do.

But all that changed in 1819. The British and the Dutch had been jockeying for position in the area. The British were thinking about moving out of the neighborhood and leaving it for the Dutch, if the Dutch would give them a nice bit of property in India that the English had been coveting for a while. Sir Thomas Stamford Bingley Raffles was the English lieutenant-governor of Java and he hated the idea.

Raffles invited the exiled oldest son of the Sultan of Johor to return to Singapore. Raffles then declared the son the rightful heir to the throne of the recently deceased Sultan—a proclamation that Raffles made over the claim of the Prince's younger brother, who had already taken a seat on the royal seat. Then Raffles signed a deal with his new Sultan to set up a British trading post. Three thousand Spanish dollars a year went to the Sultan and five thousand dollars to his local chief.

Raffles had been able to obtain an important site for British trade in the area, and now he drew up a plan for the development of his new town. It was divided into areas for each of the major immigrant groups, and its commercial strength was to rest on the town's location as a port. His plan has set the basis for the history of Singapore during the past two centuries.

CHICKEN

Barbecued Chicken with Papaya Salsa and Corn Pancakes

COSTA LINDA BEACH RESORT, ARUBA

MAKES 4 SERVINGS

FOR THE STUFFING:
1 clove garlic, minced
1/2 cup chopped scallions
1 tablespoon minced hot
   chili pepper
1/4 cup toasted sesame
   seeds
Salt and freshly ground
   black pepper
2 tablespoons sesame oil

4 boneless half chicken
   breasts, skin on

FOR THE BARBECUE
SAUCE:
1 cup tomato ketchup
1/4 cup dry mustard

FOR THE PAPAYA
RELISH:
1 cup papaya, cut into
   1-inch cubes
1 red onion, minced
1/2 teaspoon minced hot
   chili pepper
(cont. on next page)

1. Preheat the oven to 400° F. or prepare a grill.

2. **To make the stuffing:** In a mixing bowl, combine all of the ingredients into a paste. Stuff the mixture between the skin and the meat of the chicken breast.

3. **To make the sauce:** Combine the ingredients in a bowl and coat the chicken on all sides. Bake the chicken in the oven for 20 minutes, or on the grill, until fully cooked. The skin should be crispy.

4. **To make the relish:** While the chicken is cooking, combine all of the ingredients in a mixing bowl and hold aside.

5. **To make the pancakes:** In a mixing bowl, combine all of the ingredients except the corn oil. Heat the corn oil in a nonstick frying pan. Pour 1/2 cup of the pancake batter into the center of the pan and spread it out to a diameter of about 6 inches. As soon as the surface of the pancake looks dry, turn the pancake over and cook it for an additional 2 minutes. Use this technique to make 4 pancakes.

6. To serve, place 1 pancake on each of 4 plates. Place a chicken breast onto half of the pancake and fold the other half of the pancake over the chicken to make a sandwich. Serve the papaya relish on the side.

SUGGESTED MENU:

**Barbecued Chicken with Papaya Salsa and Corn Pancakes
Mixed Vegetable Salad with Peanut Dressing (page 211)
Lemon Tart (page 297)**

ABOUT ALOE VERA

During the middle of the 1800s, the farmers of Aruba began to produce aloe plants on a commercial scale. Aloe, also called aloe vera, was brought to the Caribbean by traders from the Mediterranean. By the early years of this century, Aruba was a major producer of aloe and famous for supplying the best quality in the world.

What makes the aloe plant interesting is the ability of the plant's juice to heal and protect our skin. The fresh sap from the plant can help heal small cuts and scrapes. It also seems to have a remarkable ability to heal burns. Cosmetic companies use it in hand and face creams, suntan lotions, and shampoos. During the 1950s, scientists discovered that aloe helped heal burns from radiation and there was a story going around that the U.S. Defense Department was stocking up on aloe as part of its nuclear program.

Aloe's fame goes back a long way. It's mentioned in the Bible, and the word among Egyptologists is that Cleopatra used it in her own beauty creams. I keep an aloe plant in my kitchen. Whenever I get a burn I submerge the burned area in cold water to take the heat away, then I break off a little of one of the plant's leaves and rub some of the sap on the burn.

2 tablespoons minced fresh
   cilantro
Salt and freshly ground
   black pepper
1 tablespoon white vinegar
2 tablespoons olive oil

FOR THE PANCAKES:
1 egg
½ cup milk
½ cup pureed frozen or
   canned corn
½ cup flour
½ cup cornmeal
1 teaspoon sugar
½ teaspoon baking
   powder
½ red bell pepper, minced
2 tablespoons corn oil

ROAST CHICKEN WITH GARLIC, GINGER, AND THYME

CHILE

MAKES 4 SERVINGS

FOR THE MARINADE:
2 tablespoons fresh lemon
    juice
2 tablespoons vegetable oil
2 tablespoons low-sodium
    soy sauce
1 tablespoon Dijon-style
    mustard
1½ teaspoons chopped
    fresh thyme, or ½
    teaspoon dried
1 tablespoon minced fresh
    ginger
1 clove garlic, minced
Pinch of white pepper

1 fryer chicken (3½ to 4
    pounds), cleaned and
    patted dry

1. To make the marinade: In a bowl, combine all the ingredients.

2. Place the chicken in a stainless-steel, glass, or ceramic mixing bowl. Starting with the breast, carefully slip your fingers under the skin to loosen, making sure not to tear it. Put the marinade under the skin and smear any remaining marinade on the outside of the bird. Cover the chicken and marinate for at least 30 minutes in the refrigerator.

3. Preheat the oven to 450° F.

4. Place the chicken, breast side up, on a rack in a roasting pan, then into oven. After 15 minutes of roasting, lower the oven temperature to 350° F. Continue roasting the chicken for 45 minutes to 1 hour, or until the juices run clear when the thigh is pierced with a small knife. Let the chicken rest for 10 minutes before carving.

SUGGESTED MENU:

Chilean Seafood Soup (Paila Marina) (page 5)
Roast Chicken with Garlic, Ginger, and Thyme
Spicy Mashed Potatoes (page 144)
Lima Beans with Lemon (page 184)
Glazed Applesauce Cake (page 273)

TORRES DEL PAINE NATIONAL PARK

The most impressive reason to travel to the Magallanes region of Chile is the Torres del Paine National Park. *Paine* is a native tribal word for "blue," and *torres* means "towers." The particular towers in question are the peaks that stand near the end of the chain of the Andes mountains, and the blue is a reference to the waters of the area's many lakes. The park was originally set up in 1959 and was designated a Biosphere reserve by the United Nations in 1978. Torres del Paine is nature at its most untouched.

Gray glacier pours out of a mountain pass and breaks up into huge blocks of blue ice that float into Lago Grey, and you can walk right up to the edge of the ice. Beautiful waterfalls crop up every few miles, and views of the snow-tipped mountains are everywhere. During the summer months, the fields are filled with wildflowers. Since all this is in the southern hemisphere, the summer months are December, January, and February. The park is also home to a considerable amount of wildlife. Guanacos wander along the roads and seem to be totally unfazed by the arrival of human beings. Andean condors glide above the ridges looking for dinner, and sheep constantly sample the grass.

The thing to do in the park is walk. There are over 150 miles of walking trails and serious walkers who can cover a little over 20 miles a day, complete the entire circuit in about seven days. The rough-and-ready group bring their own backpacks and stay in tents or small shelters that have been set up at key points by the National Park Service. Less rough types stay at one of the five hotels in the park and conduct their walks on a daily basis. They cover the same trails, but they do them one at a time, through the simple technique of being driven to the starting point each morning and back from the end of that day's trail each night.

Huge ice blocks that float out of the Grey Glacier and up to the beach on Lago Grey in Torres del Paine National Park in southern Chile. The ice block in the photograph is over 100 feet high.

HOTEL EXPLORA

The Hotel Explora sits on a cliff next to a waterfall on the Rio Paine, right smack in the center of one of the world's great national parks. Permission to construct the hotel was awarded to the owners after they won an international competition conducted by the Chilean Forest Service. They had to come up with a design that did not conflict with the natural beauty of the environment. From the outside it's a simple white clapboard structure. It looks like it could be the totally functional outpost for an Antarctic expedition.

But once you get inside there is pampering in Patagonia. Directly inside the front door are a series of wooden lockers that are used by the guests to store their outdoor clothing and hiking gear, and the lockers are heated. The public space has an open curving flow that feels like the inside of an elegant private yacht. The construction materials were all selected to go along with the natural feel of the park—local woods, slate, native rock—and everywhere there are windows that face out on the spectacular wilderness. There are only thirty rooms, and each has an interesting view of the surroundings. My room looked out on the Cuernos del Paine, one of the most dramatic peaks in the area.

The hotel's guides speak English, Spanish, French, and German, and will arrange daily trips. You can take a nature walk, do some serious hiking, ride along the horse trails, mountain bike, or you can pick out a really comfortable spot and just take it all in.

CHICKEN WITH MUSTARD SAUCE

HOTEL CERTOSA DI MAGGIANO, SIENA, ITALY

1. Season the pounded chicken breasts with the salt and pepper. In a large sauté pan, heat the olive oil. Sauté the chicken breasts until browned and cooked through. Remove them to a heated platter.

2. Into the same sauté pan, over medium heat, pour in the Cognac and chicken broth. Scrape the pan with a spoon to loosen the drippings. Stir in the mustard and the cream. Heat the sauce for 2 minutes, then strain.

3. Place the chicken breasts on individual dinner plates. Spoon the sauce on top. Garnish with the mustard seeds and chopped tomato, if desired.

SUGGESTED MENU:

Cheese Polenta with Wild Mushrooms (page 186)
Chicken with Mustard Sauce
Pear Tart (page 302)

MAKES 4 SERVINGS

2 boneless skinless chicken
  breasts, split and
  pounded, cut in half
½ teaspoon salt
⅛ teaspoon freshly ground
  black pepper
1 tablespoon olive oil
¼ cup Cognac
¼ cup chicken broth
1 tablespoon Dijon-style
  mustard
3 tablespoons heavy cream
1 teaspoon mustard seeds
  as a garnish
1 plum tomato, chopped,
  as a garnish (optional)

✳

THE FOOD OF TUSCANY

During the past three thousand years, hundreds of different ethnic groups have immigrated to the peninsula that is presently called Italy. Each immigration made some contribution to the cooking of the land, but there were three groups that set the foundations which eventually became what we now call Italian cooking. They were the Greeks, the Saracens, and the Etruscans. The Greeks sailed over from ancient Greece and took control of the south. During the 700s the Saracens came in from the Mideast and added a series of elements on top of the Greek base. The Etruscans came from somewhere in the eastern Mediterranean, they came during the thirteenth century B.C., and they dominated the north. Eventually the center of the area controlled by the Etruscans became known as Tuscany.

Tuscany is the heartland of Italy, the very center of its culture and tradition, both artistically and gastronomically. Michelangelo, Leonardo da Vinci, Botticelli, all came from Tuscany.

The great food writer Waverly Root once pointed out that the heartland of a country, the place where the nation's essence has existed for the longest time, is the place where the people speak the purest form of the national language and where they cook the most robust form of the national diet, and they do their cooking in the simplest way. No fuss, no frills. He gave a few examples: Touraine speaks the purest French and is famous for its roasted meats; Castille speaks the purest Spanish and is famous for its roasted meats. Tuscany also conforms to his theory. The people of Tuscany speak the purest Italian and they are famous for their grilled and roasted beef.

Steak Florentine is a perfect example of the Tuscan style. A thick slice of steak is salted and goes onto the grill. As it reaches the desired point of doneness, a little more salt and some pepper are mixed together with olive oil. The mixing is sometimes done with a sprig of rosemary. The mixture is brushed onto the steak, and that is it. At home, Tuscans love simple food, prepared without complication.

Tuscans have a long history of loving things that are simple but of high quality. They also have a fear and dislike of things that are extravagant and ornate. Tuscany was the center of the Renaissance, a time of great wealth and power, a time when it would have been very easy for the population to develop a devotion to gluttony in all things. But that did not happen, especially when it came to food.

The people of the Tuscan city of Florence actually passed a series of laws regulating the number of people who could be invited to a dinner party and how many courses could be served. Forty was the top number for guests and only three courses were allowed. *(cont. on following page)*

Every time the wealthy started to move toward a more extravagant food style, the government would pass new and more restrictive laws. They were reshaping their food pyramid into an obelisk. There is an old Tuscan saying that expresses the Tuscan dislike of excess: "We were better off when we were worse off."

During the 1500s, many new foods were brought back to Italy from the New World. The first tomatoes to come in were yellow and about the size of a cherry. They were called *pomo d'oro,* which translates as "golden apple." They were considered good to look at but poisonous to eat.

It took over two hundred years for the Italians to turn the tomato into what it is today. And even with all those years, they were still the first Europeans to really consider the tomato as an edible part of their general diet. Different foods had different levels of success in different parts of Italy. The tomato was the star in southern Italy, but not so in the north, especially in the Italian region of Tuscany.

The New World food that had the most influence in Tuscany was the bean. Tuscans have so many bean recipes and eat so many beans that they are sometimes referred to as *mangiafagioli,* the "bean eaters." The name is not meant as a compliment, but I disagree. Once you have tasted the bean dishes of Tuscany, it is an honor to be called a *mangiafagioli,* especially if you know anything about good nutrition.

LEFT
The great cathedral of Siena, Italy.

RIGHT
Tiles in front of the cathedral.

Chicken Rice

SINGAPORE AIRLINES, SINGAPORE

MAKES 4 SERVINGS

FOR THE FLAVORED
OIL:
¼ cup peanut oil
¼ cup sliced red onion
¼ cup sliced fresh ginger
¼ cup sliced garlic

FOR THE DIPPING
SAUCE:
¼ cup chopped fresh
  ginger
4 cloves garlic, minced
1 teaspoon chili paste or
  sambal oelek, or more to
  taste
4 tablespoons ketchup
1 tablespoon sugar
1 teaspoon salt
1 tablespoon rice or wine
  vinegar
1 tablespoon fresh lime
  juice

1. To prepare the flavored oil: In a saucepan over low heat, place the oil, red onion, ginger, and garlic. Heat for 2 minutes. Pour the mixture through a strainer to remove the solid ingredients, then discard the solid ingredients. Set the oil aside.

2. To prepare the dipping sauce: In a blender or food processor, puree the ginger and garlic. Add the chili paste or sambal and ketchup and process again. Then add the sugar, salt, vinegar, and lime juice. Process until blended. Remove the sauce from the blender and set aside.

3. To prepare the chicken: In a deep sauté pan over high heat, bring enough water to a boil to cover the chicken breasts. Lower the heat to a simmer, add the chicken breasts, and simmer until cooked through, about 10 minutes. Place the cooked chicken breasts in ice water to stop the cooking. Remove and pat dry. Slice the chicken breasts crosswise into strips about 1 inch thick.

4. In a bowl, combine the oyster sauce, oil, and cilantro. Reserve the oyster sauce mixture until ready to serve.

5. To prepare the rice: Cook the rice in the chicken broth according to the package directions. When the rice is thoroughly cooked, stir in the flavored oil. Let the rice sit for 5 minutes before serving.

6. To serve: Place the rice and the chicken on dinner plates. Spoon a little of the oyster sauce mixture onto the chicken. Serve the dipping sauce for the chicken on the side. Garnish with the cucumber and tomato slices.

With chicken, rice, and dipping sauce, this is a meal in itself

FOR THE CHICKEN
2 boneless, skinless
  chicken breasts, split
  (4 pieces)
2 tablespoons oyster sauce
1 tablespoon peanut oil
1 tablespoon chopped
  fresh cilantro
1 cup rice
2¼ cups chicken broth to
  cook the rice
Cucumber and tomato
  slices as a garnish

The maintenance center at Singapore Airlines, one of the reasons that the airline is often chosen as one of the world's best.

Chicken with Mushrooms

BANFF SPRINGS HOTEL, ALBERTA, CANADA

MAKES 4 SERVINGS

2 tablespoons vegetable oil
1 pound boneless, skinless
   chicken breasts, cut into
   small strips
2 shallots, chopped, or 2
   tablespoons chopped
   onion
1 cup sliced mushrooms
1/3 cup chopped dried
   porcini or morel
   mushrooms, softened in
   hot water, then drained
1 cup chicken broth
1/4 cup dry white wine or
   vermouth
1/4 teaspoon salt
1/8 teaspoon freshly ground
   black pepper
1/2 cup nonfat sour cream
Chopped fresh parsley for
   garnish

1. In a large sauté pan, heat 1 tablespoon of the oil. Add the chicken, brown on all sides, and cook thoroughly. Remove the chicken from the pan and set aside.

2. In the same pan, heat the remaining tablespoon of oil. Add the shallots and cook for 1 minute. Add the sliced and chopped mushrooms and cook for 3 minutes more. Pour in the chicken broth and the wine or vermouth, then over high heat reduce the liquid to 1 cup. Season the mixture with salt and pepper. Return the chicken to the pan and heat thoroughly. Reduce the temperature to low heat and stir in the sour cream. Serve immediately. Do not boil or the sauce will break. Garnish with chopped parsley.

SUGGESTED MENU:

Chicken with Mushrooms
Swiss Potato Pancake (page 148)
Peas with Dill (page 187)
Carrot Cake (page 278)

ABOUT THE ROCKY MOUNTAINS

The Canadian Rockies are part of an enormous mountain system that runs along the western edge of both North and South America.

Scientists who study the geology of the earth tell us that we are all going about our lives on a group of huge plates that sit on top of the molten center of our planet. About 150 million years ago, the plate on which North America sits began to move to the west. As it did so, it eventually banged up against a pile of rocks that were sitting in its path. As it pushed against the rocks, it *folded* them into the Rocky Mountains. On a somewhat smaller scale, it's what would happen if you took a newspaper, placed it flat on a desk and slowly pushed it against a wall—lots of folds and layering. That is one of the processes that formed the Rockies.

Eventually the pressure caused the rocks to break along the weakest edges. The broken fault blocks began to push upward to form peaks. Add to those forces the effects of millions of years of rain, wind, snow, and ice and you have some idea of the importance of erosion. Erosion is what gives the Rockies their rugged look. In terms of the geological clock, the Canadian Rockies are very young, and their beauty seems to have a rejuvenating effect on visitors.

Old postcard of Canada.

Chicken Satay

SINGAPORE AIRLINES, SINGAPORE

**MAKES 4 MAIN
COURSE SERVINGS
OR 8 APPETIZERS**

FOR THE MARINADE:
1 tablespoon soy sauce
2 tablespoons water
1 tablespoon fresh lime
   juice
2 tablespoons peanut oil
1 tablespoon sugar
1 clove garlic, chopped
2 tablespoons chopped
   fresh ginger
3 stalks lemon grass, thinly
   sliced (optional)
2 shallots, thinly sliced
1 tablespoon ground
   turmeric

2 boneless, skinless
   chicken breasts, cut into
   2- × 1-inch strips

1. **To prepare the marinade:** In a bowl, combine all the ingredients.

2. Place the chicken in the marinade, tossing to coat. Cover the bowl and refrigerate for 3 hours or longer, turning the chicken in the marinade every hour.

3. **To prepare the peanut sauce:** In a saucepan, combine the peanut butter, ginger, shallots, garlic, and chili paste or sambal. Stir in the chicken broth, sugar, and salt. Over medium heat, bring the mixture to a boil and boil for 3 minutes. Remove the sauce from the heat. Transfer the sauce to a serving bowl and let it cool to room temperature before serving. Preheat the broiler or grill.

4. Remove the chicken from the marinade and gently pat it dry with paper towels. Thread the chicken onto 8-inch bamboo or metal skewers. Broil the meat 4 inches from the flame for 4 or 5 minutes. Turn the skewer over and broil for another 4 to 5 minutes, or until the chicken is thoroughly cooked.

5. Serve the skewers of chicken with the peanut dipping sauce on the side.

NOTE: If using bamboo skewers, soak them in water for a couple of hours so they will not burn on the grill or under the broiler.

Chicken Satay
Shrimp Sambal with Rice (page 66)

FOR THE PEANUT
SAUCE:
1 cup peanut butter
1 tablespoon chopped
   fresh ginger
1 tablespoon chopped
   shallots
1 clove garlic, chopped
1 teaspoon chili paste or
   sambal oelek
$\frac{1}{2}$ cup chicken broth
1 cup sugar
1 teaspoon salt

✳

THE MALAYS OF SINGAPORE

When Lord Raffles showed up in 1819, Singapore was little more than a Malay village. The majority of the small population were Malaysian Muslims who had drifted down the peninsula, but their cultural influence has always been greater than their numbers. The Malay Annals contain the mythic legends of their people, including the story of how Singapore got its name.

King Sang Nila Utama was looking for a place to locate a new city. He and the menfolk set forth in the golden yacht, the women in the boat of silver. So vast was the fleet that there seemed to be no counting it. The masts of the ships were like a forest of trees. At one point they came ashore to hunt and gather food for a meal.

While following a deer, the King came to a hill from which he could see across a body of water to a magnificent white beach, and he determined to visit that beach. As they sailed over, a storm arose and his ship began to fill with water. The captain tried to lighten the vessel, but it kept sinking deeper into the ocean. At one point the captain addressed his master. "It seems to me, your Highness, that it is because of your crown of kingship that our boat is foundering. All else has been thrown overboard, and if we do not do likewise with the crown we shall all be helpless." So his Highness threw the crown overboard. At which point the seas quieted down and the ship came safely to shore.

As the king walked over the land, he beheld a strange animal. It moved with great speed, had a red body, and a black head. He asked those who were with him what animal it was. One of his companions said, "Your Highness, I have heard it told that in ancient times it was a lion that had that appearance. I think that what we saw must have been a lion."

And so the king called his new city *Singapura,* which in the Sanskrit language means "Lion City." Today, 7 percent of the population of Singapore is Malay. They are very much part of this modern city and the fact that they were there first is reflected in many subtle ways, including the fact that the national anthem is sung in Malay.

CHICKEN CACCIATORE

ROYAL VIKING SUN

The Royal Viking Sun, following the tradition of the great ocean liners, places considerable importance on the quality of its food. But the staff has also set up a program to take advantage of the fact that their kitchen actually travels around the world. When the ship gets to a port where there is a talented chef with a well-respected restaurant, that chef is invited on board to teach. An example of the program is this chicken cacciatore, prepared by the ship's executive chef, Manfred Jaud.

1. In a large skillet over medium-high heat, heat the oil and 1 tablespoon of the butter until just bubbling. Add the chicken strips and sauté until the chicken is cooked through, 5 to 10 minutes. Remove the chicken and drain on paper towels.

2. Melt the remaining tablespoon of butter in the same skillet. Add the chopped onions, mushrooms, both types of olives, and the pearl onions. Cook, stirring frequently, until the onions are translucent, about 5 minutes.

3. Sprinkle on the flour, stir well, and cook for 2 minutes. Pour in the chicken broth, stir well, and bring the mixture to a boil. Add the tomato and red wine and return the chicken to the pan. Stir well. Reduce the heat to medium and simmer until the sauce thickens enough to coat the back of a wooden spoon, about 5 minutes.

4. Serve with potato pancakes and steamed fresh vegetables.

SUGGESTED MENU:

Chicken Cacciatore
Potato Pancakes (page 149)
Peanut Butter Cookies (page 285)

MAKES 6 SERVINGS

1 tablespoon vegetable oil
2 tablespoons unsalted butter
4 boneless, skinless chicken breast halves (about 1½ pounds total), cut into ½-inch strips
½ cup finely chopped onion
½ cup sliced mushrooms
¼ cup sliced stuffed green olives
¼ cup sliced black olives
12 pickled pearl onions
1 tablespoon all-purpose flour
One 13¾-ounce can chicken broth
1 large tomato, cut into 6 wedges
1 cup red wine

THE ROYAL VIKING APPROACH
TO FOOD SHOPPING

Each day, the chefs on the Royal Viking Sun whip up dinner for just over a thousand people. They also whip up the same number of breakfasts and lunches. Plus a midnight snack. For their annual 103-day round-the-world cruise they do some rather heavy shopping: 130,000 eggs; 15,000 pounds of beef; 3,300 pounds of shrimp; 600 tons of fruits and vegetables; and 900 pounds of chocolate. Since they must do their shopping every week in different cities all over the planet, they end up with some complex logistical problems. Everything that is dry is fairly easy. But fresh products are much more difficult to handle. They use a very sophisticated computer system to estimate their needs and plan the purchasing months ahead. They also try to take advantage of what is going to be in season when they eventually get to a particular location.

Eduardo Ellis, owner of Papiamento Restaurant.

CUBIST CHICKEN

PAPIAMENTO RESTAURANT, ARUBA

Eduardo Ellis was born in Aruba. His wife Lenie was born in Holland. Together they run one of the best restaurants in the Caribbean called Papiamento. The Dutch have been in business on Aruba for over three hundred years, so the relationship between Lenie and Eduardo has considerable historical precedent. To keep that history running, they have brought their sons, Edward, Jaap, and Antoine, into the business. The following is Antoine's recipe for a dish he calls Cubist Chicken.

1. Salt and pepper the chicken on both sides. Sprinkle with the Worcestershire sauce. Mix 2 tablespoons of the vegetable oil together with the garlic and spread the mixture on top of the chicken. Dip the chicken into the flour to give each side a light coating.

2. In a sauté pan over medium heat, heat the remaining 2 tablespoons of oil together with the butter until the butter is melted and starts to bubble. Add the chicken to the pan and cook for 3 to 5 minutes on each side, or until the chicken is cooked through and its juices run clear. Remove the chicken to a serving dish and keep warm.

3. Add the fruit to the pan and cook for 2 minutes. Turn the heat to high, carefully add the Grand Marnier, and cook for 2 minutes. Pour the fruit and Grand Marnier sauce over the chicken and serve.

SUGGESTED MENU:

Cubist Chicken
Asparagus with Orange Sauce (page 177)
Mashed Gingered Sweet Potatoes (page 153)
Aruban Bread Pudding with Rum Sauce (page 248)

MAKES 4 SERVINGS

2 boneless, skinless
  chicken breasts,
  cut in half
Salt and freshly ground
  black pepper
2 tablespoons
  Worcestershire sauce
4 tablespoons vegetable oil
2 cloves garlic, minced
1/2 cup all-purpose flour,
  on a flat plate
2 tablespoons butter
1 mango, peeled, pitted,
  and cut into bite-sized
  pieces (about 2 cups)
1 papaya, peeled, seeded,
  and cut into bite-sized
  pieces (about 2 cups)
2 kiwis, peeled and cut
  into bite-sized pieces
1/2 pineapple, peeled,
  cored, and cut into
  bite-sized pieces
  (about 2 cups)
1 cup Grand Marnier
  liqueur

THE VENEZUELAN INFLUENCE IN ARUBA

During the early 1800s, much of South America was involved in a revolutionary movement designed to free itself from the Spanish crown. One of the leaders of that movement in Venezuela was Francisco de Miranda. Whenever things were not going well for Miranda in Venezuela he would sail over to Aruba, which was just off the coast and was Dutch. A safe place to rest up. Miranda had promised to pay the Dutch commander for what he and his three hundred revolutionary troops used, but when he left Aruba, his payment consisted of a letter in which he agreed that he owed 528 pesos. That letter still exists and so does the debt. In a way, Miranda's behavior is not untypical for revolutionaries of the time. They were usually very short of cash and whatever they had they needed for guns. You know all those little inns in the States that have signs telling you that "George Washington slept here, during the American Revolution"? I'll bet you that George didn't pay either. It's something about politicians.

Over the years, Aruba became the place to seek refuge when things were not going well in Venezuela. In general, these political refugees were rather wealthy, and since they had no business to do in Aruba, they literally became Aruba's earliest tourists. They often stayed for such long periods that many Venezuelan-Aruban families were formed and much of Aruban life took on a Spanish quality. Even today, Aruba is still the favorite getaway for the people of Venezuela, but only for vacations.

Natural Bridge, Aruba.

CHICKEN BREASTS WITH SUN-DRIED TOMATO STUFFING

THE CLIFT, SAN FRANCISCO, CALIFORNIA

Ruth Waltenspiel runs Timber Crest Farms in Healdsburg, California. Her farm is one of the world's most important producers of dried tomatoes. I stopped in to take a look at how her process works and as I was leaving, Ruth sent me off with some samples to test. That is precisely what I did that evening when I got back to Martin Frost's kitchen at the Clift Hotel in San Francisco. The following recipe is the result.

1. Preheat the oven to 350° F.

2. Cut a pocket in each chicken breast. In a blender, puree the basil leaves with 1 tablespoon of the olive oil. You may also use prepared pesto sauce. Spoon a quarter of the sauce into the pocket of each chicken breast. Then put 3 of the sun-dried tomatoes into each pocket.

3. In a large sauté pan with an ovenproof handle, heat the remaining tablespoon of oil and the butter. (If you are not sure about the handle, wrap it in aluminum foil or transfer the chicken to an ovenproof dish before baking.) Brown the chicken on each side for about a minute. Place the pan in the preheated oven for 10 to 12 minutes, until the chicken is cooked through and its juices run clear.

SUGGESTED MENU:

Chicken Breasts with Sun-Dried Tomato Stuffing
Roasted Bell Pepper Risotto (page 166)
Romaine Lettuce and Pears with
   Parmesan Dressing (page 204)
Flourless Chocolate Cake (page 266)

MAKES 4 SERVINGS

2 whole boneless, skinless chicken breasts, cut in half
1/2 cup basil leaves, tightly packed, about 20 leaves
2 tablespoons olive oil
12 sun-dried tomatoes, softened in boiling water
1 tablespoon butter

FORT ROSS, CALIFORNIA

During the 1500s and 1600s, European governments sent their ships across the Atlantic to establish colonies in the New World. At the same time that the Europeans were expanding their influence across the Atlantic, the Russian Czar, Peter the Great, started moving his explorers to and across the Pacific. Vitus Bering, a Danish navigator in Peter's employ, sailed across the area that is now called the Bering Straits, and claimed Alaska for his Czar. Russian trading companies began to make big money in Pacific seal and otter fur.

In 1799, the Czar, his family, his friends, and his friends' friends invested in an organization called the "Russian-American Company." The Czar granted a monopoly to the company for all trade and settlement in North America. The most southerly outpost of the Russian-American Company was just north of San Francisco in a facility known as Fort Ross.

Fort Ross was a difficult post to sustain and the Russian government made plans to close it. A last-ditch effort to save the fort was made in the 1830s when Russian Baron von Wrangell went to Mexico for help. The Mexicans, who had just won their freedom from Spain in the Mexican Revolution, were willing to help Fort Ross, and they only wanted one simple thing in exchange. They wanted the Russian government to recognize the new Mexican government. But Russia was under the control of Czar Nicholas I, who was an unwavering believer in the absolute power of a king, and could not handle the idea of revolutionary change. He would not agree to recognize Mexico and so he lost his foothold in North America.

In 1841, the fort was sold to Captain Sutter, and everyone pulled out and went back to Russia. Bad move. Just seven years later, in 1848, gold was discovered at Sutter's Mill and the California gold rush began. Today, Fort Ross is a state historic park where you can see how the Russian colonists lived during the early years of the nineteenth century.

ABOUT HONEY

Honey has been part of the human diet for over 3 million years and has always had a special spot on the menu. In ancient Egypt, it was a form of money. It was also used as an offering to the gods and as a food for sacred animals.

Honey has always been a favorite ingredient for bakers. It not only sweetens a recipe, but because honey has a high fructose content, it has a higher sweetening power than standard sugar. It also retains moisture, so the final product stays fresher longer.

When you are substituting honey for granulated sugar there are a few things you should do. First, start by selecting a mild-flavored honey, and substitute it for only half the sugar in the recipe until you see how things work out.

Reduce the amount of liquid in the recipe by a quarter cup for each cup of honey used. Obviously honey is a liquid ingredient and granulated sugar a dry one, and you need to adjust the recipe accordingly.

Add an extra half teaspoon of baking soda for each cup of honey that you use and reduce the oven temperature by 25 degrees to make sure that whatever it is you are baking won't overbrown.

The trick to measuring honey accurately and easily is to spray a little cooking oil into the measuring cup or spoon before you pour in the honey. The oil sets up a non-stick surface and the honey comes out easily and accurately measured.

Breast of Chicken with Honeyed Red Onion and Spinach

JASPER PARK LODGE, ALBERTA, CANADA

MAKES 4 SERVINGS

3 tablespoons vegetable oil
2 boneless, skinless
   chicken breasts, cut in
   half
½ cup flour
Salt and freshly ground
   black pepper
2 cups sliced red onions
¼ cup honey
2 tablespoons red wine
   vinegar (balsamic or
   raspberry)
1 clove garlic, crushed
4 cups spinach, cleaned
   and pulled into bite-
   sized pieces
4 slices Brie cheese (1 inch
   square × ¼ inch thick)

Slices of red onion and spinach are cooked with a little honey and then placed on sautéed chicken breasts. A small piece of Brie cheese is melted on top. The ingredients go in and out of the pan a number of times, but the recipe is really very fast and easy. The slightly sweet and pungent flavor is excellent.

1. Heat 2 tablespoons of the oil in a nonstick frying pan. Dredge both sides of the chicken breasts in the flour. Place the chicken into the heated oil. Lightly salt and pepper the chicken and cook for 4 minutes on each side, or until the chicken is fully cooked. Remove the chicken from the pan and hold aside.

2. Add the onion to the pan and cook, stirring, for 3 minutes. Add the honey and the vinegar and cook and stir for 2 minutes. Remove the onion mixture from the pan and hold aside.

3. Add the remaining tablespoon of vegetable oil to the pan. As soon as it is hot, add the garlic and cook for 1 minute. Add the spinach and cook and stir for 2 minutes, until wilted. Return the onions to the pan and mix them into the spinach. Remove the onion and spinach mixture from the pan and hold aside.

4. Return the chicken to the nonstick frying pan and heat for a minute. Place some of the onion and spinach mixture on top of each chicken breast. Place one piece of cheese on top of the onion and spinach mixture. Cover the pan and cook for 2 minutes, allowing the cheese to melt.

SUGGESTED MENU:

Breast of Chicken with Honeyed Red Onion and Spinach
Roasted New Potatoes with Roasted Garlic Sauce
   (page 141)
Lemon Ginger Cake (page 281)

Chef Jeff O'Neill of the Jasper
Park Lodge out on a short climb.

Chicken Breasts Stuffed with Fontina and Sun-Dried Tomato Sauce

PALLISER HOTEL, CALGARY, ALBERTA, CANADA

MAKES 4 SERVINGS

FOR THE CHICKEN:
2 whole boneless, skinless chicken breasts, cut in half
4 ounces fontina cheese, cut into finger-sized pieces
8 sun-dried tomatoes in olive oil, chopped
1 tablespoon chopped fresh basil
2 tablespoons olive oil
1/2 teaspoon salt
1/3 cup flour for dredging

FOR THE SUN-DRIED TOMATO SAUCE:
1 tablespoon olive oil
1 tablespoon chopped shallots
2 cloves garlic, chopped
4 sun-dried tomatoes in oil, chopped
1 1/2 cups chicken broth

As the Canadian Pacific Railway pushed west, it passed through some of the most spectacular scenery in North America, scenery that it could make available to everyone by building hotels and resorts at its major railheads. Today there are over 25 properties in the group, and they include some of Canada's grandest hotels and resorts. The Empress in Victoria, Château Whistler, Jasper Park Lodge, The Royal York in Toronto, and in Calgary, The Palliser.

The Palliser was originally built in 1914 and named after Captain John Palliser, an Englishman who spent a considerable amount of time exploring western Canada. Over the years, the hotel has become a major social center for the city. The hotel's restaurant is well-respected and the following is one of their most popular dishes.

1. Preheat the oven to 375° F.

2. **To make the chicken:** Cut a pocket in each chicken breast. Place the cheese, sun-dried tomato, and basil in the pocket. In a large sauté pan over medium heat, heat the oil. Season the chicken breasts with salt, then lightly dredge them in the flour. Sauté the chicken breasts until lightly browned on both sides. Transfer the chicken to a baking sheet and bake for 20 minutes.

3. While the chicken is baking, prepare the sun-dried tomato sauce: In a medium saucepan over medium heat,

heat the oil. Add the shallots and sauté for 1 minute. Then add the garlic and the sun-dried tomatoes and cook for 5 minutes. Add the chicken broth, and bring it to a boil, and continue boiling until the liquid is reduced to half the original volume, about $3/4$ cup. Place the mixture in a blender. Add the basil and cayenne or ground red pepper, then process until smooth. Add the butter, if desired, $1/2$ tablespoon at a time, processing in the blender after each addition. Serve the sauce immediately with the chicken. Do not reboil this sauce or it will break.

1 tablespoon chopped
   fresh basil
$1/8$ teaspoon cayenne or
   ground red pepper
2 tablespoons butter
   (optional)

SUGGESTED MENU:

Chicken Breasts Stuffed with Fontina and Sun-Dried Tomato Sauce
Gratin of New Potatoes, Celery, and Red Onion with Rosemary (page 145)
Chopped Vegetable Salad with Basil Vinaigrette (page 213)
Chocolate Pizza (page 242)

THE CANADIAN RAILROAD

In 1883, Calgary was just a row of tents on the Elbow River, and 90 percent of those tents were either a rooming house or a restaurant. But on August 11, 1883, the character of Calgary underwent a colossal change. The first Canadian Pacific Railway train pulled into Calgary, and life was never the same.

The Canadian government decided that they had to build a railroad from the Atlantic to the Pacific in order to pull their young nation together. The United States had just constructed a transcontinental railroad and Canada felt that if it did not do the same thing and bring its western territories into the Canadian federal system there was a good chance that the United States would take a crack at pulling those areas into the United States.

Along with the right of way to build the train tracks, the railroad got the rights to a considerable amount of land. They soon realized that a fortune could be made by importing settlers from Europe and the United States. The railroads got paid by selling both the train tickets to where the settlers were going and the land which they settled when they arrived.

Canadian railroads and the steamship companies advertised all over Europe, and the immigrants began to come in by the thousands. The settlers were attracted to places that reminded them of home. Many of the Europeans were frightened off by the open prairie land in southern Alberta and they tended to go north to Edmonton. Homesteaders coming up from Montana, Utah, and other western states already understood the demands of the wide-open prairie, and the land around Calgary looked just fine.

Engineer on the Canadian Pacific Railroad.

THE ORIGIN OF THE CALGARY STAMPEDE

At the beginning of this century, western Canada still had a reputation as being a little too rough and ready for many settlers. To dispel this image, the farmers of Calgary took a railroad car, filled it with examples of the wheat and vegetables that were grown in Alberta, and sent it back east as the Calgary Exhibition. They hoped to entice farmers to come out. The traveling Calgary Exhibition eventually evolved into an annual summer event of international fame.

In 1912, Guy Weadick, a Wild West show star from the United States, and his wife Flores LaDue, a champion trick roper, showed up in Calgary. They convinced a group of local investors to fund a week-long rodeo that was called the Calgary Stampede. These days it is held every July and attracts visitors from all over the world.

Beef, Lamb, Pork, and Veal

Steak Pizzaiola

ANTICA TRATTORIA MARTELLA, AVELLINO, ITALY

MAKES 4 SERVINGS

FOR THE STEAKS:
1 tablespoon olive oil
4 boneless shell steaks
    (about 6 ounces each)
½ teaspoon salt
⅛ teaspoon freshly ground
    black pepper

FOR THE SAUCE:
2 tablespoons olive oil
3 cups chopped tomatoes
½ teaspoon salt
1 clove garlic, chopped
2 tablespoons chopped
    fresh basil, or
    2 teaspoons dried
½ teaspoon dried oregano

The Antica Trattoria Martella was opened in 1921 as a neighborhood *cantina* making simple food for the people who worked in the neighborhood. Soup, codfish—good, uncomplicated dishes for good, uncomplicated people. These days it is run by the third generation of the founder's family and it has become *the* place to eat in the region. This steak dish is a local favorite, easy to prepare and even easier to enjoy.

1. **To make the steak:** In a large sauté pan over medium heat, heat the olive oil. Season the steaks with the salt and pepper, then brown for 2 minutes on each side. Remove the steaks to a heated platter.

2. **To make the sauce:** Drain the oil used to cook the steaks from the sauté pan. Add the olive oil for the sauce and heat over medium heat. Add the remaining ingredients and cook, stirring occasionally, for 5 minutes. Return the steaks to the pan with the sauce and cook until the steaks are heated through, about 3 minutes.

3. Place the steaks on dinner plates and spoon the sauce on top.

SUGGESTED MENU:

Stuffed Artichokes with Parmesan and Capers (page 176)
Steak Pizzaiola
Poached Peaches with Cinnamon and Marsala (page 230)

Beef Stroganoff

ROYAL VIKING SUN

The Russian city of St. Petersburg is a major port. Paintings from the 1700s show docks and trading houses all along the waterfront. It is a regular port of call for the Royal Viking Sun, and an ideal spot for chef Manfred Jaud to brush up on his Russian recipes.

1. In a large, heavy sauté pan over medium-high heat, heat the oil. Add the beef and sauté, stirring frequently, 4 to 6 minutes until just cooked. Remove the beef and drain on paper towels.

2. Melt the butter in the same sauté pan. Add the onions and mushrooms and cook, stirring frequently, until the onions are translucent, about 5 minutes.

3. Sprinkle the flour over the onion-mushroom mixture. Stir well and cook for 3 minutes.

4. Stir in the beef broth, and bring the mixture to a boil. Stir in the mustard, Cognac, and paprika. Return the beef to the pan. Cover and simmer until the beef is tender, about 5 minutes.

5. Stir in the sour cream, and season with salt and pepper to taste. Serve over freshly cooked noodles or rice.

SUGGESTED MENU:

Beef Stroganoff served with noodles or rice
Cucumber Salad (page 199)
Baked Apples (page 228)

MAKES 4 TO 6 SERVINGS

2 tablespoons vegetable oil
2 pounds beef tenderloin, cut into $1/2$-inch strips
1 tablespoon unsalted butter
2 cups coarsely grated onions
1 cup sliced mushrooms
3 tablespoons all-purpose flour
Two $13^3/4$-ounce cans beef broth
1 tablespoon Dijon mustard
2 tablespoons Cognac
2 teaspoons paprika
2 tablespoons sour cream
Salt and freshly ground black pepper
Cooked noodles or rice for serving

Beef with Prunes

THE CLIFT, SAN FRANCISCO, CALIFORNIA

MAKES 4 SERVINGS

FOR THE PRUNE
TOPPING:
1 tablespoon unsalted
   butter, softened
8 pitted prunes, chopped
¼ cup cooked barley or
   rice
¼ cup bread crumbs
2 tablespoons chopped
   fresh chives
2 tablespoons chopped
   fresh parsley
1 tablespoon chopped
   fresh tarragon or mint,
   or 1 teaspoon dried

1¼ pounds fillet of beef or
   round steak, cut into
   eight 1-inch-thick slices
1 teaspoon salt
½ teaspoon freshly ground
   black pepper
1 tablespoon vegetable oil

The farmers and ranchers of California have made their state one of the world's most important areas for the production of foodstuffs. Not only do they supply many of the things that we eat in the United States, but they have become major exporters to international markets. Back home, the chefs of California seem to take a particular delight in preparing dishes that utilize a number of local products in one recipe. Martin Frost at San Francisco's Clift Hotel makes the point in this dish of medallions of beef with a sauce made with California prunes.

1. Preheat the oven to 375° F.

2. **To make the topping:** In a small bowl, combine the ingredients. Season the beef slices on both sides with salt and pepper. In a large sauté pan with an ovenproof handle, heat the oil until hot. Add the beef and sear the meat on both sides. Put a tablespoon of the prune mixture on each piece of beef. Place the pan with the beef into the preheated oven for 10 minutes.

3. While the beef is cooking, make the sauce: Put the sherry and the shallot in a small saucepan, over high heat, and reduce to 1 tablespoon. Add the beef broth and simmer over low heat. Strain out the shallots and return the broth to the saucepan. Whisk in the arrowroot and heat briefly. Keep the sauce warm. Just before serving, whisk in the butter.

4. **To make the vegetables:** In another large sauté pan, heat the butter. Add the yellow squash, zucchini, and mushrooms. Season with the salt. Quickly stir in the spinach and cook until wilted.

5. To serve, divide the vegetables equally among 4 dinner

plates. Arrange the beef on the vegetables and top with a little of the sauce.

SUGGESTED MENU:

Beef with Prunes
Sautéed Mixed Vegetables (page 102)
Barley Pilaf with Toasted Pecans, Ginger, and Herbs (page 170)
Fresh Fruit Tart in a Cornmeal Crust (page 300)

FOR THE SAUCE:
2 tablespoons sherry
1 tablespoon shallot, minced
$1/2$ cup beef broth
$1/2$ teaspoon arrowroot
1 teaspoon unsalted butter

FOR THE VEGETABLES:
1 tablespoon unsalted butter or vegetable oil
1 cup yellow squash cubes
1 cup zucchini cubes
$1/4$ pound shiitake mushrooms, sliced
$1/2$ teaspoon salt
2 cups spinach leaves, washed and torn into small pieces

CALIFORNIA DRIED PLUMS

The discovery of gold in 1848 was clearly the most important thing that had ever happened in the area of San Francisco. In the month before gold was found, the population of San Francisco numbered 812. Two years later, the population was over 25,000.

Many of the fortune hunters came from France and were nicknamed *Keskeydees* because they were always saying, *"Qu'est-ce qu'il dit?"* to each other. *Qu'est-ce qu'il dit* is a French phrase that means, "What is he saying?" The Frenchmen who couldn't speak English were always asking that of the Frenchmen who could speak English.

Two of the French who arrived in the hope of finding gold were the brothers Louis and Pierre Pellier. At one point, Pierre wanted to go back to France to get his childhood sweetheart and bring her to California. Louis agreed to the plan but only on the condition that Pierre return with cuttings from a particular French plum tree that Louis wanted to plant in California. Pierre was a good brother and kept to the deal. He married his childhood sweetheart and returned to San Francisco with her and the plum cutting.

Louis grafted the cuttings onto the rootstock of wild American plums, and the California dried plum industry was born. Today, California is the world's largest producer of dried plums, also known as prunes. The state supplies about 70 percent of the world's prunes and it's proud of it.

And why not? Prunes are a good source of fiber, potassium, vitamin A, iron, and complex carbohydrate. They are totally free of fat and sodium. And, if it makes you feel better, you can call them dried plums, because that's what they are.

Flowers at the Singapore Botanical Gardens, one of the world's most beautiful botanical gardens.

BEEF WITH APPLES AND PEPPERS

MADAME NG SIONG MUI, SINGAPORE

1. **To prepare the marinade:** In a bowl, combine the cornstarch and water. Stir in the soy sauce, sugar, and vegetable oil. Add the beef to the marinade, tossing to coat, and let the beef sit in the marinade for 10 minutes.

2. In a wok or sauté pan over high heat, heat half of the peanut oil. Add half each of the shallots, ginger, and garlic and stir-fry for 1 minute. Add the bell peppers and stir-fry for 1 minute. Add the apple and stir-fry for 1 minute more. Remove the mixture from the wok and set aside.

3. Add the remaining peanut oil to the wok. When the oil is hot, add the remaining shallots, ginger, and garlic and stir-fry for 1 minute. Add the beef and stir-fry for 2 to 3 minutes. Return the peppers and apples to the wok and toss. Add the soy sauce and cashews and stir-fry for 1 minute more. Finally add the sesame oil and toss.

4. Serve with the white rice.

SUGGESTED MENU:

Carrot and Walnut Soup (page 3)
Beef with Apples and Peppers
Fresh Fruit

MAKES 4 SERVINGS

FOR THE MARINADE:
1 teaspoon cornstarch
1 teaspoon water
1 tablespoon soy sauce
1 tablespoon sugar
1 tablespoon vegetable oil

1 pound beef round, cut
    into thin strips
3 tablespoons peanut oil
2 shallots, minced
2 tablespoons minced fresh
    ginger
2 cloves garlic, minced
1 yellow bell pepper,
    cored, seeded, and sliced
    into strips
1 green bell pepper, cored,
    seeded, and sliced into
    strips
1 red bell pepper, cored,
    seeded, and sliced into
    strips
1 apple, peeled, cored, and
    sliced
2 tablespoons soy sauce
1 cup cashews
1 teaspoon sesame oil
Cooked white rice for
    serving

Beef Braised in Red Wine

LA CONTEA, NEIVE, ITALY

MAKES 6 SERVINGS

FOR THE MARINADE:
2 cups dry red wine,
    preferably Barolo or
    Barbaresco
2 carrots, chopped
1 medium onion, chopped
1 stalk celery, chopped
1 bay leaf
1 sprig rosemary, or
    1 teaspoon dried
2 whole cloves

FOR THE BEEF:
3 pounds bottom round or
    rump roast of beef
2 tablespoons olive oil
1 cup beef broth
3 tablespoons tomato
    paste
1 teaspoon salt

1. To make the marinade: In a large pot, combine the ingredients. Add the beef, then cover the pan and refrigerate. Marinate the meat, turning it every half hour for at least 2 hours.

2. Remove the beef from the marinade and pat it dry with paper towels. Save the marinade. In a Dutch oven or casserole, heat the olive oil. Add the beef and brown on all sides.

3. Pour the marinade into the pot with the beef. Add the beef broth. Cover the pan and simmer for $2^{1}/_{2}$ hours, adding more water or stock, if necessary. Stir in the tomato paste and season with salt. Simmer 30 minutes more.

4. To serve, slice the beef and spoon the sauce on top.

SUGGESTED MENU:

Beef Braised in Red Wine
Deviled Potatoes (page 142)
Chocolate Chestnut Cream Puffs (page 240)

THE WINES OF THE PIEDMONT

The Piedmont region of Italy is one of the world's great areas for the production of wine, and some of the greatest wines of the Piedmont come from the land around the town of Alba.

The most highly prized is Barolo. To be called a Barolo, the wine must be made from grapes grown in a small, clearly defined area. The variety of grape must be a Nebbiolo, and the wine must have spent at least three years in a wooden cask. It is a rich and full-bodied wine.

Two of the most famous producers of Barolo are Marcello and Bruno Ceretto. As a matter of fact, they are often referred to as "the Barolo Brothers." As Italy's most majestic red wine, Barolo comes with a lot of tradition, tradition that often has more to do with what people liked in the past rather than what we enjoy today. The old Barolos would often overpower the flavor of the food with which they were served.

During the 1960s, the Ceretto brothers decided that it was time to lighten things up. They wanted to make a Barolo that reflected the taste of the land, and the real flavors of the grape, as opposed to the heavy tannins and the oak of the barrels in which the wine is aged. They shortened the amount of time that the juice of the crushed grape stayed together with the grape skins. They shortened the amount of time that the wine stayed in the wooden barrels. But they lengthened the time that the wine rested in the bottle. This is a gentler aging process and the result is a wine that adds to the taste of a food. This new style of Barolo frees the flavor of the Nebbiolo grape and makes a much more enjoyable drink.

The Nebbiolo grape is also used to produce Barbaresco, which is the second great wine of the Piedmont. Wine professionals often point out that even though Barolo and Barbaresco start out with the same grape, they are clearly different by the time they get to the glass. They are both wines with strength and power, but the Barolo is more massive, like Mr. Schwarzenegger, the Barbaresco more stylish, like Mr. Eastwood.

The southernmost districts of the Piedmont produce the Dolcetto grape. It is used to make a dark red wine that has a light body and is called Dolcetto d'Alba. Dolcetto is the wine that is taken to the table every day by the families of the Piedmont. One additional grape of the Piedmont that is of considerable importance is the Arneis, which is used to produce Arneis Blange, a straw-colored wine that has a slight spritz.

THE HISTORY OF THE CINZANO FAMILY

The Cinzano family came from a small village in Piedmont called Pecetto, which has a long history of growing vines that are used for the making of medicinal infusions and elixirs. For more than five hundred years the Cinzano family has been involved in this craft. So vast were their land holdings in the area, that the old maps actually describe the district as "the Cinzano region."

During the 1780s, a drink came into fashion that was known as vermouth. Soon the Cinzanos began to experiment with a series of formulas for their own version of this flavored wine. By the middle of the 1880s, Cinzano Vermouth had become quite popular and was already being exported to other countries.

When the Cinzanos first started their business, Italy was not yet united as Italy. The Cinzanos were really living in the Kingdom of Savoy. The King was Charles Albert and he was very interested in setting up a business for the production of high-quality wine. His special interest was in something with bubbles, so he could stop pouring French Champagne and start drinking his own stuff.

The king took part of his royal land holdings south of Turino and set up a winery. The facility was called Santa Vittoria and the king asked Francesco Cinzano to go there and help with the work. Francesco was soon producing top-quality vermouth and a sparkling wine based on the Muscato grape that grew nearby. They called their sparkling wine Asti Spumante.

In the early years, the sweetness of the Muscato grape made the wine famous as "champagne on a budget." It was the drink for celebrations with millions of Italians who immigrated to North America. But as the Italian population moved up from settlers to socialites, so did Asti. The producers took advantage of newly developed techniques to modify their Spumante until it presented a delicate sweetness. Both products were quite popular and Francesco realized that he could develop a substantial international clientele.

He organized a group of salesmen to represent his products around the world. Two of his first representatives were the Carpaneto brothers. Lots of sibling rivalry: the standing Carpaneto on the page to the right is using this photo op to sneak a look at his brother's sales notes.

Giuseppe Lampiano, pictured on the opposite page, traveled for the Cinzanos from 1878 to 1922. Giuseppe was very skillful at fitting in with the locals while introducing them to the joys of his drinks.

ABOUT VERMOUTH

A vermouth is basically a wine that has been fortified to the strength of a sherry by the addition of alcohol, and sweetened and flavored by the addition of caramelized sugar, herbs, and spices. Vermouth making goes all the way back to the Middle Ages when wine that had begun to turn sour was reflavored with honey and various herbs to bring back a positive taste.

One of the most common flavoring agents was wormwood. The German word for wormwood is *Wermut,* and that is where the modern word *vermouth* comes from. In Italy, the idea of flavored wine became popular on its own, and eventually it became a major industry with its own source of good wine. In general, there are three types of vermouth on the market. There is a dry white, a sweet white, and a sweet red. The dry white is nice with a little ice or club soda as a before-dinner drink. The most famous role for the dry white is the flavoring addition to the martini, which thanks to James Bond is probably the most famous cocktail in the world. The traditional martini cocktail is 4 or 5 parts of dry gin to 1 part dry vermouth. Bond used vodka instead of gin, and he shook, rather than stirred. The sweet white is usually served by itself with a few cubes of ice, also as a before-meals drink. The sweet red is best known as an ingredient in various cocktails, such as the Manhattan.

The Carpaneto brothers were among the first traveling salesmen for Cinzano. In this photo the older brother is stealing a peek at his younger brother's sales book.

Guiseppe Lampiano traveled around the world for Cinzano. He had a unique gift for fitting in with the local culture.

BEEF RENDANG

VIOLET OON, SINGAPORE

MAKES 4 SERVINGS

FOR THE RED CHILI
PASTE:
2 cloves garlic, sliced
2 shallots, sliced
1-inch piece fresh ginger,
    sliced
1 stalk lemongrass, sliced
    (optional)
2 tablespoons tomato
    paste
2 teaspoons chili paste or
    sambal oelek

2 tablespoons vegetable oil
3 cups coconut milk
1/2 cup sugar
2 pounds beef chuck, cut
    into 1-inch cubes
2 Kaffir lime leaves
    (optional)
Cooked white rice for
    serving

1. To make the paste: In a food processor, combine the garlic, shallots, ginger, and lemongrass, if using, and puree until smooth. Add the tomato paste and chili paste or sambal. Puree until well blended.

2. In a sauté pan over medium heat, heat the oil. Add the red chili paste and cook, stirring occasionally, until the aroma of the paste is very strong. Pour in the coconut milk and sugar and cook for 3 minutes. Lower the heat to a simmer and add the beef and the lime leaves. Simmer uncovered for 1 1/2 hours. Lower the heat again, cover the pan, and simmer for 30 minutes longer. The sauce will be very thick.

3. Serve with white rice.

SUGGESTED MENU:

**Beef Rendang with white rice
Turmeric Sweet Potatoes (page 156)**

Violet Oon is one of the leading food authorities in Singapore. She taught me the history, recipes, and cooking techniques of the Paranakans, a group of Chinese traders who eventually settled on the Malay Peninsula.

THE NONYA FOOD OF THE MALAY PENINSULA

The Paranakan culture resulted from the intermarriage of Chinese men and Malay women and has produced a unique cooking style known as *nonya*. A Paranakan man is called a *babas;* and a Paranakan woman a *nonya*. Since the women have done most of the cooking for the past five hundred years, the cuisine is known as *nonya* cooking. Its origins can be traced back to the 1400s, but it had a difficult time getting started.

The Malay women who did the cooking often came from Muslim families that did not eat pork, or drink alcoholic beverages. They did season their foods with the powerful spices and herbs available on the Malay Peninsula. Most of the Chinese husbands came from a southern province of China, where pork was a major food, alcohol was used, and in general, the seasoning was rather quiet. All that set the stage for a bit of conflict in the kitchen. But as in most marriages, there was an exchange of values. The seasonings of the Malay women took over the taste buds of the men; the Chinese cooking methods of the men took over the kitchen techniques of the women; and, ingredients were taken from both cultures.

It was not a food easily available to people outside the Paranakan community and at one point in the 1960s the *nonya* style was disappearing. But thanks to a growing interest in Singapore for the preservation of its ethnic history, *nonya* cooking has become one of the most popular foods in the restaurants of the city. Sometimes the history of a cuisine is like a wide tie, if you keep it in your closet long enough it will come back into fashion.

Beef with Beans (Carne Mechada con Porotos)

TERMAS DE CAUQUENES, CHILE

MAKES 8 SERVINGS

FOR THE BEEF:
6 pounds beef round or
    rump roast
6 firm thin carrots, peeled
18 cloves garlic, sliced in
    half lengthwise, plus 2
    cloves, minced
Salt and freshly ground
    black pepper
3 tablespoons vegetable oil
2 cups chopped onions
3 cups chopped tomatoes
    with their juices
1 tablespoon each chopped
    fresh oregano, rosemary,
    and parsley
2 cups boiling water

FOR THE BEANS:
2 cups canned, frozen,
    or freshly cooked corn
    kernels
1/2 cup chopped fresh basil
    leaves, or 2 tablespoons
    dried

1. **To prepare the beef:** Using a thin slicing knife, poke 6 holes lengthwise into each side of the beef. Fill 3 of the holes on each side with the carrots and the other 3 with the sliced garlic cloves. Salt and pepper all sides of the meat. In a casserole over medium heat, heat the oil. Add the meat to the casserole and sear for about 2 minutes on each side. Add the chopped onions, minced garlic, chopped tomatoes and their juices, herbs, and boiling water. Cover and simmer on top of the range for 1 hour and 20 minutes.

2. **For the beans:** In a food processor or blender, puree the corn together with the basil and hold aside. In a saucepan over medium heat, melt the butter. Add the chopped onions and sauté for 2 minutes. Add the pumpkin or squash and cook for 2 minutes. Add the tomato, then the white beans. Add the pureed corn and basil. Salt and pepper to taste. Cover and simmer for 20 minutes. After the cooking time, keep the bean mixture warm over a low heat.

3. **To assemble:** When the cooking of the roast is complete, remove it from the casserole and place it on a cutting board to rest for 10 minutes. Slice it into 1/4-inch-thick slices. Place 2 slices on each serving dish. Place some of the bean mixture next to the meat. Pour some of the sauce from the cooking pot onto the meat.

Beef with Beans (Carne Mechada con Porotos)
Spinach with Almonds and Garlic (page 189)
Sweet Empanadas (page 226)

2 cups pumpkin or other
    squash, such as butter-
    nut or acorn, cut into
    $1/2$-inch cubes
1 cup chopped tomato
4 cups cooked white beans
Salt and freshly ground
    black pepper

These ovens on the coast of
Chile were used to heat
cannonballs, which were then
fired at wooden ships, causing
the sails and decks to burst
into flame. The cannonballs
were called "shots." When
they were heated, they were
known as "hot shots," which
is where the phrase originated.

BUTCH CASSIDY AND THE SUNDANCE KID IN SOUTH AMERICA

Sometime after their robbery of the First National Bank in Winnemucca, Nevada, in September of the year 1900, Butch Cassidy and the Sundance Kid, along with the beautiful but deadly Etta Place, headed off to South America.

At one point they ended up in Patagonia and actually spent five rather peaceful years, running a country store. They played at being good neighbors and appeared to have become respected members of the community. But when things got boring and their cash ran low, they turned back to their old and evil ways.

In 1905, they started robbing banks again. Etta was right in there, having cut her hair short to look like one of the guys. Two years of their old tricks and things were getting too hot. The Pinkerton agency was working with the local police and it looked like it was only a question of time, and not much time at that, before they would be under attack or under arrest. So they headed out, but first they sold their holdings to a beef company. The final steps in their biographies are somewhat conflicting. One story says that they were killed in South America by local soldiers. Another tale has them ending up near New York City. But Butch's sister has gone on record with the fact that Butch came back to Circleville, Ohio, in the fall of 1925 to have blueberry pie with her. Must have been a heck of a pie. She thinks that Butch died in Washington State in the late 1930s.

CHILEAN WINE

The missionaries who traveled with the Spanish conquistadors in the 1500s planted the first grape vines in Chile. The wines that were made from those grapes were used as altar wines in the services of the church.

That was more or less the story of Chilean wines for over a hundred years. Then in 1851, a man named Silvestre Ochagavia realized that Chile had the soil and the climate to be one of the world's great wine-producing nations, and he set about importing vines and wine experts from France. His experiments were very successful, and he soon became known as the "Father of Chilean Wine." Which really annoyed his children, but that's life.

The most successful wine-growing areas are just outside Santiago. Three of the most famous Chilean producers are Undurraga, Concha y Toro, and Santa Rita. Undurraga holds the distinction of being the first Chilean to export wine to the United States in the year 1912. Concha y Toro is the largest and probably the best-known in North America. Finally, Santa Rita makes excellent wine on one of Chile's most beautiful estates.

Traditional Chilean dancers, Santiago, Chile.

NEAPOLITAN MEAT LOAF

LE SIRENUSE, POSITANO, ITALY

MAKES 6 SERVINGS

FOR THE MEAT LOAF:
5 slices white bread, crusts
    removed
$1/3$ cup milk
2 pounds lean ground beef
3 eggs
2 cloves garlic, chopped
2 tablespoons freshly
    grated Parmesan cheese
$1/4$ cup chopped fresh
    parsley
$1/2$ teaspoon salt
$1/4$ pound cooked ham,
    thinly sliced
$1/4$ pound fresh mozzarella
    cheese, sliced
$1/3$ cup olive oil
$1/4$ cup white wine

FOR THE OMELET:
2 eggs
1 teaspoon water
1 tablespoon butter

Positano is a village on the Amalfi coast of Italy that clings to a semicircle of cliffs rising up from a cove in the Mediterranean Sea. It is picture perfect and contains a picture-perfect hotel called Le Sirenuse. Le Sirenuse has a cooking school that teaches the traditional dishes of the area. The director of the school is Antonio Sersale and the following is his recipe for a Neapolitan meat loaf.

The idea of making an omelet and placing it inside the loaf before it is cooked is unusual and creates a very attractive contrast in both color and texture when the loaf is sliced.

1. Preheat the oven to 375° F.

2. To make the meat loaf: In a large bowl, soak the bread in the milk. Add the ground beef and mix together. Add the eggs, garlic, Parmesan cheese, parsley, and salt. Mix everything together. On a damp cloth or on a lightly buttered piece of aluminum foil, roll or pat the mixture into a large rectangle, approximately 8 × 10 inches and 1 inch thick. Place the ham slices down the middle of the rectangle of meat, then lay the mozzarella cheese on top of the ham. Set aside.

3. To prepare the omelet: In a small bowl, beat together the eggs and the water. In a 10-inch skillet over medium-low heat, melt the butter. Add the eggs, tilting the pan to coat evenly. Turn the omelet over and cook the second side. Turn the omelet out of the pan on top of the mozzarella cheese that is on the rectangle of meat.

4. Using the damp cloth or foil, roll the meat loaf into a cylinder. Seal the seam by pressing it together gently with your fingers.

5. Into a large baking pan, place the olive oil, then put the meat loaf into the baking pan and gently roll it in the olive oil. Sprinkle the meat loaf with the white wine. Bake in the oven for 50 minutes.

6. Remove the meat loaf from the oven and allow it to rest for 10 minutes before slicing.

SUGGESTED MENU:

Neopolitan Meat Loaf
Sautéed Escarole with Garlic and Golden Raisins
  (page 183)
Tangerine Granita (page 244)

A sign pointing the way to the hotel Le Sirenuse on the steps leading up from the beach in Positano, Italy.

View from the patio attached to my room at the hotel Le Sirenuse, Positano, Italy.

A BRIEF HISTORY OF THE ITALIAN PROVINCE OF CAMPAGNA

The province of Campagna is situated on the southwest coast of the Italian peninsula. The ancient Greeks had settled in the area as early as 800 B.C. and by the first century A.D. everybody who was anybody in the Roman Empire wanted to have a vacation home in Campagna. It had a style somewhere between the Hamptons of Long Island, and Los Angeles's Malibu, with a light dusting of Aspen, Colorado. Horace, Virgil, Ovid, even Cicero had a place there, and the traffic from Rome on a summer weekend was murder.

But the area was not just a spot for holidays. The main city of the province was Naples, and from the very beginning of its history it was a major port. If you were going to do business, or make war in the ancient world, controlling Naples was a primary objective. The Romans hung on for a few centuries, but when Rome fell, so did the fortunes of the region.

At that point, the German tribes came through and sacked everything. Then the Moslem Saracens came over from the eastern Mediterranean. Next up were the Norman Knights. They were passing through the neighborhood in 1027, on their way home from their Crusades in the Holy Land. When they got a look at the area around the Bay of Naples, well, there was just no going home for those boys.

After a while the Normans lost control and the Germans of the Holy Roman Empire took over. The French had a crack at running the place. Spain controlled the area for a time, through the great power of the Bourbons, and the Austrians ruled for a while through the Habsburgs.

For almost three thousand years, Campagna was just a pawn for foreign powers. But all that changed in the mid-1800s, when Garibaldi united the districts of this peninsula into modern Italy. Of course, more foreigners go there than ever before, but they are no longer tyrants, just tourists.

GRILLED SONOMA LAMB CHOPS

SONOMA MISSION INN, BOYES HOT SPRINGS, CALIFORNIA

1. **To make the marinade:** In a glass or stainless-steel pan large enough to hold the chops, combine the marinade ingredients. Add the lamb and coat on both sides. Marinate for at least 1 hour, turning the meat over after 30 minutes. Heat the grill or a broiler.

2. Remove the chops from the marinade. Grill or broil to the desired degree of doneness.

3. **To make the sauce:** In a small saucepan over high heat, combine the wine, shallots, and garlic and boil briefly until the liquid is reduced to 1 tablespoon. Add the beef broth and simmer over low heat for 5 minutes. Strain out the shallots and the garlic. Return the broth to the saucepan. Whisk in the arrowroot and heat briefly until slightly thickened. Keep the sauce warm over low heat. Just before serving, whisk in the butter, if desired.

4. When the chops are finished, divide them among 4 dinner plates and spoon some of the sauce on each chop.

SUGGESTED MENU:

Lemon Rice Soup (page 7)
Grilled Sonoma Lamb Chops
Vegetable Gratin (page 193)
Eggplant Puree with Roasted Garlic (page 182)
Orange Bars (page 237)

MAKES 4 SERVINGS

4 loin lamb chops, 1½ inches thick

FOR THE MARINADE:
¼ cup olive oil
¼ cup water
2 cloves garlic, smashed
2 tablespoons chopped fresh thyme, or
  2 teaspoons dried

FOR THE SAUCE:
2 tablespoons dry red wine
1 tablespoon minced shallots
1 clove garlic, minced
½ cup beef broth
½ teaspoon arrowroot
1 teaspoon butter (optional)

✳

SONOMA MISSION INN, BOYES HOT SPRINGS, CALIFORNIA

Beneath the surface of Sonoma Valley are a series of hot springs that have been boiling to the surface for thousands of years. The Native American tribes who live there were well aware of the springs and considered them to be sacred ground. The tribes used them to practice their religious rights, to heal themselves, and because no conflicts were allowed in these special locations, to rest in a safe place. Because the water was over 100 degrees as it came to the surface, it was also used for cooking.

The first European colonists to arrive in the area were shown to the hot springs by the local tribes and soon joined in for the cure. During the 1880s, coming to a hot spring for a little rest and relaxation became the thing to do. The visits worked well for a number of reasons. First of all, the guests got away from the stress of the cities in which they lived. Hot springs are almost always in relaxed rural areas. Many locals were in attendance and recommended the drinking of the waters for whatever was bothering the guests. Whether the mineral waters actually had any medical value is seriously in doubt, but it made everybody think they were getting better, and state of mind had a great deal to do with improving one's health. The most famous classical spa of the area is the Sonoma Mission Inn at the Boyes Hot Springs, just north of San Francisco.

In 1895, a young Englishman named H. E. Boyes was drilling a well on his land in the Sonoma Valley. As he passed through the seventy-foot mark he hit water, which came to the surface at 112° F. Boyes had a good commercial sense and he immediately realized that he had just entered the hot mineral water business. Within five years he was able to construct the Boyes Hot Springs Hotel. The who's who of San Francisco came up to "take the waters" at what had become the finest hot mineral water resort in California. It boasted the largest mineral water swimming tank in the world. The advertisements recommended the waters as a cure for rheumatism, stomach trouble, and nerve problems. Which was a pretty nervy claim. The original hotel was destroyed by fire in 1923. In 1927, the current Sonoma Mission Inn was built on the same spot. The building is an architecturally accurate replica of a California mission, and it became even more popular than the earlier Boyes Hotel. Ferries and trains connected San Francisco to the area and people considered it an easy trip. Today, the Sonoma Mission Inn & Spa is a Four Star, Four Diamond luxury resort. *(cont.)*

When guests arrive at the inn the staff gently recommends that they stop for a "Stress Reducer" massage in order to get into the proper Sonoma state of mind. Remember, northern California is the land of the laid-back.

Without anyone pushing in any direction, you can choose from a selection of aerobic classes, indoor and outdoor exercise pools. The outdoor pool is kept at a nice, warm 85 degrees. There are tennis courts, access to a nearby golf course, and all kinds of spa treatments, including their famous seaweed body wrap, which gives you a great insight to what it feels like to be a sushi.

LEFT AND BELOW
The Sonoma Mission Inn at the turn of the century.

Grilled Lamb Chops with a Ginger and Tomato Salsa

JASPER PARK LODGE, ALBERTA, CANADA

MAKES 4 SERVINGS

FOR THE SALSA:
2 tablespoons olive oil
2 tablespoons red wine
    vinegar
2 cloves garlic, minced
2 cups chopped tomatoes
    with their juices
1 yellow bell pepper,
    seeded and chopped
    into small pieces
1 green bell pepper, seeded
    and chopped into small
    pieces
3 tablespoons minced fresh
    cilantro
1 tablespoon chili paste
1 cup sliced scallions
¼ cup minced Japanese
    pickled ginger
1 tablespoon sugar
Salt and freshly ground
    black pepper

For over 100 years the Canadian province of Alberta has been producing some of the world's finest lamb, and quite naturally it has become a regular part of the menu at many of the finer restaurants. Jeff O'Neill, the executive sous chef at the Jasper Park Lodge, prepared the following dish on an outdoor grill alongside a small secluded lake on the lodge's property. It is an ideal recipe for a cookout because all of the elements except the lamb can be prepared before you go out.

1. **To prepare the salsa:** In a glass or stainless-steel bowl, mix all of the ingredients. Cover the bowl and let the mixture rest in the refrigerator for 1 hour or longer.

2. Ready your outdoor or indoor grill for cooking or preheat your oven broiler. Lightly salt and pepper the chops and cook them 5 to 7 minutes on each side, or to the point of doneness that you like.

3. When the chops are done they are served with the salsa on top.

NOTE: *Frenching* is a technique that removes some of the meat and fat from between the bones. The cut usually runs down for about an inch from the tip of the meat. The frenching can be done for you by your butcher (just ask), or you can do it yourself at home.

Grilled Lamb Chops with a Ginger and Tomato Salsa
Garlic Mashed Potatoes (page 150)
Broccoli with Lemon Sauce (page 178)
Chocolate Waffles (page 239)

2 racks of lamb chops,
tips frenched, cut
into individual chops
(see Note)
Salt and freshly ground
black pepper

✳

MOUNTAINEERING IN CANADA

By the end of the 1800s, most of the important mountains in Europe had been conquered by climbers, and serious mountaineers were looking for new challenges. When word of the Canadian Rockies reached climbing clubs in Europe and the eastern cities of North America, the climbers started heading to Canada's western provinces. The railroads quickly realized that catering to mountain climbers could be a very profitable business.

They also discovered that the press coverage of the mountaineers brought hundreds of general tourists who just wanted to stay in hotels owned by the railroads and look at the mountains that were being climbed. The railroads began bringing in mountain guides from Switzerland and assigning them to the hotels. Eventually it got to a point where any tourist who wanted to climb a mountain could safely do so. They set up climbs that were more like uphill hikes for the amateur, as well as the real stuff for the real climbers.

Broiled Lamb Chops Stuffed with Mint and Basil Pesto

ITALY

MAKES 4 SERVINGS

3 tablespoons toasted
  pine nuts
1/2 cup fresh basil leaves,
  snugly packed
1/2 cup fresh mint, snugly
  packed
2 cloves garlic, chopped
2 tablespoons extra-virgin
  olive oil
1/2 teaspoon salt
1/4 teaspoon freshly ground
  black pepper
8 loin lamb chops

1. In a food processor, puree the pine nuts, basil, mint, garlic, olive oil, and half the salt and pepper. The result is the basil pesto stuffing.

2. Using a small sharp knife make an incision between the "tail flap" of loin and the bone of the chops, with the knife follow along the line of the bone to make an interior pocket. Repeat this with all the chops. Stuff the chops with the pesto. Snip off a corner of a plastic bag to make a pastry-type bag. Fill the bag with the pesto stuffing. Pipe the pesto into the chops. Rub whatever leftover pesto you have over the chops.

3. Heat a broiler and cook the lamb chops for 4 to 5 minutes per side, or to desired state of doneness. Serve immediately.

SUGGESTED MENU:

Eggplant Parmesan (page 180)
Broiled Lamb Chops Stuffed with Mint and Basil Pesto
Baked Apples with Figs, Apricots, and Raisins (page 229)

Roast Pork with Rosemary and Garlic

ITALY

1. Preheat the oven to 350° F.

2. With the wide blade of a knife smash the garlic and then combine with half the salt to make a rough paste. In a small bowl, combine the garlic paste with the rosemary, olive oil, and black pepper. Rub this mixture over the pork roast to coat evenly.

3. In a medium roasting pan, spread the onions evenly over the bottom of the pan and season with the remaining salt. Place the pork roast on top and cook for 1½ hours. Stir the onions occasionally, so they are coated with the juices from the pork and cook evenly.

4. Turn the heat up to 450° F. and cook the pork roast for 15 to 25 minutes more, basting occasionally. The roast is done when it is rich golden brown and has an internal temperature of 160° F.

5. Remove from the oven and let rest, loosely covered with foil, for 10 minutes before you slice it. Serve the pork on a bed of the roasted onions.

SUGGESTED MENU:

Ribollita (Tuscan Vegetable Soup) (page 8)
Roast Pork with Rosemary and Garlic
Chocolate Biscotti (page 284)

MAKES 4 SERVINGS

8 cloves garlic
1 teaspoon salt
2 tablespoons minced fresh rosemary
2 tablespoons olive oil
1 teaspoon freshly ground black pepper
One 8-bone pork rib roast
6 cups sliced onions

Mung Bean Sprouts with Pork

MADAME NG SIONG MUI, SINGAPORE

MAKES 4 SERVINGS

MARINATED PORK
1½ teaspoons salt
1½ teaspoons sugar
1½ teaspoons soy sauce
¾ teaspoon freshly ground
    black pepper
1½ tablespoons cornstarch
1 tablespoon vegetable oil
¾ pound pork loin,
    cut into ¼-inch dice

FOR THE MUNG BEAN
SPROUTS:
3 tablespoons oil
3 tablespoons minced
    ginger
3 tablespoons minced
    shallot
6 cups mung bean sprouts,
    coarsely chopped
1½ teaspoons salt
1½ teaspoons sugar
1½ teaspoons soy sauce
1 tablespoon cornstarch
3 tablespoons water
3 tablespoons minced fresh
    coriander
¾ cup sliced scallions,
    white and green parts,
    cut into ½-inch pieces

1. **To marinate the pork:** In a medium bowl, combine all the ingredients for the marinade except the pork, and mix together to make a thick paste. Add the pork and stir with a spoon so the pork is thoroughly coated with the paste. Set aside to marinate for ten minutes.

2. When ready to cook, heat a wok or large skillet. Add 1 tablespoon of the oil. Add half the ginger and shallot and stir-fry for 1 to 2 minutes. Take care not to burn the shallots. Add the sprouts, salt, sugar, and soy sauce. Stir-fry over high heat for 3 minutes to wilt the sprouts. Remove the sprouts from the pan and set aside.

3. Reheat the wok and add the remaining oil. When the oil is hot, add the remaining ginger and shallot and cook until fragrant, about 1 minute. Add the marinated pork and stir-fry over high heat for 4 to 5 minutes, until the pork is cooked.

4. When the pork is cooked, return the sprouts to the pan, and cook for 2 minutes to heat through. Dissolve the cornstarch in the water and add to the pan. Cook for 2 minutes more so the cornstarch thickens. Add the coriander and scallions, mix well, and serve.

SUGGESTED MENU:

**Mung Bean Sprouts with Pork
Cauliflower Salad (page 198)**

THE CHINESE OF SINGAPORE

Thousands of years ago Chinese traders started sailing down through the South China Sea, turning west at Singapore and heading for the Bay of Bengal to do a little business in India. Over the centuries a few of those traders settled into Singapore, but when Singapore became part of the British Empire in the early 1800s, the number of Chinese living there began to increase rapidly. By the middle of the 1800s, over 60 percent of the population of Singapore was Chinese.

Most of the Chinese immigrants had come as indentured workers. Their plan was to earn as much money in Singapore as they could and then head back to their hometowns in China. When Singapore became a crown colony under the direct control of England, it began to play a key role in Britain's world trade. Commercial sailing vessels were on their way out and steamships were taking over. When England opened the Suez Canal in 1869, Singapore became *the* place to refuel when steaming between Asia and Europe. Much of the work associated with the port fell on the backs of the Chinese laborers.

The Chinese who settled in Singapore are known as Straits Chinese, Straits being a reference to the waters that surround Singapore. Straits Chinese have a history that goes back for hundreds of years. Originally their families lived mostly in the southeastern part of China. Over the centuries they began to move down along the coasts of Vietnam, Thailand, and Malaysia, until they came to Singapore. They are as Chinese as any other Chinese.

The Straits Chinese of Singapore keep the same lunar calendar as traditional Chinese all over the world. They share the same cultural influences of great thinkers like Confucius and Lao-tzu, they write with the same pictorial language, and sign their important documents with the same type of chop.

As more and more Chinese came into Singapore during the 1800s, Singapore became a city that is predominantly Chinese. For the most part, laborers stopped arriving. The newer immigrants were shopkeepers, traders, and businessmen, and they came to stay. A government policy has encouraged all Chinese to learn to speak the mother language of China, known as Mandarin, and slowly all the Chinese have learned to speak to each other. And with so many people using English as a second language, they can even speak to me.

THE INDIGENOUS FOOD OF SINGAPORE

The indigenous food of Singapore was originally the cooking of Malaysia and Indonesia. In Singapore these foods are presented as four different cuisines.

The first is *Sumatran Nasi Padang*. It originated in the Padang area of western Sumatra. Many of the dishes consist of coconut cream combined with various spices and chilies to produce a sauce which is then used as the cooking base for fish, poultry, and vegetables. White rice comes in to damp down the heat of the chilies.

Second is *Javanese*. The most famous of the Javanese dishes is *satay*. *Satay* is made by marinating bite-sized pieces of lamb, chicken, or beef; placing them on wooden skewers; and then grilling the meat over coals. The cooked food is then presented with a peanut sauce. There is a *satay* recipe on page 82.

Next up are the *Malayan* dishes. There is a considerable similarity between Malayan and Javanese cooking, but the approach to spicing is somewhat different. One of the best of the Malay dishes is *pepisan*—seafood coated with a sauce made from coconut milk and spices, then grilled in a banana leaf.

The fourth of the traditional cuisines is called *Nonya*. *Nonya* cooking combines many of the classic ingredients and cooking techniques of both the Chinese and the Malaysians. *Laska* is a good example, thick noodles and shrimp drawn from a Chinese recipe then blended together with Malaysian coconut milk and spices.

When you take these four indigenous food styles and add them to the eight regional cuisines that were brought by the Chinese immigrants, and the two forms imported by the settlers from India, you can see why Singapore is famous for its good food. Of course, you must also give the Singaporeans credit for *not* being influenced by English food during their British colonial period.

A stand of bamboo, one of the basic building blocks for the architecture and gastronomy of southeast Asia.

ROASTED SPICY PORK RIBS

SANTIAGO PARK PLAZA HOTEL, CHILE

This is one of the down-home country-style recipes of Chile that is often prepared for a family gathering. Having tasted it a number of times on my visit to Chile, I decided to join a family just for the food of it.

1. Combine the vegetable oil and smashed garlic to make a garlic oil. Let stand for at least 30 minutes, the longer the better. In a small bowl, combine the oregano, salt, and pepper and set aside.

2. **To prepare the sauce:** In another small bowl, stir together the ketchup and Chinese chili paste and set aside.

3. Preheat the oven to 375° F.

4. Cut the ribs into serving-sized pieces. Place the ribs on a large baking sheet lined with aluminum foil. Rub both sides of the ribs with the garlic oil mixture and coat with the chopped garlic. Then cover both sides with the chili sauce. Sprinkle the ribs with the oregano mixture and bake for 1½ hours.

SUGGESTED MENU:

Roasted Spicy Pork Ribs
Sweet Potatoes with Dates (page 154)
Tomato Salad with Parsley Sauce (page 209)
Strawberry Shortcakes (page 238)

MAKES 4 SERVINGS

¼ cup vegetable oil
1 clove garlic, smashed, plus 5 cloves, chopped
1 tablespoon dried oregano leaves
1¼ teaspoons salt
⅛ teaspoon ground white pepper, or ¼ teaspoon freshly ground black pepper
4 to 5 pounds pork spareribs

FOR THE CHILI SAUCE:
1 cup ketchup
2 to 3 tablespoons Chinese chili paste or Chinese chili paste with garlic

❋

A SHORT INTRODUCTION
TO CHILE'S GEOGRAPHY

The word Chile comes from one of the ancient languages of South America's native tribes. It means "the place where the land ends," and that's a pretty good description. Chile has over 2,500 miles of coastline where the west side of South America ends and the Pacific Ocean begins. The southern tip of Chile is on the island of Tierra del Fuego, which is the most southerly point in South America, and right opposite the polar ice of Antarctica; clearly the point where the land ends.

If you take a look at a map of South America you see Chile running down the western side of the continent like a ribbon, 3,000 miles from top to bottom but only 100 miles wide. Chile is so narrow that you can stand on the peaks of the Andean mountains that represent the country's eastern frontier with Argentina and see the beaches on the Pacific Ocean that make up the western border.

The Atacama Desert in the north is the driest place on earth. As far as anyone knows, there are parts of Atacama that have never had a single drop of rain. In the middle of the country is the nation's agricultural center, with thousands of acres of exceptional soil. The area's farms, orchards, and vineyards are constantly being irrigated by a flow of fresh water from the melting snow in the Andes. To the south of the farms is the Lake District with some of the most beautiful scenery in the world. Finally, as Chile comes to an end, the land breaks up into a thousand islands. Chile also has 2,085 volcanoes. Two thousand and thirty are quietly sleeping. Fifty-five are awake, active, and very busy doing their thing.

The Central Market,
Valparaiso, Chile.

VEAL SCALLOPINE WITH PARMESAN AND TOMATOES

ITALY

1. **To prepare the sauce:** In a bowl, combine all the ingredients and set aside.

2. **To make the scallopine:** In a food processor, combine the bread and the thyme together to make a fine crumb. Add the cheese and pulse to mix evenly. Place the flavored bread crumbs on a piece of waxed paper or a large flat plate. Place the flour on a piece of waxed paper or on a large flat plate for dredging the scallopine. Mix the egg in a rimmed plate or broad bowl with the water and a pinch of salt and pepper. Dry off the veal scallopine and season with the salt and pepper. Dredge the scallopine in the flour and shake off the excess. Then dip the scallopine in the egg, let any excess drip off. Then coat the scallopine in the flavored bread crumbs. Repeat with all of the veal.

3. Heat a large skillet and add enough of the oil to coat the bottom of the pan. Sauté the scallopine over medium-high heat until golden brown, 2 to 3 minutes per side. Do this in batches, if necessary, and replenish the oil as needed.

4. Place the cooked scallopine on a warm platter. When all the scallopine are done, add the tomato sauce to the pan and cook over high heat for 1 minute, until heated through. Spoon the sauce over the scallopine, garnish with basil leaves, and serve immediately.

SUGGESTED MENU:

Risotto with Red Wine (page 167)
Veal Scallopine with Parmesan and Tomatoes
Hazelnut Cake (page 280)

MAKES 4 SERVINGS

FOR THE SAUCE:
2 ripe medium tomatoes, diced
2¹/₂ tablespoons minced fresh basil
2 tablespoons extra-virgin olive oil
2 teaspoons white wine vinegar
1 clove garlic, minced
¹/₂ teaspoon salt
¹/₄ teaspoon freshly ground black pepper

FOR THE SCALLOPINE:
4 slices white bread
1¹/₂ teaspoons dried thyme
¹/₄ cup finely grated Parmigiano-Reggiano cheese
Flour for dredging
1 egg
1 tablespoon water
¹/₂ teaspoon salt
¹/₈ teaspoon freshly ground black pepper
8 scallopines of veal (about 3 ounces each)
2 tablespoons olive oil
Basil leaves for garnish

Pasta, Potatoes, and Grains

SPAGHETTI WITH OLIVES AND CAPERS

LE SIRENUSE, POSITANO, ITALY

MAKES 4 SERVINGS

4 quarts water
2 tablespoons olive oil
2 anchovy fillets, chopped
2 cloves garlic, chopped
½ teaspoon crushed red
    pepper
¼ cup sliced pitted black
    olives, preferably Greek
    or Italian
1 tablespoon capers
2½ cups chopped
    tomatoes and their
    juices
¼ cup chopped fresh
    parsley
½ teaspoon dried oregano
1 pound spaghetti

Positano is on the coast of Italy just south of Naples, and it is home to a resort named Le Sirenuse, which means "the sirens." Ancient Greek legend has it that the sirens could infatuate sailors with their singing. The hotel infatuates its guests with its cooking, an example of which is this recipe for pasta with olives and capers.

1. In a large saucepan, bring the water, lightly salted, to a boil.

2. In a sauté pan over medium heat, heat the olive oil. Add the anchovies, and cook, stirring, for 1 minute. Add the garlic and the crushed red pepper and cook for 1 minute more. Stir in the olives, capers, tomatoes and their juices, parsley, and oregano. Simmer the sauce for 10 minutes.

3. Add the spaghetti to the boiling water and cook according to the package directions. Drain the spaghetti.

4. Add the spaghetti to the sauce in the saucepan. Heat thoroughly and serve.

AN INTRODUCTION TO THE FOOD OF CAMPAGNA

Both the ancient Greeks and the Romans were impressed with the quality of Campagna's soil. It was an ideal place for growing fruits and vegetables; olive trees produced excellent oil. The hills were planted with vineyards that yielded highly respected wines. The climate was mild enough for the planting of citrus crops and the growing season lasted all year round. At about A.D. 600, water buffalo were brought to the area from India, and today, great herds of their descendants are used to produce the finest mozzarella cheese.

For the past thousand years or so, foreign rulers made Campagna a difficult environment for the average person, and when the chance came to immigrate to North America millions did so. During the period from 1880 to 1920, almost 4 million Campagnese moved to the United States and Canada, many of them from the area in and around Naples. But, unlike many of the immigrant groups that came to North America before them, the Italians held on to their approach to food. As a result, when Americans talk about Italian food, what they are often talking about is the food of Campagna.

Perhaps the most important food from Campagna is pasta. When you talk about pasta there are two basic types. There is fresh pasta, traditionally made everyday at home, usually flat, a specialty of the northern part of the country, and until very recently not very common in North America. Then there is dry pasta, produced in factories, and hard and round instead of soft and flat. This is the specialty of the southern part of Italy. Its most common form is spaghetti, and it has become as basic to the diet of North Americans as hamburgers and hot dogs. The factories of Campagna have been producing dry pasta in the form of spaghetti or one of its variations since the 1400s.

Campagna also played an important role in the story of ice cream. The Campagnese city of Naples has a worldwide reputation for ice cream, and it was an Italian immigrant from Naples, one Philip Lenzi, who in 1777 ran the first advertisement for commercially made ice cream. It ran in a New York City newspaper. Before Breyers, Sealtest, Häagen-Dazs, even before Ben or Jerry, there was Lenzi. Also, it was from Campagna that North America received its first pizza. Pasta, ice cream, and pizza. Not bad for one neighborhood.

THE WINES OF MASTROBERARDINO

Campagna is one of the world's oldest regions for the production of wine. Historians tell us that the ancient Greeks planted vineyards in Campagna, and there is clear evidence that the ancient Romans produced some of their best wines in the soil of this area. Part of the reason that the soil is so productive is that it is filled with nutrient-rich volcanic ash from Mount Vesuvius. I guess every volcanic cloud has a silver lining. The ancient Romans had some favorite grape varieties from the area, too. One was called Aglianico. The Romans had called this grape *Vitis hellenica* meaning "Greek vine." Another variety was called Fiano.

For years the Fiano was thought to be extinct. Then, in 1952, a local wine expert named Antonio Mastroberardino discovered a small group of Fiano growing wild, and decided to try and bring the vines back to the level of quality that they had some two thousand years ago.

Today, Mastroberardino uses these ancient grape varieties to produce some of Italy's finest wines. In a time when we are losing many of our agricultural varieties, and have fewer and fewer species to choose from, it is wonderful to see someone preserving our heritage.

Pasta and tomato sauce by the pool at the hotel Le Sirenuse, Positano, Italy.

TAGLIATELLE WITH CHICKEN SAUCE

HOTEL CERTOSA DI MAGGIANO, SIENA, ITALY

In the year 1314, Cardinal Riccardo Petroni ordered the construction of a Carthusian Monastery on the outskirts of the city of Siena. For hundreds of years these buildings functioned as an important monastery. But when the religious aspects of the estate began to wane, it was turned into a 17-room resort with an excellent restaurant. The property is known as Certosa Di Maggiano. The following recipe comes from the hotel's restaurant and is unusual in that it uses a traditional meat sauce, but instead of a beef base it uses ground chicken.

1. In a large sauté pan over medium heat, heat the olive oil. Add the ground chicken or turkey and cook until brown, about 4 minutes, stirring occasionally. Add the salt and pepper.

2. Add the carrot, onion, and celery and cook for 5 minutes more. Pour in the wine, chopped tomatoes, bay leaf, rosemary, and broth. Simmer over low heat for 1 hour.

3. In a saucepan, bring the water, lightly salted, to a boil. Add the pasta and cook according to the package directions. Put 2 tablespoons of the pasta cooking water into the sauce. Drain the pasta.

4. Remove the bay leaf and rosemary sprig from the sauce. Add the drained pasta to the pan with the sauce. Toss the pasta with the sauce and heat through. Serve with grated Parmesan cheese on top.

MAKES 4 SERVINGS

1 tablespoon olive oil
1 pound ground chicken or turkey
½ teaspoon salt
⅛ teaspoon freshly ground black pepper
1 carrot, chopped
1 small onion, chopped
1 stalk celery, chopped
½ cup dry white wine
1 cup chopped tomatoes; or 4 plum tomatoes, chopped
1 bay leaf
1 sprig rosemary, or 1 teaspoon dried
2 cups chicken broth, or 1 cup beef broth and 1 cup chicken broth
4 quarts water
1 pound tagliatelle or fettuccine pasta
2 tablespoons pasta cooking water
Freshly grated Parmesan cheese

Pasta with Meat Sauce

Tornavento Ristorante, Treiso, Italy

MAKES 4 SERVINGS

2 tablespoons olive oil
1 sprig rosemary, or
    1 teaspoon dried
1 bay leaf
1 clove garlic, chopped
1 carrot, chopped
2 stalks celery, chopped
1 medium onion, chopped
1 pound ground beef
1/2 teaspoon salt
1 cup red wine
3 cups pureed tomatoes
2 cups boiling water, plus
    4 quarts water
1 pound spaghetti or
    linguine
Freshly grated Parmesan
    cheese

As Piedmont towns go, Treiso is tiny. If you blink while you are passing through, you will miss it. Which would be a shame, because Treiso is home to an interesting restaurant called Tornavento. *Tornavento* means "weathervane," and in this case it will point you to a restaurant with a very contemporary look. Open and bright, with a wonderful attention to detail, it is owned by Leila Gobino and Marco Serra and they are reworking the traditional recipes of the region. An example is this dish of pasta with meat sauce.

1. In a large sauté pan over medium heat, heat the olive oil. Add the rosemary, bay leaf, garlic, carrot, celery, and onion. Cook, stirring occasionally, for 3 minutes. Add the ground beef. Cook, stirring for 5 minutes. Add the salt.

2. Pour in the red wine and cook until the wine is completely absorbed by the meat. Finally, add the tomatoes and boiling water. Simmer uncovered for 1 hour.

3. In a large saucepan, bring the 4 quarts of water, lightly salted, to a boil. Add the pasta and cook according to the package directions. Drain the pasta.

4. Remove the bay leaf and rosemary sprig from the sauce. Add the pasta to the sauce and heat thoroughly. Serve with grated Parmesan cheese on top.

THE FOOD OF PIEDMONT

The Po and Tanaro rivers flow through Piedmont creating a fertile plain, a plain that has produced crops of the highest quality for thousands of years. Some of our most ancient crops—barley, wheat, rye, and oats—are grown there and used to produce magnificent breads. Corn is ground into meal and used to make polenta. Polenta is an ancient corn pudding that for centuries was the food of the rural poor. There are apples, pears, grapes, pomegranates, walnuts, chestnuts, and the famous hazelnuts of Alba.

The area is also famous for its rice. During the 1780s, Thomas Jefferson traveled through Europe making friends and drumming up business for the newly formed United States of America. Jefferson, like so many gentlemen of the time, was extremely interested in farming and was always on the lookout for something new and valuable to bring back home. As he passed through Piedmont he collected samples of the local seed rice, which was already famous as the best rice in Europe. He took the samples back to the United States and made a profitable contribution to the rice industry in North America. Actually, to say he "took" the rice back home is not totally accurate. What he did was "smuggle" the rice back home. The people of Piedmont knew how important their rice was and had passed laws against having it exported.

The cooking of Piedmont is often similar to the type of cooking that you find in the Alpine areas of France and Switzerland. The older recipes took the heat that was being generated in the hearth to warm the home and gave it an additional role as the fire for cooking—roasting on spits, long, slow cooking in big pots that hold the heat. It is the cooking of mountain families, cooking that is filling and healthful for the lifestyle of the people who created it.

Noodles in Butter Sauce

CALIFORNIA

MAKES 4 SERVINGS

¹/₂ pound broad noodles
2 tablespoons unsalted
  butter
Salt and freshly ground
  black pepper

1. In a large saucepan of lightly salted boiling water, cook the noodles for 7 minutes or until tender.

2. Drain the noodles and return them to the saucepan. Add the butter and toss well. Season to taste with salt and pepper.

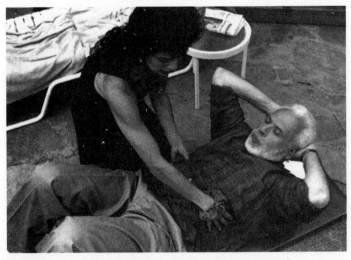

Yvonne Esquer, the trainer at the Sonoma Mission Inn, teaching me a couple of techniques for flattening my stomach. Of course, the one that works best is limiting my calorie intake.

ROASTED NEW POTATOES WITH ROASTED GARLIC SAUCE

CANADA

1. Preheat the oven to 350° F.

2. In a bowl, combine the potatoes, olive oil, salt, pepper, and thyme. Toss to coat the mixture evenly.

3. Place the potatoes and the unpeeled garlic cloves on a baking sheet and into the oven. Bake for 35 minutes, or until the potatoes are tender.

4. **To prepare the sauce:** After 25 to 30 minutes of baking time, remove the garlic cloves. The cloves will be softened and can be easily popped out of their skins. In a blender, place the roasted garlic cloves, balsamic vinegar, olive oil, and salt. Puree until smooth. Remove the sauce from the blender. Stir in the chives.

5. When the potatoes come out of the oven, toss evenly with the sauce.

MAKES 4 SERVINGS

1 pound new potatoes, washed and sliced in half or in quarters if they are large
1 tablespoon olive oil
1/2 teaspoon salt
1/8 teaspoon freshly ground black pepper
3/4 teaspoon chopped fresh thyme, or 1/4 teaspoon dried
6 cloves garlic, unpeeled

FOR THE ROASTED GARLIC SAUCE:
6 cloves roasted garlic, above
1/2 teaspoon balsamic vinegar
3 tablespoons olive oil
1/2 teaspoon salt
1 tablespoon chopped fresh chives

DEVILED POTATOES

ITALY

MAKES 6 SERVINGS

3 pounds red potatoes,
   or other waxy-style
   potatoes, cut into
   1-inch pieces
3 tablespoons olive oil
2 cloves garlic, minced
1/2 teaspoon red pepper
   flakes
Salt

1. Preheat the oven to 400° F.

2. Place the potatoes in a roasting pan and coat them with half the olive oil. Roast the potatoes in the oven for 40 minutes, stirring occasionally.

3. While the potatoes are cooking, mix the remaining olive oil with the garlic and the red pepper flakes. After the potatoes have cooked for 40 minutes and are tender and lightly browned, stir in the seasoned oil and garlic, and roast for 10 minutes more. Season to taste with salt and serve.

The fog-shrouded vineyards at Ceretto Wineries in Piedmont, Italy. The fog plays a key role in controlling the effects of the sun on the vines.

TURMERIC POTATOES WITH GREEN BELL PEPPERS

SINGAPORE

1. In a pot of water, boil the potatoes in their jackets until cooked but still firm. Plunge them into cold water for a minute and peel. (The peeling is optional.) Cut into 1-inch cubes.

2. Quarter the peppers; remove the stems and seeds. Cut into 1-inch pieces.

3. In a large frying pan, heat the oil over a moderately high flame. When the oil is very hot, add the turmeric, and immediately add the potatoes and peppers. Sprinkle with salt, if used, and sauté, turning and tossing for 3 to 4 minutes. Sprinkle the water over the vegetables, reduce the heat, and cook, covered, until the peppers are cooked but still very crisp, 5 to 10 minutes.

4. Uncover, and raise the heat to evaporate any excess moisture remaining in the pan and to brown the vegetables. Cook and stir for about 5 minutes.

MAKES 6 SERVINGS

8 medium boiling potatoes
4 medium bell peppers (red, green, and/or yellow; the more colors the better)
3 to 4 tablespoons vegetable oil
1½ teaspoons ground turmeric
1½ teaspoons kosher salt (optional)
2 to 3 tablespoons water

✳

SPICY MASHED POTATOES

CHILE

MAKES 4 SERVINGS

4 medium potatoes, peeled
    and cut into chunks
1/3 cup milk, heated
1 tablespoon butter
3/4 teaspoon salt
1 to 2 teaspoons Chinese
    chili paste or Chinese
    chili paste with garlic

1. In a large pot, boil the potatoes in plenty of water until they are tender, about 20 minutes.

2. Put the potatoes through a potato ricer or food mill. Stir in the heated milk and butter. Add the salt and the chili paste, stirring briefly to blend evenly.

GRATIN OF NEW POTATOES, CELERY, AND RED ONION WITH ROSEMARY

CANADA

1. Preheat the oven to 375° F.

2. In a bowl, place the potatoes, onion, and celery. Add the olive oil, rosemary, salt, and pepper and toss to coat evenly.

3. Arrange the vegetables, slightly overlapping them, in an 8-inch square baking dish. Pour in the chicken broth. Bake for 50 minutes, then remove the dish from the oven.

4. Preheat the broiler. Sprinkle the top of the potatoes with the Parmesan cheese and broil for 3 minutes, or until the cheese is lightly browned. Serve the gratin using a slotted spoon.

MAKES 4 SERVINGS

1 pound new potatoes, sliced
1 medium red onion, thinly sliced
2 stalks celery, thinly sliced
2 tablespoons olive oil
1 tablespoon dried rosemary
3/4 teaspoon salt
1/8 teaspoon freshly ground black pepper
1/3 cup chicken broth
1 tablespoon freshly grated Parmesan cheese

LAYERED POTATOES AND ONIONS WITH BASIL

CALIFORNIA

MAKES 4 SERVINGS

1½ pounds potatoes,
    peeled and thinly sliced
1 teaspoon salt
¼ teaspoon freshly ground
    black pepper
2 tablespoons chopped
    fresh basil,
    or 1 tablespoon dried
2 medium onions, thinly
    sliced

FOR THE SAUCE:
2 tablespoons butter
1 tablespoon all-purpose
    flour
1 cup milk, warmed

1. Preheat the oven to 350° F. Lightly grease an 8-inch round, heatproof pan.

2. In the prepared pan, make a layer of half of the potatoes, season with half of the salt and pepper, sprinkle half of the basil on top, then add a layer of all the onions. Finally, layer the rest of the potatoes. Season with the remaining salt and pepper, ending with a sprinkling of chopped basil.

3. To make the sauce: In a saucepan over low heat, melt the butter. Add the flour, whisking constantly. Gradually pour in the warm milk, whisking constantly so there are no lumps. Pour the sauce into the pan with the potatoes and onions.

4. Bake for 1 hour. Let the potatoes stand for 5 minutes before serving.

Curried Potatoes and Vegetables

ARUBA

1. Into a pot of lightly salted cold water, place the potatoes and parboil them for 5 to 7 minutes, until they are almost tender. Drain the potatoes and set them aside.

2. In a saucepan fitted with a steamer, steam the cauliflower and string beans for 2 to 3 minutes, until almost tender.

3. In a sauté pan over medium heat, heat the vegetable oil. Add the onion and garlic and cook for 2 minutes. Stir in the curry powder and cook, stirring constantly, for another minute. Add the chicken broth or water and the salt to the pan, then add the potatoes and the vegetables. Cover the pan and simmer gently for 5 minutes, or until the potatoes and vegetables are tender.

4. Stir in the sour cream and heat gently over low heat. Serve immediately.

MAKES 4 SERVINGS

2 medium potatoes, peeled and cubed
1½ cups cauliflower florets
1 cup sliced green beans
1 tablespoon vegetable oil
1 medium onion, chopped
1 clove garlic, chopped
1 tablespoon curry powder
½ cup chicken broth or water
½ teaspoon salt
½ cup nonfat sour cream

Swiss Potato Pancake

BANFF SPRINGS HOTEL, ALBERTA, CANADA

MAKES 4 SERVINGS

2 to 3 large whole baking
  potatoes, such as Idaho
  (about 1 pound total),
  unpeeled
3 tablespoons vegetable oil
1/3 cup thinly sliced onions
1/2 teaspoon salt
1/4 teaspoon freshly ground
  black pepper

1. In a pot, boil the potatoes for 12 to 15 minutes, or until they are almost but not quite cooked. Cool completely. Peel the potatoes and grate coarsely.

2. In a 10- or 12-inch nonstick skillet, heat the oil. Add the onions and sauté for 1 minute. Add the grated potatoes in a thin, even layer. Season with salt and pepper. Lightly press the potatoes together with a spatula. Cook over medium heat for 5 minutes, until a crust forms on the bottom. The potato pancake is then turned over in order to brown on the other side. Place a plate that is slightly bigger than the pan over the top of the pan. Turn the pan upside down so the pancake is resting on the plate. Slide the pancake back into the pan. The cooked side will now be facing up. Cook until the second side is brown and crisp, about 5 minutes. This pancake can be made ahead and reheated briefly in a 425° F. oven until crisp.

3. Cut into pie-shaped wedges to serve.

POTATO PANCAKES

ROYAL VIKING SUN

1. In a medium mixing bowl, beat together the eggs, flour, salt, pepper, and onion.

2. Place the grated potatoes on a piece of cheesecloth or a clean kitchen towel, gather the ends together, and wring the potatoes to extract their moisture. Add the grated potatoes to the egg mixture and stir well. Shape the mixture into 6 thin potato pancakes.

3. In a large, heavy frying pan over medium-high heat, heat the oil until almost smoking. Add 3 of the pancakes and cook for 2 to 3 minutes on each side, or until golden brown. Repeat with the remaining 3 pancakes. Drain on paper towels and serve hot.

MAKES 6 PANCAKES

2 eggs
1/3 cup all-purpose flour
1 teaspoon salt
1/2 teaspoon freshly ground
   black pepper
1/4 cup grated onion
2 cups coarsely grated
   potatoes
2 tablespoons vegetable oil

Garlic Mashed Potatoes

CANADA

MAKES 4 SERVINGS

1½ pounds potatoes,
   peeled and cut into
   chunks
3 tablespoons olive oil
2 to 3 cloves garlic,
   crushed and finely
   minced
¾ cup chicken broth or
   milk
¾ teaspoon salt

1. In a saucepan of cold lightly salted water, boil the potatoes for 20 minutes or until tender.

2. Drain the potatoes and press them through a potato ricer or food mill or mash them with a masher. Stir in the remaining ingredients and blend well.

Bell pepper vendor,
Valparaiso Market,
Chile.

Baked Sweet Potato Chips

CHILE

---

1. Preheat the oven to 400° F.

2. Lightly oil a baking sheet and set it aside. In a bowl, combine the olive oil, salt, and ginger.

3. Peel the potatoes and cut them into $1/8$-inch slices. Put the potatoes in a bowl, add the oil and ginger mixture. Toss to blend evenly.

4. Arrange the slices on the baking sheet. Bake for 25 to 30 minutes, turning every 10 minutes, until the potatoes are tender and lightly browned.

MAKES 4 SERVINGS

$1/4$ cup olive oil
1 teaspoon salt
$1/2$ teaspoon ground ginger
2 large sweet potatoes

The Central Market, Valparaiso, Chile.

THE VOLCANO OF CHILE

The most dramatic element in the landscape surrounding the town of Pucon is the local volcano. It is considered an active volcano but is sufficiently mellow to have become a major tourist attraction.

In town there are a number of agencies that will supply you with guides and gear for an ascent to the top of the volcano. You'll drive to the foot of the mountain, be equipped with the proper gear, and guided up. Assuming that you are in good condition, the climb to the top will take about five hours. If you are not in good condition, schedule about two years. And get in shape. This is not something you do by yourself. The trip will take you into some serious terrain, and a professional guide from the area is absolutely essential. If you are up to it, it is an amazing experience. At the top you will be looking right down into the center of the earth.

Volcanoes are formed as a result of plate tectonics. The outer shell of the world is made up of a series of giant sheets of rock that are called tectonic plates. The plates sit next to each other, on top of a core of partly melted rock. But the plates also slide around on the melted rock. They move from a half inch to eight inches a year. Sometimes they bang into each other. Sometimes they slide against each other. Sometimes one plate drifts under another. Most volcanoes that are on land are formed when two plates collide and one is forced under the other. The friction between them causes an enormous amount of heat—heat that is so intense that it actually melts rocks that are some fifty to a hundred miles inside the earth.

The melted rock is forced to the surface of the earth and the first thing you know, you have a volcano. The melted rock is called magma, and it contains a great deal of gas. From time to time the pressure of the gas and the magma is just too much and the whole thing blows its stack. When the magma reaches the surface, it is called lava. The actual mountain is usually built up around the opening into the center of the earth by lava that was pushed out during repeated eruptions.

Once a volcanic mountain is formed, the lava flows and eruptions don't always take place at the top of the central vent. At this point it is possible for the magma and gases to break through on the side of the mountain.

MASHED GINGERED SWEET POTATOES

ARUBA

1. Preheat the oven to 400° F.

2. Bake the sweet potatoes for 50 to 60 minutes, or until the potatoes are tender when pierced with a knife.

3. Scrape the flesh out of the potatoes. Press the potatoes through a potato ricer or food mill or mash them with a masher. Stir in the remaining ingredients.

MAKES 4 SERVINGS

2 pounds sweet potatoes
2 tablespoons unsalted
  butter
1/3 cup orange juice or milk
2 teaspoons fresh ginger
  (about one 3-inch piece),
  peeled and finely
  minced
1/4 teaspoon ground
  cinnamon
1/2 teaspoon salt

Town square in Oranjestad, Aruba's capital city.

Sweet Potatoes with Dates

CHILE

MAKES 4 SERVINGS

FOR THE DRESSING:
1 tablespoon balsamic, red
  wine, or raspberry
  vinegar
2 tablespoons olive or
  vegetable oil
½ teaspoon salt
½ cup chopped dates
½ cup toasted slivered
  almonds

1½ pounds sweet
  potatoes, peeled and
  cut into 1-inch cubes

1. **To prepare the dressing:** In a mixing bowl, combine the ingredients, then set aside.

2. In a large saucepan fitted with a steamer, place the potatoes and steam for 7 to 10 minutes or until just tender. Do not overcook.

3. Place the sweet potatoes in the bowl with the dressing and toss to mix evenly.

Riverside, Valdivia, Chile.

THE MAPUCHE NATIVES OF SOUTH AMERICA

The original cooks in Chile were the Mapuche, which means "people of the earth." Their family groups have lived on the land that is now called Chile for thousands of years. They lived in huts that were moved from one area to another. The moves allowed them to take advantage of the best hunting, fishing, and gathering in each season. But each of the areas that they moved to was considered part of their tribal lands.

The central political and economic unit is an extended family that can easily number five hundred individuals. The head of the family is called the Cacique. His power and importance are based, not only on his material possessions, but also on the quality of his wisdom as expressed in the advice he gives to the younger members of his family.

The women of the group play a particularly important role as the head of all things mystical. A girl is identified during her childhood as having the necessary skills to be able to communicate with the gods, and she takes on this responsibility. The women known as Machi are in contact with the gods of life. The women known as Kalku communicate with the gods of death.

They feel that all life exists in a perfect balance of positive and negative forces, similar to the yin and yang powers of Buddhism.

TURMERIC SWEET POTATOES

SINGAPORE

MAKES 4 SERVINGS

3 tablespoons vegetable oil

1 teaspoon yellow mustard
  seeds

1 teaspoon curry powder

1 onion, chopped (about
  ³/₄ cup)

1 tablespoon minced fresh
  ginger

3 jalapeño chilies, seeded
  and chopped

3 sweet potatoes (about
  1¹/₂ pounds), peeled,
  washed, and cut into
  1-inch cubes

¹/₂ teaspoon salt

¹/₂ teaspoon ground
  turmeric

3 tablespoons water

3 tablespoons shredded
  coconut

1. Heat a wok or large skillet. Add the oil, and when it is hot, add the mustard seeds and curry powder. Stir-fry for 1–2 minutes, until the mustard seeds brown and begin to pop. Add the onion, ginger, and chilies, and stir-fry until the onion is soft, about 3 minutes.

2. Add the sweet potatoes and mix well. Stir in the salt, turmeric, and the water. Cover and cook over medium heat for 10 to 12 minutes, or until all the water has evaporated and the sweet potatoes are tender.

3. Add the shredded coconut and mix to combine. Serve immediately.

Spices in Singapore's Chinese Market.

THE HAWKER FOOD OF SINGAPORE

For the majority of its early history, Singapore was a trading port with a mostly male society. A large segment of the population was made up of laborers who lived in communal rooming houses. No real homes and, accordingly, no real home cooking. Their meals were taken from street vendors who would set up a stove.

Eventually the owners of these peripatetic pots and pans equipped themselves with tables and chairs, and became roving restaurants. They announced their daily specials at the top of their lung capacity and became known as "hawkers." The hawkers had a series of favorite locations and the eaters had a series of favorite hawkers. In 1987, the Hawkers gathered into a series of Food Centers. The centers are filled with talented cooks who prepare Malay, Indian, and Chinese dishes.

Even today, Hawker food is the favorite food for many of the people of Singapore. When I asked one of the cooks if he would ever like to work in a traditional restaurant, his answer was a hard and fast "No." He felt that when people came to a restaurant they were responding to many factors—decoration, service, status, location. When people come to his hawker stand they are there only because of his cooking. And he liked the uncompromised compliment. Don't we all.

Chefs at the Satay Club in Singapore. They are cooks at a hawker center, an area filled with small stands at which skilled cooks prepare their favorite foods.

INDONESIAN-STYLE SAUTÉED RICE

COSTA LINDA BEACH RESORT, ARUBA

MAKES 4 SERVINGS

FOR THE RICE:
2 tablespoons vegetable oil
½ cup chopped onion
1 cup chopped carrots
1 cup chopped celery
1 cup chopped cabbage,
    bok choy, or savoy
    cabbage, if available
½ cup scallions cut into
    ½-inch strips
1 cup cooked chicken, cut
    into bite-sized pieces
1 cup roast pork, cut into
    bite-sized pieces
1 cup cooked ham, cut into
    bite-sized pieces
1 tablespoon oriental
    sesame oil
1 tablespoon curry powder
1 tablespoon chili powder
1 tablespoon soy sauce
4 cups cooked long-grain
    rice

FOR THE OMELET AND
GARNISH:
2 eggs
2 tablespoons water
1 tablespoon vegetable oil
1 cup shredded lettuce

The seventeenth century was the golden age of Dutch history—great wealth, great architecture, great art. The great houses that line the canals of Amsterdam, the furniture inside those magnificent buildings, and the works of art that were commissioned by the people who lived in those buildings—works painted by artists like Rembrandt and Frans Hals—were all funded, to a great extent, by the enormous wealth made from Holland's trade with Indonesia.

That trade also introduced Indonesian cooking to Holland and to its other colonies, including the Caribbean island of Aruba. Chef Scott Scheuerman at Aruba's Costa Linda Beach Resort carries on the tradition with this recipe for Indonesian rice.

1. To make the rice: Heat the vegetable oil in a hot wok or frying pan. Add the vegetables and stir-fry for 3 minutes. Add the chicken, pork, and ham and stir-fry for 3 minutes. Add the sesame oil and stir-fry for 1 minute. Add the curry powder, chili powder, and soy sauce and stir-fry for 1 minute. Add the cooked rice and stir-fry for 2 minutes. Hold aside and keep warm.

2. To make the omelet: In a small mixing bowl, scramble together the eggs and the water. Heat the oil in a large nonstick frying pan. Pour the egg mixture into the pan and spread it to the edges in order to be able to cook a very thin omelet. When one side is cooked, flip the omelet over and cook the other side until done. Remove the cooked omelet to a cutting surface, roll it into a tube, and slice crosswise into thin strips.

3. Place the rice onto a serving plate. Put the strips of omelet on one side and the shredded lettuce on the other.

HERBED WILD RICE

SONOMA

1. Place the rice in a strainer and run cold water over it, then drain thoroughly.

2. In a medium saucepan over high heat, bring the rice, chicken broth, and salt to a full boil. Lower the heat to a simmer and cook for 45 to 50 minutes, until the rice is just tender. The rice should not be too soft.

3. Drain the rice and transfer to a bowl. Add the parsley, chives, thyme, and butter or margarine and toss gently. Season to taste with the black pepper.

MAKES 4 SERVINGS

1 cup wild rice
4 cups chicken broth
1 teaspoon salt
1/4 cup chopped fresh
    parsley
1/4 cup chopped fresh
    chives
1 teaspoon chopped fresh
    thyme, or 1/4 teaspoon
    dried
1 tablespoon butter or
    margarine
Freshly ground black
    pepper

ABOUT SONOMA, CALIFORNIA

Drive north from San Francisco across the Golden Gate Bridge, past the houseboats of Sausalito, through the hills and shopping centers of Marin County, and in about an hour you will arrive in the valley called Sonoma.

There are two theories about the meaning of the word *Sonoma*. One says that it is a Native American word that translates as "the land of Chief Nose," a reference to a local chief who had a very big sniffer . . . the Cyrano de Bergerac of his neighborhood. Eventually, Sonoma became the birthplace of the California wine industry, where a big nose is still important. The other story claims that Sonoma is a native word, from a different tribe, meaning "valley of the moons," the validity of which can be confirmed on any clear night.

The first European to take up residence in the Sonoma Valley was Father Jose Altimira, a Franciscan missionary who established himself in the Mission Solano de Sonoma. The year was 1823, and the mission was the most northerly outpost of all the Spanish colonies on the west coast of the New World. They stretched from the bottom of South America all the way up to Sonoma.

In 1834, the Mexican government sent General Mariano Vallejo to Sonoma. His orders were to secularize the mission and establish a Mexican settlement. That was just a polite way of saying . . . take out the guys with the God and put in the guys with the gun. Vallejo immediately set up a system of land grants for his friends and relatives.

I can just see Vallejo poring over his map of Sonoma and making his plan. "Okay, this spot by the creek . . . very nice. I give it to my sister, no charge. And this place with the hill overlooking the valley . . . perfect for Uncle Carlos. Also no charge. This land by the lake is good for my brother-in-law's brother. But I don't like him so much, so we charge him; but just a little."

Of course, the fact that this land had been occupied for the past thirty-five thousand years or so by the native tribes was one of those little subtleties that was lost in the "bigger picture." Governments love "bigger pictures" . . . it lets them ignore "little people."

The very first vineyards in northern California were planted by the Franciscan missionaries so they could make sacramental wine. When General Vallejo secularized the mission he also secularized the vineyards and planted additional vines behind the army barracks. General Vallejo was able to combine making war with making wine, and in 1841 became Sonoma's first commercial vintner.

ISLAND WHITE RICE WITH LIME

ARUBA

1. In a saucepan, bring the water to a boil. Add the rice, salt, butter, lime juice, and garlic. Cover the pan and lower the heat. Simmer for 18 to 20 minutes, until all the liquid is absorbed. Remove the clove of garlic.

2. Place the rice in a serving bowl. Stir in the lime zest and chives, if desired.

MAKES 4 SERVINGS

1³/₄ cups water
1 cup white rice
¹/₂ teaspoon salt
1 tablespoon butter
2 tablespoons fresh lime
    juice
1 whole clove garlic,
    peeled
2 teaspoons finely grated
    lime zest
1 tablespoon chopped
    fresh chives (optional)

Dutch hurdy-gurdy. Oranjestad, Aruba.

Island Confetti Rice and Beans

ARUBA

**MAKES 4 TO 6
SERVINGS**

2 cups water
1 cup white rice
1 teaspoon salt
1 tablespoon vegetable oil
1 small onion, finely
    chopped
2 cloves garlic, finely
    chopped
1 small green or red bell
    pepper, diced
1 stalk celery, diced
1 carrot, diced
1 small zucchini or yellow
    squash, diced
1/2 teaspoon ground
    allspice (optional)
1 cup cooked red, pink,
    or black beans
Chopped fresh cilantro or
    parsley as a garnish

1. In a saucepan, bring the water to a boil. Add the rice and 1/2 teaspoon of salt, then cover the pan and lower the heat. Simmer for 18 to 20 minutes, until all the liquid is absorbed.

2. Meanwhile, in a sauté pan over medium heat, heat the oil. Add the onion, and cook for 2 minutes. Add the garlic, and cook for 1 minute longer. Then add the vegetables and cook for 2 minutes. Stir in the allspice and remaining 1/2 teaspoon of salt. Stir in the cooked beans and over low heat keep warm until the rice is cooked.

3. In a large bowl, combine the rice with the vegetables and beans.

Aruba is traditionally short of wood. As a result, farmers plant cacti to make fences.

BACON FRIED RICE

SINGAPORE

---

1. In a skillet, fry the bacon until crisp and drain on paper towels.

2. In a wok or large skillet, heat 1 tablespoon of the oil. Add the eggs and cook, stirring, just until firm. Remove from the pan and reserve.

3. Heat the remaining 2 tablespoons of oil in the pan and add the rice. Mix well. Add the soy sauce and mix well. Mix the eggs into the rice, breaking them into smaller pieces as you stir. Add the scallions and bacon. Mix again to combine, and serve.

NOTE: The rice should be cooked at least several hours ahead, or the day before, and refrigerated. It should be completely cold to be used for fried rice.

This dish can be kept in a casserole in the oven at 140° F. for about 40 minutes without drying out. It makes a good dish to serve with a main course that needs last-minute preparation.

MAKES 4 SERVINGS

½ pound bacon, cut into
   ½-inch pieces
3 tablespoons vegetable oil
2 eggs, beaten
3 cups cold cooked rice
   (see Note)
1½ tablespoons soy sauce
½ cup coarsely chopped
   scallions, green part only

Risotto with Pumpkin and Rosemary

Hotel Cipriani, Venice, Italy

MAKES 4 TO 6 SERVINGS

6 cups homemade or low-sodium chicken broth
3 tablespoons olive oil
2 cups cubed pumpkin or other squash
1 tablespoon minced garlic (2 to 3 cloves)
1 tablespoon dried rosemary, crumbled
1 teaspoon salt
1/4 teaspoon freshly ground black pepper
2 tablespoons unsalted butter
1/2 cup diced onion
2 cups arborio rice
1/2 cup freshly grated Parmigiano-Reggiano cheese
whole small pumpkin, seeded and cleaned out, to be used as a serving bowl (optional)

1. In a medium saucepan, slowly heat the chicken broth to a simmer.

2. In a 10- or 12-inch skillet or saucepan, heat the oil. Add the pumpkin, garlic, rosemary, and 1/4 of the teaspoon salt and half the pepper. Cook, over medium heat, stirring frequently until the pumpkin is tender, about 10 minutes. Remove the cooked pumpkin from the pan and set aside.

3. In the same pan, melt half the butter. Add the onion and cook over medium heat, for 2 to 4 minutes, until softened. Add the rice, stir to coat with the butter, and cook for 3 to 4 minutes.

4. Pour 1/2 cup of the hot broth into the rice and stir with a wooden spoon, until absorbed. Continue with the rest of the broth, adding 1/2 cup at a time and letting each addition be absorbed completely into the rice before adding more liquid. The constant stirring ensures that the rice will release its starch into the cooking liquid, resulting in the characteristic creamy risotto texture. When half the liquid has been used, about 10 to 12 minutes, add the pumpkin. Finish adding the remaining broth, 1/2 cup at a time, until all the broth is absorbed and the rice is cooked but slightly al dente.

5. Swirl in the remaining butter and the cheese and season with the remaining salt and pepper. Serve the risotto immediately in warm bowls or in the hollowed-out pumpkin.

THE HOTEL CIPRIANI, VENICE

In 1956, Giuseppe Cipriani, the owner of Harry's Bar, decided to build a hotel across the Grande Canal from his restaurant. The location he chose was the quiet tip of the island of Giudecca, which is a four-minute boat ride from the steps of St. Mark's Square. Guests make the trip in the hotel's private motor launches, which run up and back every ten minutes.

I cannot think of a more beautiful or efficient hotel in the world. If Ed McMahon ever comes to my door with *the* $10 million check, I'm retiring to The Cipriani. Actually, there is a special part of the hotel that I like best. It is a fifteenth-century residence linked to the main building by an ancient, flower-covered courtyard. The building is called the Palazzo Vendramin. It is divided into seven apartments, each with a bedroom, sitting room, dining area, kitchen, and palatial bathroom. Private butler service comes along with the rooms.

Since 1977, the managing director of the hotel has been Dr. Natale Rusconi, whose attention to detail and demanding standards have made him famous. During my visit, Dr. Rusconi asked Sandro Fabris, the director of food and beverage, to take me on a tour of the markets of Venice and have the chef, Renato Piccolotto, teach me a few of the hotel's signature recipes.

The Hotel Cipriani, Venice.

ROASTED BELL PEPPER RISOTTO

THE CLIFT, SAN FRANCISCO, CALIFORNIA

MAKES 4 SERVINGS

1 yellow, red, or orange
   bell pepper
2 tablespoons olive oil
3 cups chicken broth
1 tablespoon butter
½ cup chopped onion
1 cup arborio rice

1. Preheat the oven to 375° F.

2. Put the pepper on a baking sheet and bake for 25 minutes, turning every 5 minutes until the skin is lightly browned. Remove the pepper from the oven and put it immediately into a paper or plastic bag, closing the bag tightly. When the pepper is cool enough to handle, remove the pepper from the bag and remove the skin; it should peel off easily. Discard the stem and the seeds. Then put the pepper and 1 tablespoon of oil into a blender and puree. Set the mixture aside until later.

3. In a large saucepan, heat the chicken broth. In another saucepan over medium heat, heat the remaining oil and the butter. Add the onion and cook for a minute, then add the rice to the pan and cook for another minute. Add half of the hot chicken broth, stirring constantly. When the broth has been absorbed, add the other half of the broth. Continue this process until all the broth has been used and the rice is cooked. This should take about 20 minutes. Stir in the reserved pepper puree. Serve immediately.

RISOTTO WITH RED WINE

LA CONTEA, NEIVE, ITALY

Neive is a small, picturesque Piedmont hill town that looks the way a Piedmont hill-town would look if it was built by a set decorator in Hollywood—a main street with structures that have been standing on it for hundreds of years, an ancient church, and a good restaurant called La Contea. La Contea is owned by Claudia and Tonino Verro, a husband-and-wife team who do the cooking for the restaurant, and run the small inn that is part of the establishment. The following recipe for rice cooked in red wine combines Piedmont's tradition as a major rice producing area with its history for great wine making.

1. In a saucepan over medium heat, bring the chicken broth to a simmer.

2. In a 2-quart sauté pan over medium-low heat, heat the oil. Add 1 teaspoon of the rosemary and the garlic. Cook for 1 minute. Add the vegetables and cook for 2 minutes more. Stir in the rice and cook for 2 minutes. Raise the heat to medium, then add the wine, and stir until all the liquid is absorbed.

3. Add ½ cup of the simmering broth, and stir constantly until all the broth is absorbed. Continue the process, adding ½ cup of broth at a time. Before adding the last ½ cup of broth, add the remaining ½ teaspoon of rosemary. The entire cooking time should be 25 to 30 minutes. The rice should be tender, but al dente, not mushy.

4. Serve immediately with freshly grated Parmesan cheese.

MAKES 4 SERVINGS AS A MAIN COURSE; 6 SERVINGS AS AN APPETIZER

4 to 5 cups chicken broth
2 tablespoons olive oil
1½ teaspoons chopped fresh rosemary (crushed if dried)
2 cloves garlic, chopped
1 stalk celery, chopped
1 small onion, chopped
1 small carrot, chopped
1½ cups arborio rice
½ cup dry red wine
Freshly grated Parmesan cheese

THE WHITE TRUFFLES OF ALBA, ITALY

A truffle is a fungi, like a mushroom. But unlike a mushroom, truffles grow completely underground. They start to form during the summer and are ready for eating by the beginning of October. The trick, of course, is to find them. The truffle hunters of Piedmont use trained dogs that have graduated from the truffle dog university of Italy. Honest! And they are worth a fortune, both the dogs and the truffles.

The dogs have learned to pick up the scent of the truffle and lead their masters to the spot in which they are growing. The hunting is done at night, for a number of reasons: The aroma of the truffle is stronger. The dogs are not distracted by other visual signs. And, though no one talks about it, the darkness hides the location of the truffle area from poachers, who might come along later and try stealing the harvest. The secrecy of a truffle location is very important, and that is one of the reasons the hunters use small flashlights. There is no need to let anyone know where they are hunting. The less light that is shed on the subject, the better.

The truffles of Alba like to grow in the same soil that hosts the great vineyards of the area that produce the Barolo and Barbaresco wines. Now you would think that having truffles in your vineyard would be great for the vineyard owner, but that is not the case. You need lots of rain during the late summer to have top-quality truffles, but lots of rain during the late summer can damage the grape harvest.

Lea, a top truffle-hunting dog from Piedmont, Italy, with Dario Rinaldi, a top truffle-gathering man.

AN INTRODUCTION TO THE HISTORY AND GEOGRAPHY OF PIEDMONT

The Piedmont district of Italy is in the northwest corner of the country, bordering both France and Switzerland, at the foot of the Alpine mountain range. The word *Piedmont* translates into English as "foot of the mountain," which is an excellent description of the terrain.

During the 1500s, Turino, the capital city of Piedmont, was also the capital city of the Kingdom of Savoy. Savoy was a small independent dukedom that was constantly battling its neighbors in order to stay alive. In addition to whatever else you did for a living, you also needed to be a part-time soldier. It was a tough neighborhood and it toughened up the people who lived in it. The mountains and the military shaped the local mentality. The people of the Piedmont ended up with a serious approach to hard work, balanced by the love of a good time. A lot of that good time is based on good food and good wine, in moderation, of course.

Marcello and Bruno Ceretto, known as "the Barolo brothers" because of the excellence of their wines.

BARLEY PILAF WITH TOASTED PECANS, GINGER, AND HERBS

CALIFORNIA

MAKES 4 SERVINGS

4 cups water or chicken
   broth
1 cup medium pearled
   barley
1/3 cup chopped toasted
   pecans
1 1/2 teaspoons grated fresh
   ginger
3 tablespoons chopped
   fresh parsley
1 tablespoon chopped
   fresh mint or tarragon,
   or 1 1/2 teaspoons dried
3/4 teaspoon salt
1 tablespoon butter

1. In a saucepan, bring the water to a boil. Stir in the barley, reduce the heat, then cover the pan. Simmer gently for 45 to 50 minutes, or until tender. Remove the pan from the heat and let the barley stand for 5 minutes.

2. Reserve 1/4 cup of cooked barley if you are making Beef with Prunes (page 102). In a large mixing bowl, combine the cooked barley, pecans, ginger, parsley, mint, and salt. Stir to mix evenly. Finally, stir in the butter. This dish can be served hot, or as a cold salad on a bed of mixed greens.

Spiced Almond Couscous

CANADA

1. In a saucepan over high heat, bring the chicken broth or water and the butter to a boil. Stir in the couscous and cover the pan. Remove the pan from the heat and let stand for 5 minutes.

2. Transfer the couscous to a bowl. Using a fork, fluff the couscous lightly. Add the remaining ingredients and stir with a fork to mix.

MAKES 4 SERVINGS

1½ cups chicken broth or water
1 tablespoon unsalted butter
1 cup quick-cooking couscous
¼ cup toasted sliced almonds
¼ cup golden raisins
2 tablespoons chopped fresh mint, parsley, or cilantro
¼ teaspoon ground cumin
¼ teaspoon ground cinnamon
½ teaspoon salt
Pinch of cayenne pepper

VEGETABLES, SALADS, AND DIPS

Artichokes Stuffed with Ratatouille

QUAIL LODGE, CARMEL, CALIFORNIA

**MAKES 4 SERVINGS AS
AN APPETIZER OR
SIDE DISH**

FOR THE ARTICHOKES:
1 head garlic,
 cut in half horizontally
1/2 lemon, sliced
1 teaspoon salt
4 large artichokes

FOR THE
RATATOUILLE:
1 tablespoon olive oil
2 cloves garlic, chopped,
 then blended with 1/2
 teaspoon salt
1 small onion, chopped
1 red bell pepper, chopped
1 green bell pepper,
 chopped
2 tablespoons chopped
 fresh basil, or
 2 teaspoons dried
2 medium yellow squash,
 cut into 1/2-inch cubes
 (about 2 1/2 cups)
1 tomato, chopped
(cont. on next page)

1. To make the artichokes: Fill a large pot with water, then add the garlic, lemon, and salt. Bring the water to a boil. While the water is coming to the boil, cut off the stems of the artichokes, then trim about 1 inch off the top. Remove any withered outer leaves. Place in the boiling water, cover the pot, and cook for 30 to 40 minutes, or until an outer leaf pulls off easily. Drain the artichokes upside down. Using tongs, open the artichoke and pull out the center leaves. Scoop out the inedible choke with a spoon.

2. While the artichokes are cooking, make the ratatouille: In a large sauté pan, heat the oil. Add the garlic and salt and cook for 1 minute. Add the onion and the red and green bell peppers and cook for 3 minutes. Add the basil. Stir in the yellow squash and tomato and cook for 5 minutes more. Then stir in the tomato paste and wine and cook for another 3 minutes. Just before serving, season with salt and pepper and stir in the black olives and lemon juice.

3. To serve: Spoon the ratatouille into the center of each artichoke, allowing it to cascade over the opened leaves onto the plate.

CARMEL, CALIFORNIA

In 1602, three Carmelite missionaries stood on the hills about 125 miles south of what was to become San Francisco, and looked out on the magnificent coast in front of them. Rolling surf, white sandy beaches, the deep green tree-covered landscape. A river near them ran to the sea and they named it Rio Carmelo after their Carmelite order and then they moved on. Not much else happened in the neighborhood for the next three hundred years, and when it happened, it happened in San Francisco.

What happened was the Earthquake of 1906. For just under a minute the city shook. Every steeple bell was set ringing by the force. The streets twisted and turned, and the buildings crumbled. The fires started by the quake raged for three days, and when they finally burned out, San Francisco was devastated.

A few years before the quake a man by the name of Frank Devendorf had filed a map to set up a subdivision for the town of Carmel, and the earthquake was the perfect excuse for him to bring his plan to the attention of the people of San Francisco, many of whom were now living in tents.

A few of the earliest residents of Carmel had been artists and writers who had moved to the area from San Francisco. After the quake, they urged their fellow artists to join them in this quiet, safe, and beautiful community by the sea. Ever since then, writers, painters, and musicians have been coming to the area. More recently, however, the most famous creative talents to move to Carmel have come from the movie business. Clint Eastwood lives there and so does Doris Day.

1 tablespoon tomato paste
1/4 cup dry white wine
1 teaspoon salt
1/2 teaspoon freshly ground black pepper
1/4 cup sliced pitted black olives
1 tablespoon fresh lemon juice

STUFFED ARTICHOKES WITH PARMESAN AND CAPERS

ITALY

MAKES 4 SERVINGS

1 cup bread crumbs
½ cup Parmigiano-
   Reggiano cheese
1 stalk celery, minced
3 tablespoons minced fresh
   parsley
2 anchovies, minced to a
   paste
2 tablespoons capers
⅓ cup extra-virgin olive oil
2 cloves garlic, minced
½ teaspoon salt
¼ teaspoon freshly ground
   black pepper
4 large artichokes
3 tablespoons lemon juice
3 to 4 cups water
1 bay leaf

1. In a bowl, combine the bread crumbs, Parmigiano-Reggiano, celery, parsley, anchovies, capers, olive oil, and garlic. Season with half the salt and all the pepper.

2. To prepare the artichokes for stuffing: With a sharp knife cut off the upper third of each artichoke, break off the tough lower leaves and cut off the bottom stem. With scissors, trim off the tips of the outer 2 or 3 layers of the leaves to form a staggered floral effect. Brush the cut artichokes with some of the lemon juice. To spread the artichoke leaves for stuffing, gently pound them on the corner of a table and pull back the leaves. With a spoon, evenly pack the artichokes with the stuffing.

3. Place the artichokes in a heavy-bottomed pan that will accommodate them comfortably. Add the water to come up to the bottom of the stuffing. Add the remaining lemon juice, salt, and bay leaf. Cook, covered, for 40 to 50 minutes over low heat, or until the artichoke leaves are tender. Serve warm or at room temperature.

Asparagus with Orange Sauce

ARUBA

1. Cut the tough ends off the asparagus and peel the stalks. Bring a shallow skillet of water to a boil, add the salt and asparagus. Cook for 5 to 7 minutes, until tender, then drain.

2. Meanwhile, prepare the sauce: In a bowl, combine the sour cream and mayonnaise until blended. Stir in the orange juice, orange zest, and thyme leaves.

3. To serve, place a dollop of the sauce on the asparagus or serve the sauce on the side.

MAKES 4 SERVINGS

1 pound fresh asparagus
½ teaspoon salt

FOR THE SAUCE:
¼ cup nonfat sour cream
2 tablespoons low-fat mayonnaise
¼ cup orange juice
½ teaspoon freshly grated orange zest
¼ teaspoon chopped fresh thyme leaves

The divi-divi trees of Aruba always point west. Since the hotels of Aruba are almost exclusively on the west side of the island, the divi-divi trees will direct you to your accommodations.

Broccoli with Lemon Sauce

CANADA

MAKES 4 SERVINGS

1 pound broccoli spears

FOR THE SAUCE:
1 tablespoon fresh lemon
   juice
1 teaspoon grated lemon
   zest
1/2 teaspoon salt
3 tablespoons olive oil
2 tablespoons diced red
   bell pepper

1. In a saucepan with a steamer, steam the broccoli for 4 minutes, or until the stems are tender.

2. Meanwhile, prepare the sauce: In a bowl, combine the lemon juice, lemon zest, and salt. Gradually whisk in the olive oil, then stir in the red bell pepper.

3. Toss the cooked broccoli in the sauce.

Red Cabbage with Apples and Caraway

CANADA

1. In a large sauté pan over medium heat, melt the butter and sauté the cabbage for 3 minutes.

2. Add the remaining ingredients and mix together. Cover the pan and simmer for 7 minutes, until tender but still crisp.

MAKES 4 SERVINGS

2 tablespoons butter
1¼ pounds red cabbage (1 medium), shredded
2 Granny Smith apples, peeled, cored, and sliced
2 tablespoons sugar
¼ cup white wine
¼ cup chicken broth or water
½ teaspoon caraway seeds
1 teaspoon salt

EGGPLANT PARMESAN

ANTICA TRATTORIA MARTELLA, AVELLINO, ITALY

MAKES 4 SERVINGS

FOR THE TOMATO
SAUCE:
1 tablespoon olive oil
2 cloves garlic, chopped
2¹/₂ cups chopped
    tomatoes and their
    juices
1 tablespoon chopped
    fresh basil, or
    1 teaspoon dried
¹/₂ teaspoon salt

FOR THE EGGPLANT:
3 eggs
¹/₄ teaspoon salt
1 cup all-purpose flour
2 medium eggplants (about
    2 pounds), peeled and
    sliced lengthwise ¹/₄ inch
    thick
¹/₄ cup olive oil
¹/₂ pound fresh mozzarella
    cheese, cut into ¹/₄-inch
    cubes
¹/₄ cup freshly grated
    Parmesan cheese
1 tablespoon chopped
    fresh basil

1. **To prepare the sauce:** In a medium saucepan, heat the olive oil. Add the garlic and cook for 1 minute. Add the tomatoes, basil, and salt. Cook for 15 minutes.

2. Preheat the oven to 375° F. Lightly grease an 8-inch square baking dish.

3. To make the eggplant: In a medium bowl, whisk together the eggs and salt. Place the flour in another bowl. Dip the eggplant slices first into the eggs, then into the flour. In a large sauté pan, heat the olive oil. Fry the eggplant until golden brown on both sides. Make sure not to crowd the pan. Drain the eggplant on paper towels.

4. To assemble: Put ¹/₂ cup of the tomato sauce in the bottom of the prepared dish. Place a layer of fried eggplant, then some of the mozzarella cheese, and then some basil. Repeat the layering process, substituting the Parmesan cheese for the mozzarella in the second layer. Continue layering until the dish is filled. Top with a little tomato sauce.

5. Bake for 20 minutes. Let stand for 5 minutes before slicing.

THE FOOD OF ANCIENT CAMPAGNA

Two thousand years ago Campagna was a very important spot in the ancient Roman Empire. It was part of the largest metropolis on the west coast of Italy, busy and growing. The volcanic Mount Vesuvius had always stood nearby, but the people who had the job of predicting the future by looking at the entrails of animals told everybody that Vesuvius was asleep, and not to worry. Well, those guys should have used those chicken livers to make pâté.

On the twenty-fourth of August, A.D. 79, Vesuvius blew its stack. Pliny the Younger, a writer of the time, described the event as a blast that sent flaming lava and hot earth into a cone that rose up into the sky for some fifty thousand feet. The hot gases and ash that came down into the towns suffocated the inhabitants and buried the area under more than twenty feet of debris.

The ancient buildings lay hidden until the 1700s, when they were rediscovered. Today, the research is still going on and we are constantly finding out more and more about the way the ancients lived, especially when it comes to eating and drinking.

Baking was a very important business at the time, and one of the most elaborate houses excavated from the ruins was the home of a man who appears to have been a very rich baker, kind of the Sara Lee of his day. In one of the bakeries a series of traditional round breads were found. They had actually been baked on the day of the explosion, and were made from hard wheat and barley. Some had been scored across the top so they could be easily divided into individual pieces.

Scientists have also found the home of a fellow named Scaursu, who lived during the first century A.D. and made a great fortune as the manufacturer of a popular sauce. It was used the way we use ketchup in the United States or the way the Japanese use soy sauce. It was called garum and was made from fish, salt, and spices that sat around in a barrel for a few months.

Historians who have tried to reproduce garum ended up with something that was agonizingly salty, and they believe there was a reason that the Romans liked it that way. The Romans made their cooking pots with clay that contained enough lead to give them all lead poisoning, a symptom of which is an inability to taste salt. As a result, they kept adding more and more salt to their diet. Some historians also think that the nutty behavior of the ancient Romans can be attributed, in part, to the lead poisoning. Makes a great case for watching out for lead in our own lives.

Eggplant Puree with Roasted Garlic

SONOMA MISSION INN, BOYES HOT SPRINGS, CALIFORNIA

MAKES 4 SERVINGS

1¼ teaspoons salt
1 large eggplant, sliced in
    half lengthwise
3 cloves garlic, roasted (see
    Note)
1 small potato (about 2
    ounces), peeled
1 tablespoon chopped
    fresh basil, or
    1 teaspoon dried
⅛ teaspoon freshly ground
    black pepper

1. Salt the eggplant with 1 teaspoon of the salt and place upside down on a rack for 1 hour so the bitterness will drain out.

2. Preheat the oven to 400° F.

3. Place the eggplant on a baking sheet, cut side down, and bake for 30 minutes until tender. (See Note below on roasting garlic as the garlic can be roasted at the same time.) Scoop out the meat from the skin. While the eggplant is roasting, boil the potato and set aside.

4. In a food processor or blender, combine the eggplant meat, the roasted garlic, basil, potato, the remaining ¼ teaspoon of salt, and the pepper. Process until smooth. Serve immediately.

NOTE: Roasted garlic is sweet and has a marvelous flavor. To roast the garlic: Preheat the oven to 400° F. Place a whole head of garlic on a baking sheet and bake for 20 to 30 minutes (depending on the size of the head of garlic), until tender. Separate the cloves, they should pop out of the skin.

Sautéed Escarole with Garlic and Golden Raisins

ITALY

1. In a small heatproof bowl, plump the raisins in the boiling water for about 5 minutes. Drain off the water.

2. In a large skillet over medium heat, heat the olive oil with the garlic until the garlic turns a light golden brown, about 2 minutes. Add the escarole and the raisins, cook over medium-high heat for 4 to 5 minutes, until the escarole is thoroughly wilted and the leaves are tender.

3. Season with salt and pepper and serve.

MAKES 4 SERVINGS

1/4 cup golden raisins
1/4 cup boiling water
3 tablespoons extra-virgin
  olive oil
1 1/2 tablespoons minced
  garlic
2 heads escarole, cut into
  1- to 2-inch pieces,
  cleaned and drained
1/2 teaspoon salt
1/8 teaspoon freshly ground
  pepper

LIMA BEANS WITH LEMON

CHILE

MAKES 4 SERVINGS

Two 10-ounce packages
   frozen lima beans
1 cup water
2 tablespoons fresh lemon
   juice
$1/2$ teaspoon salt

FOR THE SAUCE:
2 tablespoons butter
Grated zest of 1 lemon
6 scallions, thinly sliced
Pinch of cayenne pepper
$3/4$ teaspoon salt
1 tablespoon chopped
   fresh parsley

1. In a saucepan over medium heat, combine the beans, water, lemon juice, and salt and cook for 5 to 7 minutes, or until the beans are just tender. Drain the beans.

2. To prepare the sauce: In a small sauté pan over low heat, melt the butter. Add the lemon zest, scallions, and cayenne pepper. Cook for 2 minutes until the scallions start to soften. Stir in the salt and parsley.

3. Add the cooked beans to the sauce and heat thoroughly.

Window grate on the front door of Chile's national poet, Pablo Neruda (Santiago).

THE STRAITS OF MAGELLAN

As South America comes to its southernmost tip, it slowly trails off into the icy waters of the Antarctic Ocean. The final points of land that remain are the snow-covered peaks of the Andes mountain range as it descends to the ocean floor. The first Europeans to see this part of the world were members of the crews that sailed with Ferdinand Magellan.

Magellan was a Portuguese nobleman who convinced the King of Spain to put up the money for a voyage of exploration. Magellan felt that he could sail west from Europe, across the Atlantic, and find a passage to the Spice Islands—the same passage that Columbus had missed. Spices were still worth their weight in gold, and Spain still did not have a real piece of the business. Now mind you, the rulers of Spain were not unhappy with Columbus. Finding gold instead of finding something worth its weight in gold will always get you full credit for a right answer.

Magellan went south along the east coast of South America. On October 21, 1520, his lookouts spotted an opening along the shore. Magellan took his fleet of five ships and headed in. As they moved through the straits, they saw a series of campfires and marked the area on their charts as *Tierra del Fuego,* Land of Fire. The place is still known by that name. Walls of snow-capped mountains lined the passage. They spent thirty-eight days in the straits and sailed over three hundred miles. On the twenty-eighth of November 1520, his squadron slid past the last of the rocks and out into the great ocean that he had dreamed of. The day was so perfect and the sea so peaceful that Magellan named the ocean *Pacifico.*

Cheese Polenta with Wild Mushrooms

ITALY

MAKES 4 SERVINGS

FOR THE POLENTA:
4 cups water
1 cup instant polenta
1 teaspoon salt
½ cup grated Parmigiano-
    Reggiano cheese

FOR THE MUSHROOMS:
¾ pound button mushrooms
¾ pound cremini
    mushrooms, (or other
    wild mushrooms)
2 tablespoons olive oil
½ teaspoon salt
¼ teaspoon freshly ground
    black pepper
⅓ cup minced red onion
2 cloves garlic, minced
⅓ cup dry Marsala wine
⅓ cup beef or chicken broth
½ teaspoon minced fresh
    sage, or ⅛ teaspoon dried
1 teaspoon minced fresh
    thyme leaves, or
    ¼ teaspoon dried
2 tablespoons minced fresh
    parsley

Parmigiano-Reggiano for
    dusting (optional)

1. **To prepare the polenta:** In a medium saucepan, bring the water to a boil. Slowly whisk in the polenta and add the salt, reduce the heat to low, and cover. Cook the polenta for 15 minutes, stirring occasionally. Add the grated cheese and stir to combine thoroughly. Hold in a warm place until ready to serve. (Or, if you want to grill or fry the polenta, pour the polenta into a loaf pan, cover with plastic wrap, and let cool to room temperature. Let the polenta set in the refrigerator for 1 or 2 hours before slicing. Then grill or fry the polenta and serve with the mushrooms.)

2. While the polenta is cooking, make the mushrooms: Clean and quarter the mushrooms. Heat the oil in a large skillet, add the mushrooms and sauté until golden brown, 4 or 5 minutes. Season with the salt and pepper. Add the onion and garlic and cook for 1 minute. Add the Marsala, broth, and herbs. Cook over high heat for 3 or 4 minutes, to thicken slightly.

3. To serve, spoon the warm polenta onto a rimmed plate and ladle the mushroom mix on top. Dust with the cheese, if desired.

PEAS WITH DILL

CANADA

1. In a small bowl, mash together the softened butter, dill, and lemon juice.

2. Place the peas in a saucepan and cover with water. Over high heat, bring the water to a boil, cover the pan, and reduce the heat. Simmer gently for 5 minutes.

3. Drain the peas and place them in a serving bowl. Add the dill butter and stir gently to coat evenly. Salt to taste.

MAKES 4 SERVINGS

1 tablespoon butter, softened
1 teaspoon chopped fresh dill, or 1/2 teaspoon dried
2 teaspoons fresh lemon juice
2 cups frozen green peas
Salt

SNOW PEAS AND CARROTS WITH MINT

ARUBA

MAKES 4 SERVINGS

2 tablespoons vegetable oil
or unsalted butter or
margarine, softened
1 tablespoon orange juice
2 tablespoons finely
chopped fresh mint
1/2 teaspoon salt
3 cups water
2 medium carrots, thinly
sliced at an angle
1/2 pound snow peas,
trimmed

1. In a bowl, combine the oil or softened butter, orange juice, mint, and salt, then set the mixture aside.

2. In a saucepan, bring the water, lightly salted, to a boil. Add the carrots and cook for 1 or 2 minutes. Then add the snow peas. Return the water to a boil and cook for 1 minute more. Drain the vegetables.

3. Place the cooked vegetables in the bowl with the mint mixture. Toss to coat evenly, and serve.

Aloe fields, Aruba. For many years they were a major supplier to the world.

Spinach with Almonds and Garlic

CHILE

1. In a sauté pan over low heat, heat the olive oil. Add the garlic and cook for 1 minute. Add the almonds, salt, and cayenne and cook for 2 minutes more. Remove from the heat and set aside.

2. Coarsely chop the spinach. In a large covered saucepan in a small amount of boiling salted water, cook the spinach for 4 minutes, or until tender. Drain well.

3. Mix the garlic and almond mixture into the spinach.

MAKES 6 SERVINGS

2 tablespoons olive oil
2 cloves garlic, chopped
$1/2$ cup sliced almonds
$3/4$ teaspoon salt
$1/8$ teaspoon cayenne
     pepper
2 pounds spinach, washed
     well and trimmed

Spinach Rolls

VILLA MONSANTO, CHIANTI, ITALY

MAKES 4 SERVINGS

FOR THE SPINACH
ROLLS:
1 pound fresh spinach,
    cooked, or one 10-ounce
    package frozen spinach,
    thawed
3/4 cup ricotta cheese
2/3 cup all-purpose flour
1 egg
1 cup freshly grated
    Parmesan cheese
1/4 teaspoon ground
    nutmeg

4 quarts water

FOR THE TOMATO
SAUCE:
1 tablespoon olive oil
1 clove garlic, chopped
2 cups chopped tomatoes
1/2 teaspoon dried oregano
1/2 teaspoon dried basil
1/2 teaspoon salt

This dish was taught to me by Juliana Bianchi at the Villa Monsanto in Tuscany. The spinach rolls are considered a first course, similar to pasta, but they are also excellent as a main course in a light lunch.

1. **To make the spinach rolls:** Squeeze the liquid out of the cooked spinach, finely chop, and set it aside. In a bowl, combine the remaining ingredients. Add the chopped spinach and blend evenly.

2. Divide the mixture into 12 small pieces. Using the palms of both hands, quickly roll the spinach mixture to form ovals, 1 1/2 to 2 inches long. Repeat the process until all 12 ovals are shaped. If the mixture starts to stick to your hands, dust them lightly with flour.

3. In a large saucepan, bring the water to a boil.

4. While the water is coming to a boil, prepare the sauce. In a saucepan over medium heat, heat the olive oil. Add the garlic and cook for 1 minute. Add the tomatoes, oregano, basil, and salt. Simmer the sauce gently for 5 minutes.

5. Add a pinch of salt to the boiling water, then add the spinach rolls, 4 at a time. When the water returns to a boil, remove the spinach rolls with a slotted spoon and transfer them to a warm serving platter or dinner plates. Repeat the process until the other rolls are cooked. To serve, top with the sauce. Three rolls are considered a single serving.

ABOUT CHIANTI

Starting just below the city of Florence and running south to just above the city of Siena is an ancient district known as Chianti. For centuries, the people of Florence battled against the citizens of Siena for control of this area. During the 1300s, the Florentines organized the Chianti League, which brought the small cities of Chianti into a buffer zone designed to give Florence a shield against the regular attacks of the Sienese troops.

Chianti's fame as a location for battles was short-lived in comparison to its reputation as a location for barrels—barrels of wine that is. We know that the Etruscans cultivated vineyards in this region during the ninth century B.C. The Romans, who popped in shortly thereafter, also considered this an important spot for wine production. As early as the 700s the local farmers were producing a wine they called Chianti.

When Cosimo dei Medici of Florence finally defeated Siena in 1555, the people of Chianti turned their energy to serious wine making and within a few years were exporting excellent vintages.

For many years the wicker-covered bottle of Chianti set on a red-and-white checked tablecloth was the symbol of the neighborhood Italian restaurant in North America. As more and more neighborhood Italian restaurants opened, Chianti produced more and more wine, until the district was on the verge of destroying its reputation for quality.

At which point the government decided to come in and solve the problem. The government made some rules about how wine was to be made and who was to be able to use the Chianti name. But there were still problems, so the government made more rules. But there were still problems, so the government made more rules. And by the 1970s, you had some great rules, but it was almost impossible to make great wine. Some of the wine makers of Chianti who were interested in quality decided to take matters into their own hands, or feet, as the case may be, and just make wine. They did so without reference to some of the government rules on labeling. They decided to make wine that tasted better even if that meant that they could not use the famous Chianti name.

These days, as a general rule, a bottle of Chianti that is marked Chianti Classico Riserva will be considerably better than one that is not. There are a whole series of wines that are made in Tuscany that are excellent but do not carry the government label of Chianti. The wine makers describe them as *nome di fantasia,* which means wines with fantasy names, and many of them are actually the best wines of Tuscany. A few examples are Nemo, Tinscvil, and Ghiaie della Furba.

Yellow Squash with Tarragon

CANADA

MAKES 4 SERVINGS

1 pound yellow squash
(2 medium), cut into
half-moons ¼ inch thick

FOR THE SAUCE:
2 tablespoons olive oil
1 clove garlic, pressed
¾ teaspoon chopped fresh
tarragon, or ¼ teaspoon
dried
½ teaspoon salt
4 scallions, sliced

1. In a saucepan with a steamer, steam the yellow squash for 4 minutes or until tender.

2. To make the sauce: In a bowl, combine the olive oil, garlic, tarragon, and salt. Stir in the scallions.

3. Toss the cooked yellow squash in the sauce and serve.

VEGETABLE GRATIN

SONOMA MISSION INN, BOYES HOT SPRINGS, CALIFORNIA

1. Preheat the oven to 400° F. Lightly oil an 8-inch square baking dish.

2. Evenly spread the garlic, shallots, and basil in the bottom of the prepared dish. Season with salt and pepper. Angle the yellow squash, zucchini, and tomatoes in upright layers, repeating the pattern until all the vegetables are used. Alternate each of the ingredients. Sprinkle the top with the cheese, then the bread crumbs.

3. Bake for 40 to 45 minutes, until the vegetables are tender. Let stand for 5 minutes before slicing to serve.

MAKES 6 SERVINGS

2 cloves garlic, chopped
2 shallots, chopped
1 tablespoon chopped
    fresh basil, or
    1 teaspoon dried
1/2 teaspoon salt
1/4 teaspoon freshly ground
    black pepper
2 medium yellow squash
    (about 10 ounces), thinly
    sliced lengthwise
2 medium zucchini (about
    10 ounces), thinly sliced
    lengthwise
3 tomatoes, sliced
2 tablespoons grated
    Parmesan cheese
1/4 cup dry bread crumbs

Sonoma Mission Inn, Sonoma, California.

Indian Vegetable Sauté with White Rice

MARINA MANDARIN HOTEL, SINGAPORE

MAKES 6 SERVINGS

FOR THE SAUCE:
¼ cup vegetable oil
1 bay leaf
1 stick cinnamon
1 shallot, chopped
2 cloves garlic, chopped
1 tablespoon chopped
    fresh ginger
1 teaspoon chili paste or
    sambal oelek, or more to
    taste
1 tablespoon ground
    turmeric
3 tablespoons sugar
1½ cups coconut milk
2 tablespoons fresh lime
    juice

FOR THE VEGETABLES:
2 tablespoons peanut oil
1 small potato, peeled and
    cubed
1 cup peeled baby carrots
    or sliced carrots
1 red bell pepper, cored,
    seeded, and cut into
    1-inch chunks

1. **To prepare the sauce:** In a sauté pan over medium heat, heat the oil. Add the bay leaf, cinnamon, shallot, garlic, and ginger and cook for 2 minutes. Stir in the chili paste or sambal and turmeric and cook for 1 minute. Add the sugar, coconut milk, and lime juice and bring to a boil. Remove from the heat and set aside.

2. **To prepare the vegetables:** In another sauté pan large enough to hold all the vegetables and the sauce, over medium heat, heat the oil. Add the potato and carrots and cook for 5 minutes. Add the red and green bell peppers and eggplant and cook for another 3 minutes. Stir in the broccoli, cauliflower, and reserved sauce and simmer for 3 minutes. Finally add the cabbage and simmer for 2 minutes longer. Remove the cinnamon and bay leaf.

3. Serve on a bed of white rice. Accompanied by a cucumber salad, this is a meal in itself.

Peter Wee, one of the leading authorities on the Paranakan culture of the Malay Peninsula. His antique shop in Singapore is filled with traditional Paranakan objects.

1 green bell pepper, cored, seeded, and cut into 1-inch chunks
$2/3$ cup eggplant, cut into 1-inch chunks
1 cup cooked broccoli florets
1 cup cooked cauliflower florets
1 cup shredded savoy or Napa cabbage
4 servings white rice, cooked according to the package directions

Stuffed Avocados

CHILE

MAKES 4 SERVINGS

FOR THE DRESSING:
2 teaspoons fresh lemon
    juice
$\frac{1}{2}$ teaspoon salt
$\frac{1}{8}$ teaspoon freshly ground
    black pepper
2 tablespoons olive oil

1 cup cooked and coarsely
    chopped chick-peas
    (garbanzo beans)
1 ripe tomato, seeded and
    diced
4 scallions, sliced
1 clove garlic, chopped
1 tablespoon chopped
    fresh cilantro or parsley
2 ripe avocados
1 tablespoon fresh lemon
    juice

1. To prepare the dressing: In a small bowl, combine the lemon juice, salt, and pepper. Slowly whisk in the olive oil, then set aside.

2. In another bowl, combine the chick-peas, tomato, scallions, garlic, and cilantro or parsley. Pour the dressing over the mixture, tossing gently to mix evenly.

3. Slice the avocados lengthwise into 4 halves and remove the pits. Sprinkle the lemon juice over the meat.

4. Spoon the chick-pea mixture into the center of each avocado half, and serve.

A fisherman's boat tied up in the river alongside the city of Valdivia in southern Chile.

CURRIED CARROTS IN YOGURT

SINGAPORE

1. In a medium bowl, stir the yogurt until smooth. Add the carrot and set aside.

2. In a wok or small skillet, heat the oil. When the oil is hot, add the mustard seeds and stir-fry for 2 minutes until they brown lightly. Add the curry powder, onion, chilies, and salt. Stir-fry 5 to 7 minutes, until the onion begins to turn brown. Add this mixture to the carrots and yogurt.

3. Chill at least a half hour before serving.

MAKES 4 SERVINGS

2 cups low-fat plain yogurt
2 carrots, skinned and
　　grated (about ⅔ cup)
1 tablespoon vegetable oil
1 tablespoon yellow
　　mustard seeds
2 teaspoons curry powder
1 small onion, chopped
　　(about ½ cup)
2 jalapeño chilies, seeded
　　and finely minced
1 teaspoon salt

CAULIFLOWER SALAD

SINGAPORE

MAKES 4 SERVINGS

1 head cauliflower, cut into
   florets
FOR THE DRESSING:
2 teaspoons peanut oil
2 teaspoons olive oil
1 tablespoon white wine
   vinegar
Juice of ½ lemon
Freshly ground black
   pepper
Pinch of chopped garlic
¼ cup plain yogurt
¼ cup mayonnaise
1 tablespoon chopped
   fresh mint (optional)

Lettuce leaves
Fresh chives, chopped,
   as garnish

1. In a pot, blanch the cauliflower in boiling water for 3 minutes. Drain and set aside.

2. To make the dressing: In a bowl, combine the peanut oil, olive oil, vinegar, lemon juice, pepper to taste, and garlic. Pour over the cauliflower and set aside to marinate for 30 minutes.

3. Stir in the yogurt, mayonnaise, and mint, if using.

4. Serve the cauliflower salad on a bed of lettuce leaves and sprinkle with chives.

✳

CUCUMBER SALAD

ROYAL VIKING SUN

1. Place the cucumbers in a bowl and weigh down with a plate. Let stand at room temperature for 2 hours. Drain the cucumbers.

2. In a mixing bowl, combine the vinegar, sugar, white pepper, and dill.

3. Pour the mixture over the cucumber slices, cover, and chill for 4 hours.

MAKES 4 SERVINGS

3 cucumbers, scrubbed, thinly sliced
1 cup white vinegar
¼ cup sugar
½ tablespoon freshly ground white pepper
2 tablespoons chopped fresh dill

ABOUT THE CUCUMBER

Cucumber seeds have been carbon-dated in cultivated gardens as far back as 8000 B.C. We know they were around in ancient Rome because Apicius, who was a big-deal food authority back then, used cucumbers in his recipes. He was so interested in getting the sweetest cucumbers, that his gardeners began dipping their cucumber seeds in honey, hoping that would make the final cucumbers sweeter. Cucumbers appear to have gotten their start in eastern India or Thailand, which makes them a logical ingredient in curry.

Marinated Cucumber and Carrot Salad

CALIFORNIA

MAKES 12 SERVINGS

4 carrots, peeled and thinly
    sliced
4 cucumbers, peeled and
    thinly sliced
1/4 cup chopped pimento
1/4 cup chopped fresh
    chives or parsley
2 1/2 cups water
1 cup rice or white wine
    vinegar
6 tablespoons sugar
1 1/2 teaspoons salt

1. In a mixing bowl, combine the carrots, cucumbers, pimento, and chives or parsley. Add the water, vinegar, sugar, and salt. Stir to mix.

2. Cover the bowl and refrigerate for at least 2 hours before serving.

FENNEL AND PARMIGIANO-REGGIANO SALAD

ITALY

1. Soak the red onion in cold water for about 10 minutes while you prepare the rest of the salad. This helps to mellow the harsh taste of raw onion. In another large bowl, combine the fennel with half the salt and set aside.

2. **To make the vinaigrette,** in a nonreactive bowl, combine the remaining salt and the pepper with the vinegar and optional anchovies. Whisk in the olive oil.

3. To finish the salad, drain the onions and toss with the fennel, vinaigrette, Parmigiano-Reggiano, and parsley. Serve as part of an antipasto, with black olives and cured meats, like salami or prosciutto.

MAKES 4 SERVINGS

1 red onion, thinly sliced
2 fennel bulbs, thinly sliced
1½ teaspoons salt
½ teaspoon freshly ground
    black pepper
2 tablespoons white wine
    vinegar
2 anchovies, minced
    (optional)
⅓ cup extra-virgin olive oil
½ cup freshly grated
    Parmigiano-Reggiano
    cheese
¼ cup chopped fresh
    parsley

The courtyard with the well that was dug during the 1100s at the Hotel Certosa di Maggiano, Siena, Italy.

Garden Salad with Pistachios

CHILE

MAKES 4 SERVINGS

FOR THE DRESSING:
2 tablespoons orange juice
$1/2$ teaspoon salt
$1/8$ teaspoon freshly ground
  black pepper
6 tablespoons olive oil
$1/3$ cup chopped unsalted
  pistachios

1 head romaine lettuce,
  washed, dried, and torn
  into pieces
1 medium tomato, cored
  and cut into wedges
1 small green or yellow
  bell pepper, cored,
  seeded, and cut into thin
  strips
2 tablespoons chopped
  fresh chives as a garnish

1. To make the dressing: In a small bowl, combine the orange juice, salt, and pepper. Slowly whisk in the olive oil. Stir in the pistachios and set aside.

2. In a salad bowl, combine the lettuce, tomato, and bell pepper. Add the salad dressing and toss well.

3. Divide the salad onto 4 salad plates. Garnish with the chopped chives.

WARM LENTIL SALAD

ARUBA

1. In a saucepan, put the lentils, chicken broth or water, whole cloves of garlic, bay leaf, and salt. Bring to a boil, lower the heat, and simmer for 18 to 20 minutes, until tender. Be careful not to overcook the lentils. Remove the bay leaf and garlic.

2. In a bowl, combine the cooked lentils with the vegetables, parsley, and chives or chervil.

3. **To prepare the dressing:** In a bowl, combine the vinegar, garlic, salt, and white pepper. Gradually whisk in the olive oil.

4. Pour the dressing over the lentils and vegetables, tossing to coat evenly. Serve the lentils on a bed of the lettuce.

MAKES 4 SERVINGS

1 cup brown lentils
3½ cups chicken broth or water
2 whole cloves garlic
1 bay leaf
½ teaspoon salt
1 small red onion, diced
1 stalk celery, diced
1 carrot, peeled and diced
1 small red or yellow bell pepper, cored, seeded, and diced
2 tablespoons chopped fresh parsley
1 tablespoon chopped fresh chives or chervil
8 lettuce leaves, such as curly endive, Boston, romaine, or frisée, washed and dried

FOR THE DRESSING:
1 tablespoon white wine vinegar
1 clove garlic, chopped
½ teaspoon salt
Pinch of white pepper
¼ cup olive oil

Romaine Lettuce and Pears with Parmesan Dressing

CALIFORNIA

MAKES 4 SERVINGS

1 small head romaine
   lettuce, washed, dried,
   and torn into small
   pieces
2 Bosc or Anjou pears,
   peeled, cored, and sliced

FOR THE DRESSING:
$1/2$ teaspoon Dijon-style
   mustard
2 teaspoons red wine
   vinegar
$1/4$ cup olive oil
2 tablespoons freshly
   grated Parmesan cheese

1. In a salad bowl, combine the romaine lettuce and pears.

2. To prepare the dressing: In a small bowl, combine the mustard and vinegar. Gradually whisk in the olive oil. Finally, whisk in the Parmesan cheese.

3. Pour the dressing over the salad and toss.

MANGO AND ORANGE SALAD

SINGAPORE

1. In a medium bowl, combine the red onion and the vinegar and set aside.

2. Peel the oranges and, with a paring knife, scrape off any pith left on the orange. Break the oranges into segments. With the tip of the paring knife, pop out any seeds. Add the orange segments, mango, and tomato to the red onion. Toss together and season with the salt and pepper.

3. Line a serving plate or bowl with the lettuce leaves, place the salad in the center. Refrigerate for 20 minutes and serve.

MAKES 4 SERVINGS

$1/2$ cup thinly sliced red
  onion
1 tablespoon rice vinegar
2 mandarin oranges or
  clementines
1 mango, peeled and cut
  into 1-inch cubes
1 tomato (about $1/2$ pound),
  chopped
$1/2$ teaspoon salt
$1/8$ teaspoon freshly ground
  black pepper
4 to 6 romaine lettuce
  leaves

TRICOLOR SLAW WITH BUTTERMILK POPPY-SEED DRESSING

CANADA

MAKES 6 SERVINGS

3 cups shredded green
    cabbage
3 cups shredded red
    cabbage
3 carrots, peeled and
    shredded

FOR THE DRESSING:
1 1/2 cups buttermilk
1/2 cup nonfat sour cream
    or nonfat mayonnaise
1/4 cup sugar
1 tablespoon fresh lemon
    juice (optional)
1 tablespoon poppy seeds
1 1/2 teaspoons salt

1. In a large bowl, combine the green and red cabbage and the carrots.

2. To make the dressing: In a small bowl, stir together all the ingredients.

3. Pour the dressing over the cabbage and carrot mixture. Refrigerate for at least 2 hours before serving.

The Columbia Ice Field in Alberta, Canada. There are bus tours that will take you right onto the glacier. It's hard to believe, but this was at the very edge of Alberta's cowboy country, where slaw was a common dish.

Spinach and Boston Lettuce with Grapefruit and Maple-Walnut Vinaigrette

CANADA

1. **To make the dressing:** In a bowl, mix the vinegar, maple syrup, and salt. Gradually whisk in the peanut or vegetable oil and the walnut oil, if being used. The dressing can also be made in a blender up to this point. Stir in the chopped walnuts.

2. In a salad bowl, combine the spinach, lettuce, and grapefruit.

3. Pour the dressing over the salad and toss.

MAKES 8 SERVINGS

FOR THE DRESSING:
1/4 cup white wine vinegar
2 tablespoons maple syrup
1 teaspoon salt
1/2 cup peanut or vegetable oil
1 tablespoon walnut oil (optional)
1/4 cup finely chopped walnuts

1 1/2 cups fresh spinach, washed, dried, and torn into small pieces
2 heads Boston lettuce, washed, dried, and torn into small pieces
1 1/2 cups grapefruit sections

ABOUT MAPLE SYRUP

Maple syrup is the sweet amber-colored nectar that is created when the sap from a maple tree is boiled down. True maple syrup is very expensive—as much as $10 a pint. Many of the so-called maple syrups that we pour over our pancakes are really corn syrups with a limited amount of maple syrup or maple flavoring added. Pure maple is thin, not thick.

The American Indians in New England taught the colonists how to make maple syrup. The colonists upgraded the process by boiling the sap in kettles. In March, when the days are warm and the nights still freeze, the sap begins to run in the maple forest or sugar bush. The trees are tapped with a spike and the sap is collected and boiled in a shallow metal pan over a fire fueled with wood or oil. The old way of hand gathering with buckets has been replaced with a network of plastic tubing that transports the sap from the trees to the sugarhouse.

Maple syrup is graded as light amber, medium amber, and dark amber, with medium being the most popular. The last dregs of making maple syrup are unpalatable and are often sold to tobacco companies for flavoring cigarettes. It takes 30 to 40 gallons of sap to produce 1 gallon of syrup. Maple sugar is syrup that has been crystallized. It was used by colonists to replace expensive West Indian sugar.

Mexican John, a famous frontier cook in Alberta, Canada, during the early years of this century.
Courtesy Glenbow Museum.

Tomato Salad
with Parsley Dressing

CHILE

---

1. To make the sauce: In a bowl, combine the ingredients.

2. Arrange the tomato slices on a plate. Top with the dressing.

MAKES 4 SERVINGS

FOR THE DRESSING:
1/2 cup chopped fresh
    parsley
1 clove garlic, minced
1 jalapeño or serrano chili
    pepper, seeded and
    chopped
2 scallions, coarsely
    chopped
2 tablespoons fresh lime
    juice
4 tablespoons olive oil
1 teaspoon salt

4 ripe medium tomatoes,
    cored and cut into thick
    slices

Tomato Rice Salad with Avocado and Corn

CHILE

MAKES 4 SERVINGS

1 ripe medium tomato,
   cored and cut into
   wedges
1 cup cooked corn or
   thawed frozen corn
2 cups cooked rice, at
   room temperature
1 small ripe avocado,
   peeled and cut into
   cubes
1 teaspoon fresh lemon
   juice

FOR THE DRESSING:
2 tablespoons fresh lemon
   juice
1 teaspoon salt
2 cloves garlic, minced
2 teaspoons chopped fresh
   ginger
1 tablespoon chopped
   fresh mint or parsley
6 tablespoons olive or
   vegetable oil

1. In a bowl, combine the tomato, corn, and rice. In a second bowl, toss the avocado in the lemon juice, then add to the other ingredients.

2. To make the dressing: In a third bowl, combine the lemon juice, salt, garlic, ginger, and mint or parsley. Slowly whisk in the oil.

3. Pour the dressing over the vegetables and rice, and toss gently.

MIXED VEGETABLE SALAD WITH PEANUT DRESSING

ARUBA

---

1. To make the salad: In a saucepan fitted with a steamer, steam the broccoli for 2 to 3 minutes. Immediately immerse the broccoli in iced water to stop the cooking. In a bowl, combine the broccoli with the remaining vegetables. Keep in the refrigerator until ready to serve.

2. To make the dressing: In another bowl, stir together the peanut butter, oil, water, vinegar, and honey until smooth. Then stir in the garlic and Tabasco sauce.

3. Pour the peanut dressing over the vegetables, tossing to combine well.

MAKES 4 SERVINGS

FOR THE SALAD:
2 cups broccoli florets
1/4 pound mushrooms, sliced
1 carrot, sliced
1 cucumber, sliced
1 cup cooked corn kernels (thawed, frozen, or canned)
1 tomato, cut into wedges

FOR THE PEANUT DRESSING:
2 tablespoons crunchy peanut butter
4 tablespoons vegetable or peanut oil
2 tablespoons water
2 tablespoons vinegar
2 tablespoons honey
1 to 2 cloves garlic, crushed
4 to 6 drops Tabasco or hot sauce

The old Gold Mill, Aruba.

ABOUT THE PEANUT

The peanut probably got its start in South America. Peanut seeds have been found in the ancient tribal tombs of Peru, and the Incas cultivated the plant as part of their regular diet. The early European explorers first saw peanuts in Haiti and Mexico, and Cortez and Columbus brought them back to Spain and Portugal.

The peanuts that go to make things like peanut butter are actually not nuts like almonds or walnuts; they are legumes like lentils and peas, which is why we call it a "pea" nut.

Peanuts have more protein than any other nut. They are also a good source of thiamine, niacin, iron, magnesium, and folic acid. They contain lots of dietary fiber and are considered to have a moderate amount of fat for a nut. Almost every home in America has a jar of peanut butter, and the average American eats 3.3 pounds of peanut butter each year.

Vendor of sugar-coated peanuts, the national sweet of Chile (Valparaiso, Chile).

CHOPPED VEGETABLE SALAD WITH BASIL VINAIGRETTE

CANADA

1. To make the salad: In a bowl, mix together all the ingredients.

2. In a second bowl, whisk together the vinegar, mustard, salt, and pepper. Slowly whisk in the olive oil, then whisk in the chopped basil.

3. Pour the dressing over the vegetables and refrigerate for at least 30 minutes before serving. This salad can be made a day ahead.

MAKES 4 SERVINGS

FOR THE SALAD:
1 small red bell pepper, coarsely chopped
1 small green bell pepper, coarsely chopped
1/2 cucumber, peeled, seeded, and coarsely chopped
1 cup frozen corn kernels, thawed
1 carrot, coarsely chopped
1 rib celery, coarsely chopped
4 scallions, sliced
1 tablespoon chopped fresh parsley

FOR THE DRESSING:
2 tablespoons red wine vinegar
1/4 teaspoon Dijon-style mustard
1/2 teaspoon salt
1/8 teaspoon freshly ground black pepper
4 tablespoons olive oil
2 tablespoons chopped

CHICK-PEA AND SESAME DIP

ROYAL VIKING SUN

MAKES 6 CUPS

4 cups cooked chick-peas
  (garbanzo beans)
1/4 cup cold water
1/4 cup peanut oil
2 tablespoons sesame oil
1 cup tahini (sesame paste)
1/2 tablespoon ground
  cumin
Juice of 2 limes
2 dashes of Tabasco sauce
2 garlic cloves, crushed
1 1/4 teaspoons coarse salt
1/2 to 3/4 cup red bell pepper
  strips
Pita or other bread, cut
  into triangles, warmed
  or toasted

1. In a food processor or blender, combine the chick-peas, water, oils, tahini, cumin, lime juice, Tabasco, garlic, and salt. Puree until light and fluffy. If you are using a blender, the ingredients may be divided into 2 or 3 separate batches. Taste the dip and adjust the seasoning if necessary. If the mixture is too thick, add more lime juice or sesame oil.

2. Scrape into a decorative bowl and garnish with the pepper strips.

3. Serve with triangles of warm or toasted bread.

CHILEAN SALSA (PEBRE)

HACIENDA LOS LINGUES, SANTIAGO, CHILE

1. In a bowl, mix all of the ingredients together.

2. Let the salsa stand for 15 minutes before serving.

MAKES 3 CUPS

1 cup minced onion
2 cups peeled, chopped
   fresh ripe tomatoes with
   their juices
1/2 cup minced fresh Italian
   parsley
1 hot green chili pepper,
   seeded and minced
2 tablespoons olive oil
Salt and freshly ground
   black pepper

BISCUITS, BREADS, AND EMPANADAS

WHOLE WHEAT ONION BISCUITS

CALIFORNIA

MAKES 10 SERVINGS

2 cups all-purpose flour
3/4 cup whole wheat flour
1 teaspoon salt
1 1/2 teaspoons baking
    powder
1/4 cup grated onion
1/3 cup vegetable
    shortening
2/3 cup milk, warmed
1 tablespoon vegetable oil

1. In a mixing bowl, combine the dry ingredients. Stir in the grated onion. With a knife or pastry blender, cut in the shortening until the mixture resembles coarse crumbs. Make a well in the center of the flour mixture and pour in the warmed milk, stirring quickly to blend and form a dough.

2. Place the dough onto a lightly floured board. Knead for 5 minutes. Cover the dough with a damp cloth and let it rest for 15 minutes.

3. Preheat the oven to 400° F. Lightly grease a baking sheet.

4. Shape the dough into 10 balls, 1 1/2 inches in diameter. Place the balls on the prepared baking sheet, then lightly press down on each to flatten slightly. Rub a little vegetable oil on the top of each. Bake for 12 to 15 minutes, until lightly browned. Serve immediately.

CORN CHEESE BISCUITS

CHILE

1. Preheat the oven to 400° F. Lightly butter or oil a 6-cup muffin pan and set aside.

2. In a bowl, combine the dry ingredients. Work in the butter or margarine until the mixture resembles coarse crumbs.

3. Stir in the egg and milk until just blended, then stir in the cheese.

4. Pour the batter into the prepared muffin pan, and bake for 20 minutes.

5. Cool in the pan for 3 to 5 minutes and serve warm.

Whenever we finish videotaping the preparation of a recipe, we put the finished dish aside for our final close-up, which we shoot later in the day. A number of years ago, all of the foods were eaten by the local kitchen staff before we returned to tape. Since then, we have been very careful to label the food so that it remains in place until we get back. The sign on these finished dishes reads "NO TOUCHING, NO EATING, NO LOOKING . . . THANKS."

MAKES 6 BISCUITS

$1/2$ cup cornmeal
$1/2$ cup all-purpose flour
$1/2$ teaspoon salt
2 teaspoons baking powder
2 tablespoons unsalted butter or margarine, softened
1 egg, lightly beaten
$1/2$ cup milk
$1/2$ cup finely grated Jack or Cheddar cheese

Corn Bread with Chives

CANADA

MAKES 8 SERVINGS

1 cup coarsely ground
    cornmeal
1 cup all-purpose flour
2½ tablespoons baking
    powder
1 teaspoon salt
¼ teaspoon baking soda
⅛ teaspoon cayenne
    pepper
1 tablespoon sugar
2 tablespoons chopped
    fresh chives
¼ cup vegetable oil
1 cup buttermilk
2 egg whites, lightly
    beaten

1. Preheat the oven to 400° F. Lightly grease an 8-inch square baking dish.

2. In a medium-sized bowl, combine the dry ingredients. Stir in the chopped chives.

3. Add the oil to the dry ingredients. With your fingers, work until the oil is evenly mixed with the dry ingredients.

4. In a small bowl, combine the buttermilk and the egg whites, then pour this mixture into the dry ingredients. Stir quickly to blend.

5. Spread the batter evenly in the prepared baking dish. Bake for 20 minutes, until the top is golden and a toothpick inserted in the center comes out clean. Cool on a rack before serving.

DUTCH OVEN BROWN BREAD

RAFTER SIX RANCH RESORT, SEEBE, ALBERTA, CANADA

This bread is steamed rather than baked. The molds that hold the batter are used food cans that have been cleaned. The actual preparation of the batter is very simple and though the cooking time is long, it is well worth the wait.

1. Prepare three food cans with a 20-ounce volume or four food cans with a 16-ounce volume. Remove the labels and make sure that the open tops are free of jagged and dangerous edges. Clean the cans and lightly oil the insides.

2. In a bowl, mix together the buttermilk and molasses. In a second bowl, mix together the raisins, walnuts, whole wheat and rye flours, cornmeal, baking soda, and salt.

3. Stir the dry ingredients into the wet ingredients. Add only one quarter of the dry ingredients at a time and make sure that they are fully incorporated before adding additional dry ingredients. This technique helps avoid lumps in the batter and is valuable for all baking recipes at the point where the dry and wet ingredients are brought together.

4. Divide the batter among the food cans. Cover the tops of the cans lightly with aluminum foil, and put them into a Dutch oven or stockpot, or any other pot that is deep enough to hold them. Pour boiling water into the Dutch oven until it comes up about 2 inches on the outside of the cans. Cover the Dutch oven, place it over low heat, and keep the water inside at a simmer for 3 hours. As the water level in the Dutch oven begins to drop, add more water.

5. To remove the bread from the can, cut out the bottom of the can and push out the bread through the other open end. Allow them to cool on a rack.

MAKES 3 OR 4 BREADS

2 cups buttermilk
3/4 cup molasses
1 cup raisins
1/4 cup chopped walnuts
1 cup whole wheat flour
1 cup rye flour
1 cup yellow cornmeal
3/4 teaspoon baking soda
1/2 teaspoon salt

BEEF EMPANADAS

HACIENDA LOS LINGUES, SANTIAGO, CHILE

MAKES 10 EMPANADAS

FOR THE PASTRY:
3 cups all-purpose flour
3 teaspoons baking powder
1 teaspoon salt
6 tablespoons shortening
6 tablespoons unsalted
    butter
10 tablespoons cold water

FOR THE FILLING:
2 tablespoons olive oil
1 cup finely chopped onion
1 pound ground beef
Salt and freshly ground
    black pepper
2 tablespoons minced fresh
    parsley
$1/2$ teaspoon dried oregano
$1/2$ teaspoon paprika
2 tablespoons ground
    cumin

$1/2$ cup raisins
20 stuffed olives, sliced
5 eggs, hard-boiled, sliced
    into quarters lengthwise

1 recipe Chilean Salsa
    (Pebre) (page 215)

1. To prepare the pastry: Sift the flour, baking powder, and salt together into a bowl. Cut in the shortening and butter. Mix in the water until the dough forms a ball and holds together. Wrap the dough in plastic and refrigerate for 1 hour.

2. To prepare the filling: In a sauté pan over medium heat, heat the oil. Add the onions and cook for 2 minutes. Add the beef and cook, stirring, for 3 minutes. Add the seasonings, stir, and cook for 2 minutes.

3. Preheat the oven to 400° F.

4. To assemble: Turn the dough out onto a floured surface and roll it out to a thickness of $1/4$ inch. Cut the dough into 10 circles each with a diameter of approximately 6 inches.

5. Place the circles of dough on a flat work surface. Place $1/4$ cup of the filling near the center of each circle. Place a few raisins, slices of olive, and slices of egg onto the filling. Fold the dough in half, enclosing the filling and producing a half-moon-shaped pocket. Carefully seal the edges.

6. Place the empanadas on an ungreased baking sheet and bake for 25 minutes.

7. Serve with Chilean Salsa.

A SHORT HISTORY OF CHILE

The first European to see Chile was the Portuguese explorer Ferdinand Magellan. He sailed through the straits at the bottom of Chile and gave his name to the passage. Then he sailed up along the coast, but he never settled in. I always consider Magallanes a food guy. He had been sent out by the rulers of Spain to find a short-cut to the Far East, so they could buy eastern spices at the source and resell them to other European countries at prices that would give them enormous profits.

Francisco Pizarro was one of the leaders of the Spanish conquistadors, and Pedro de Valdivia was one of his, shall we say, associates. Valdivia was given Chile as a reward for his loyalty to Pizarro. De Valdivia then became the first European to settle in Chile.

Those were the good old days when loyalty was really appreciated. I can hear Pizarro, "So, Pedro, you have been a good and loyal friend, and for that I give you Chile, and because it's Friday I throw in a nice slice of Argentina." Today if you have been a staunch supporter of the head of a country you get to be ambassador to Paris. I tell you, the whole idea of loyalty is being devalued. Anyway, in 1541, Valdivia founded the first colonial city in Chile, and he called it Santiago.

For the next two hundred years or so the Spanish fought with the native Mapuche tribes for control of the land. The Mapuches had never seen a horse, and in the early years of the conflict they thought that the Spanish soldier and his horse were one animal. Kind of like the way I felt about my son James when he got his first motorcycle.

For its first three hundred years, Chile was more or less under the control of Spain. But in the early 1800s, the ideas that led to both the American and French revolutions were filtering down to Chile, and a movement for independence got under way. It was clearly an idea whose time had come, not only in Chile but all over South America. On January 1, 1818, Chile declared its independence. Today, Chile is a democracy with a government that is freely elected by over 90 percent of the public.

LOS LINGUES

During the early 1500s, a man named Juan Jufre y Montero del Aguila traveled through South America with the conquistadors. His job was to keep a record of what was going on for the king of Spain. Juan did such a good job that the king decided to give him a bonus. And so in 1545, Carlos V, King of Spain, Ruler of the Americas, Defender of the Faith, and Holder of the Secret Formula for Making a Great Cup of Cocoa, among other things, gave to his loyal servant ten thousand acres of fabulous land just south of the Chilean city of Santiago. It's good to be king, and it's not so bad to be the king's good friend either.

Since then the land has been passed down through the family, and today it is called Los Lingues. It's owned by German Claro Lyon and his wife Maria Elena. It is a working farm that breeds Aculeguano horses, which are often described as the best horses in South America. They trace their bloodlines back to the Moors, who bred Aculeguano in Spain during the 700s. The hacienda and the nearby outbuildings have been turned into a rural guesthouse with a traditional Chilean kitchen.

Maria Gomez has been the household's cook for over thirty years, and her skill at producing the classic dishes of Chile is unbeatable.

CHEESE EMPANADAS

CHILE

1. **To prepare the dough:** In a bowl, combine the flour, salt, and baking powder. Using 2 knives or a pastry blender, cut in the shortening so the mixture resembles coarse crumbs. Stir in the egg yolk. Add water, a tablespoon at a time, stirring with a fork until a dough forms. Turn the dough out onto a floured board and knead for 1 minute. Roll the dough 1/8 to 1/4 inch thick. Cut the dough into 3-inch squares.

2. **To prepare the filling:** In a bowl, combine the ingredients, then set aside.

3. Preheat the oven to 375° F. Lightly butter a baking sheet and set aside.

4. **To make the empanadas:** Place about 2 teaspoons of the filling into each square. Fold the squares in half to form triangles, and seal the edges by crimping with a fork. Place the empanadas on the prepared baking sheet and refrigerate for 10 minutes.

5. **To make the glaze:** In a small bowl, beat the egg and water together.

6. Brush the tops of the empanadas with the glaze. Bake for 20 to 25 minutes, or until the tops are lightly browned. Cool for 2 minutes on a rack before serving.

MAKES 4 SERVINGS

FOR THE DOUGH:
2 cups all-purpose flour
1/2 teaspoon salt
1/2 teaspoon baking powder
6 tablespoons vegetable shortening or margarine
1 egg yolk
3 to 4 tablespoons ice water

FOR THE FILLING:
1/3 cup grated Swiss cheese
1/2 cup grated Cheddar cheese
1/4 teaspoon paprika
1 egg white, lightly beaten

FOR THE GLAZE:
1 egg, lightly beaten
1 teaspoon water

Sweet Empanadas

CHILE

MAKES 6 SERVINGS

2 cups orange marmalade

FOR THE DOUGH:
2 cups all-purpose flour
2 tablespoons granulated
    sugar
$1/2$ teaspoon salt
8 tablespoons vegetable
    shortening or margarine
3 to 4 tablespoons ice
    water

2 tablespoons unsalted
    butter, melted
$1/4$ cup shredded coconut
2 tablespoons granulated
    sugar
Confectioners' sugar for
    dusting

1. Place the marmalade in a strainer over a bowl. Press the marmalade with a spoon so the moisture starts to drain out. Let the mixture drain for 30 minutes.

2. To prepare the dough: In a mixing bowl, combine the flour, sugar, and salt. Using a pastry blender or 2 knives, cut in the shortening until the mixture resembles coarse crumbs. With a fork, stir in the ice water, tablespoon by tablespoon, until a dough forms. You may need to add more or less water depending on the humidity.

3. Preheat the oven to 350° F. Lightly butter a baking sheet and set aside.

4. On a lightly floured surface, roll out the dough $1/8$ to $1/4$ inch thick. Cut it into 3-inch squares. Place about 2 teaspoons of the drained marmalade on each square. Fold the squares in half to form triangles. Seal the edges by crimping with a fork.

5. Transfer the triangles to the baking sheet. Brush them with a little melted butter. Sprinkle some coconut and granulated sugar on top. Bake for 30 minutes, until lightly golden, then cool briefly on a rack.

6. Dust the tops with a little confectioners' sugar.

Desserts

BAKED APPLES

ROYAL VIKING SUN

MAKES 6 SERVINGS

³/₄ cup packed light brown
    sugar
1 teaspoon ground
    cinnamon
¹/₄ teaspoon ground
    nutmeg
¹/₃ cup raisins
¹/₃ cup cinnamon red hot
    candies
6 baking apples, cored
    but not peeled
¹/₂ cup maple syrup

1. Preheat the oven to 350° F. Lightly butter a loaf pan or square baking pan large enough to hold all the apples.

2. In a bowl, mix together the sugar, cinnamon, nutmeg, raisins, and red hot candies. Spoon this mixture into the cores of the apples.

3. Place the apples in the prepared pan. Pour the maple syrup over the apples. Bake for 30 to 40 minutes, or until the apples are tender.

NOTE: Baking time can vary slightly with the variety and size of the apples.

BAKED APPLES WITH FIGS, APRICOTS, AND RAISINS

ITALY

1. Heat the oven to 400° F.

2. Remove the stem from the apples, and with a paring knife remove the top 1½ inches of apple skin. With a melon baller remove the core of the apple. Continue to scoop out the center of the apple, to make a cavity. Save the good bits of apple to add to the stuffing. Rub the cut apple with the lemon to prevent discoloration.

3. In a small saucepan, combine the water and the dried fruits. Bring to a boil, remove from the heat, set aside to plump, 3 to 5 minutes.

4. Remove the plumped fruit from the liquid, and save the liquid. Chop the fruit. In a medium bowl, mix the fruit with the crumbled cookies, butter, and cinnamon. Stuff the filling into the prepared apples and place in a baking dish or gratin dish. Add the reserved liquid from plumping the fruit to the bottom of the dish to keep the apples moist while they bake.

5. Sprinkle the stuffed fruits with the sugar and bake for 40 minutes. Serve warm or at room temperature.

MAKES 4 SERVINGS

4 baking apples, Golden Delicious or Granny Smith
1 lemon, halved
⅓ cup water
4 dried figs
6 dried apricots
¼ cup golden raisins
4 amaretti cookies, crumbled
2 tablespoons unsalted butter, softened
¼ teaspoon ground cinnamon
1 tablespoon sugar

Poached Peaches with Cinnamon and Marsala

ITALY

MAKES 4 SERVINGS

2¹/₂ cups Marsala
1¹/₂ cups water
1¹/₂ cups sugar
2 cinnamon sticks
6 allspice berries
4 ripe peaches
1 cup ricotta cheese
(optional)

1. In a medium-sized saucepan that will accommodate the peaches, combine the Marsala, water, sugar, cinnamon, and allspice. Bring to a boil, cover, and simmer for 5 minutes.

2. With a paring knife cut an **X** in the skin of the bottom of each peach. This will make peeling the peaches much easier. Place the peaches in the poaching liquid and poach over very low heat until they're tender but not mushy, 25 to 30 minutes. Let the peaches cool in the poaching liquid.

3. When the peaches are cool enough to handle, gently remove their skins. To make a sauce, reduce the poaching liquid to a syrup and drizzle over the peaches. Or add some of the reduced syrup to the ricotta cheese. Serve the peaches with the sweetened ricotta cheese, if desired.

Wine bottles being stored, Piedmont, Italy.

Broiled Pineapple with Rum Sauce

CHILE

1. **To prepare the pineapple:** Preheat the broiler. In a bowl, combine the sugar and cinnamon. Arrange the pineapple on a broiler tray and sprinkle the top with half of the sugar-cinnamon mixture. Broil for 5 minutes, or until the pineapple is lightly browned. Turn the pineapple over, sprinkle with the remaining sugar-cinnamon mixture, and broil for 5 minutes longer, or until lightly browned. Place the broiled pineapple on dessert plates.

2. **To prepare the sauce:** In a sauté pan over medium heat, melt the butter and brown sugar, then cook for 3 minutes. Add the rum and vanilla. Spoon the sauce on the pineapple and serve.

MAKES 6 SERVINGS

FOR THE PINEAPPLE:
1/4 cup granulated sugar
1/2 teaspoon ground cinnamon
6 large slices or wedges of fresh pineapple

FOR THE SAUCE:
2 tablespoons unsalted butter
1/2 cup brown sugar
1/4 cup dark rum
1/2 teaspoon vanilla extract

✳

WINTER FRUIT OF CHILE

I once heard the country of Chile described as if it were a thin strip of land, similar to the west coast of North America, running from the top of Alaska to the bottom of California, but flipped over into the southern half of the globe. One of the effects of that flip is that when it is winter in North America, it is summer in Chile. That, in turn, results in opposite harvest seasons for many fruits and vegetables.

Somewhere along the line, someone in Chile realized that New York was directly north of Chile's major farmlands and that their summer harvest was perfectly timed for North America's winter. Nice deal for everyone. Chile is now a major exporter of apples, peaches, pears, plums, grapes, and kiwis. From December through April, the United States and Canada are the importers.

Of all the research that has come in during the last few years on the relationship of food to good health, my favorite is the material on the importance of fresh fruits. It appears that a diet high in fresh fruits is extremely important to your health. Even a single portion each day can improve your well-being in terms of your heart. I love it when something that is healthy for me, is also easy to eat and tastes good.

A fruit and vegetable market, which is set up on the banks of the river each morning in Valdivia, Chile.

POACHED FRUIT WITH CARAMEL SAUCE

CALIFORNIA

1. **To prepare the fruit:** In a saucepan, combine the wine, water, sugar, lemon zest, and vanilla. Bring the mixture to a boil and add the fruit. Lower the heat to a simmer and cook until the fruit is tender when pierced with a paring knife, but still slightly firm: 5 to 7 minutes for apples; 8 to 10 minutes for peaches; or 20 to 30 minutes for pears. The cooking times may vary depending on the ripeness of the fruit. Drain the fruit from the liquid and cool.

2. **To prepare the caramel sauce:** In a saucepan, combine the ingredients. Cook, stirring occasionally, for about 5 minutes (makes approximately 1 cup of sauce).

3. **To serve:** Place 2 halves of the fruit on a dessert plate and spoon a little of the sauce on top.

MAKES 4 SERVINGS

FOR THE FRUIT:
1½ cups white wine
1½ cups water
½ to ¾ cup granulated sugar, depending on the ripeness of the fruit
Zest of 1 lemon
1 teaspoon vanilla extract
4 medium apples, pears, or peaches, peeled, halved, cored, pits removed

FOR THE CARAMEL SAUCE:
½ cup light corn syrup
½ cup light brown sugar
¼ cup heavy cream
1 tablespoon unsalted butter
½ teaspoon vanilla extract

WINE AND HONEY–MARINATED FRUIT

ITALY

MAKES 4 SERVINGS

1 orange
1 cup white wine
½ cup honey
1 cinnamon stick
2 cups strawberries, tops
    trimmed, and halved
2 cups melon chunks
1 cup black or red seedless
    grape halves
3 sprigs mint

1. With a zester or peeler remove the zest from half of the orange. In a small saucepan, combine the wine, honey, orange zest, juice of the orange, and cinnamon stick. Bring to a boil and simmer for 1 minute.

2. In a bowl, combine the fresh fruit and mint and pour the flavored wine over the fruit. Let cool and marinate for 1 hour, or overnight in the refrigerator. Serve by itself or as a compliment to ice cream or pound cake.

A restaurant in Piedmont, Italy, where the wines are presented on the walls of the restaurant rather than on a wine list. As you come in, you walk past the shelves, select the bottle you like, and bring it to your table.

APPLE COBBLER

CANADA

1. Preheat the oven to 400° F. Lightly grease a 9-inch round cake pan.

2. **To prepare the apples:** In a bowl, mix the sliced apples, sugar, and cinnamon. Add the flour, tossing the apples to coat evenly. Stir in the nuts.

3. **To prepare the batter:** In a bowl, combine the dry ingredients. In another bowl, mix together the egg, milk, and oil. Gently stir the wet ingredients into the dry ingredients. The batter will be sticky.

4. Place the apples into the prepared cake pan. Spread the batter evenly over the apples. Bake for 30 minutes, or until the top of the cobbler is brown and crusty. Serve warm.

MAKES 8 SERVINGS

FOR THE APPLES:
4 cups Rome, Cortland, or
  other baking apples,
  pared, cored, and sliced
1/4 cup sugar
1/2 teaspoon ground
  cinnamon
2 tablespoons all-purpose
  flour
1/2 cup chopped walnuts
  (optional)

FOR THE BATTER:
1 1/2 cups all-purpose flour
2 teaspoons baking
  powder
1/2 teaspoon salt
1/4 cup sugar
1/4 teaspoon ground
  cinnamon
1 egg
1/2 cup milk
3 tablespoons vegetable oil

PEACH BERRY CRUMBLE

CANADA

MAKES 8 SERVINGS

One 20-ounce package
    frozen unsweetened
    peaches, thawed
1 cup frozen or fresh
    blueberries
1/4 cup granulated sugar
1/8 teaspoon ground
    nutmeg
1 teaspoon vanilla extract
2 tablespoons all-purpose
    flour

FOR THE TOPPING:
3/4 cup all-purpose flour
3/4 cup brown sugar
1/2 teaspoon ground
    cinnamon
6 tablespoons salted butter
1/2 cup chopped hazelnuts

1. Preheat the oven to 350° F. Lightly grease an 8-inch square baking dish.

2. In a bowl, combine the peaches, blueberries, sugar, nutmeg, and vanilla. Add the flour, tossing the fruit to coat evenly. Place the fruit in the prepared pan.

3. To prepare the topping: In a bowl, combine the flour, sugar, and cinnamon. With 2 knives, cut in the butter until the mixture resembles coarse crumbs. Stir in the chopped nuts.

4. Sprinkle the topping evenly over the fruit. Bake for 35 to 40 minutes, or until the topping is browned.

Orange Bars

CALIFORNIA

1. Preheat the oven to 375° F. Lightly butter an 8-inch square baking dish.

2. **To make the crust:** In a bowl, combine the flour and confectioners' sugar. Cut in the butter until it is absorbed. Press the mixture into the prepared pan and bake for 20 minutes.

3. **To make the filling:** In a bowl, beat together all the ingredients. Pour the mixture over the baked crust. Return the pan to the oven and bake for 20 to 25 minutes, or until the filling is set.

4. Cool on a rack, then chill. Before serving, dust the top with confectioners' sugar.

MAKES 8 SERVINGS

FOR THE CRUST:
1 cup all-purpose flour
½ cup confectioners' sugar
8 tablespoons unsalted
   butter

FOR THE FILLING:
2 eggs, lightly beaten
1 cup granulated sugar
1 tablespoon all-purpose
   flour
¼ cup orange juice
Zest of 1 orange, finely
   grated

Confectioners' sugar for
   dusting

Strawberry Shortcakes

CHILE

MAKES 8 SERVINGS

FOR THE
SHORTCAKES:
4 cups all-purpose flour
1/4 cup plus 2 tablespoons
    sugar
1 tablespoon plus
    2 teaspoons baking
    powder
1 teaspoon salt
3/4 cup unsalted butter,
    chilled and cut into bits,
    plus 2 tablespoons,
    melted and cooled
1 1/2 cups heavy cream

FOR THE FILLING:
2 pints fresh ripe
    strawberries, washed
    and stemmed
2 tablespoons sugar, or to
    taste
Heavy cream, sweetened
    and whipped

1. Preheat the oven to 425° F. Lightly butter a large baking sheet.

2. To make the shortcakes: In a large bowl, mix together the dry ingredients. Add the butter pieces, and with a pastry blender or fingertips, rub the butter into the dry ingredients until the mixture resembles coarse meal. Add the cream and mix thoroughly until a soft dough forms. Gather the dough into a compact disk and place on a lightly floured board or work surface. Knead the dough for about 1 minute, folding it end to end and pressing down and pushing forward several times with the heel of your hand. Roll out the dough into a 1/2-inch-thick circle. With a 3-inch cookie cutter, cut out 9 rounds. With a 2 1/2-inch cookie cutter, cut the remaining dough into 9 rounds. (If there isn't enough dough, gather the scraps, knead briefly, and roll out again.) Arrange the 3-inch rounds on the prepared baking sheet. Brush each with the melted butter and top with a 2 1/2-inch round.

3. Bake in the center of the oven for 15 minutes, until the shortcakes are firm to the touch and golden brown. Remove to a rack to cool.

4. Coarsely chop half the strawberries, reserving the most attractive ones for the top.

5. Pull the smaller tops away from the bottoms of the shortcakes. Spread a layer of chopped strawberries on the bottom halves, sprinkle each with sugar, and gently cover with the top halves. Garnish with the whipped cream and whole strawberries.

CHOCOLATE WAFFLES

SONOMA MISSION INN, BOYES HOT SPRINGS, CALIFORNIA

1. **To prepare the waffles:** In the top of a double boiler or in a glass bowl in a microwave oven, melt together the bittersweet and semisweet chocolates. In a bowl, whisk or beat together the egg yolks and the brown sugar until their volume is almost double. Fold the egg yolks and brown sugar mixture into the melted chocolates. Fold the flour into the chocolate mixture, ¼ cup at a time. Add in the Grand Marnier or orange juice. In another bowl, whisk the egg whites until they begin to stiffen, then add in the granulated sugar, ¼ cup at a time, while continuing to whisk. When the egg whites start to stand in peaks, fold one third of them into the chocolate mixture, then fold in the remaining whites. Cover the container and place this batter into a refrigerator for at least 30 minutes. The batter, tightly sealed, will last in the refrigerator for up to a week.

2. When you are ready to serve the waffles, preheat and lightly butter your waffle iron. Remove the batter from the refrigerator and while it is still firm, scoop about a cup of the batter onto the hot iron. Of course, you may need to adjust the amount of batter that you put on your waffle iron in accordance with its size and shape. Cook the batter on each side for 3 minutes, or until it has a firm crust.

3. To serve, cover one half of the surface of a serving plate with chocolate syrup and the other half with raspberry syrup. Place a scoop of ice cream in the center. Arrange the waffle on or next to the ice cream. Add a garnish of fresh strawberries and a light dusting of the confectioners' sugar and the cocoa.

MAKES 6 SERVINGS

FOR THE WAFFLES:
8 ounces bittersweet chocolate
4 ounces semisweet chocolate
6 eggs, separated
½ cup brown sugar
1 cup sifted all-purpose flour
2 tablespoons Grand Marnier liqueur or orange juice
1 cup granulated sugar

1 ounce butter for waffle iron

GARNISHES FOR SERVING:
½ cup chocolate syrup
½ cup raspberry syrup
1 pint ice cream
1 cup strawberries
2 tablespoons confectioners' sugar
2 tablespoons unsweetened cocoa powder

Chocolate Chestnut Cream Puffs

ITALY

MAKES 12 CREAM PUFFS

FOR THE CREAM PUFFS:
3/4 cup water
6 tablespoons unsalted butter
3/4 cup all-purpose flour
3 large eggs
Egg wash: 1 egg beaten with pinch of salt

FOR THE CHESTNUT FILLING:
1 1/3 cups peeled chestnuts (about 20)
1 cup milk
1 cup granulated sugar
4 ounces semisweet chocolate
2 tablespoons rum or brandy
1 1/4 cups heavy cream

Confectioners' sugar for dusting

1. Heat the oven to 425° F. Line a cookie sheet with parchment paper.

2. **To make the cream puffs:** In a 1 1/2-quart saucepan, combine the water and butter, and bring to a boil over medium heat, stirring occasionally. Remove from the heat and add the flour, stirring with a wooden spoon. Return to medium heat and beat constantly, until the mixture holds together and the paste pulls away from the sides of the pan, about 2 minutes. Remove the paste from the pan to a medium bowl, and cool slightly. When cool, using the wooden spoon add in the eggs, one at a time. Make sure that each egg is fully incorporated before adding the next egg.

3. Increase the oven temperature to 450° F. Transfer the dough to a pastry bag if available. Pipe the cream puff dough into 2-inch-diameter plump round balls, onto the prepared cookie sheet. If you don't have a pastry bag, use a large spoon to make the puffs. Space the cream puffs about 2 inches apart to allow for expanding when cooking. Brush with the egg wash and bake for 15 minutes. Turn the oven down to 350° F. and continue to bake until the puffs are golden brown and crisp, about 20 minutes more. Check the inside of one of the puffs, it should be hollow and somewhat dry. Remove the puffs from the oven and cool.

4. **To make the chestnut cream:** In a 1 1/2-quart saucepan, combine the chestnuts, milk, and granulated sugar. Bring to a boil, stirring to dissolve the sugar. Simmer for 15 minutes, until the chestnuts are tender. While the chestnuts are sim-

mering, melt the chocolate in a microwave for 30 seconds to 1 minute, or melt in a double boiler. Puree the cooked chestnuts, milk, chocolate, and rum or brandy in a food processor until smooth. Cool slightly. Whip the cream to soft peaks and then fold it into the chestnut-chocolate mix. Refrigerate for 1 hour.

5. When ready to serve, cut a third of the top off of the cream puffs and pipe or spoon the chocolate-chestnut mix into the cream puffs. Replace the tops and dust with confectioners' sugar.

Bakeware storage area, Sonoma Mission Inn.

Chocolate Pizza

THE PALLISER HOTEL, CALGARY, CANADA

MAKES 10 SERVINGS

FOR THE PIZZA
CRUST:
¹/₂ cup unsalted butter
¹/₂ cup brown sugar
¹/₂ cup granulated sugar
¹/₂ teaspoon baking powder
¹/₂ teaspoon vanilla extract
2 large eggs
1 cup all-purpose flour
¹/₂ cup chocolate chips

FOR THE TOPPINGS
(ALL OR ANY
COMBINATION
OF THE FOLLOWING):
¹/₂ cup peanut butter
¹/₂ cup mini-marshmallows
¹/₂ cup butterscotch chips
¹/₄ cup dark chocolate
    chips
¹/₄ cup dark chocolate
    shavings, loosely packed
¹/₄ cup milk chocolate
    shavings, loosely packed
¹/₄ cup chopped pistachio
    nuts
¹/₄ cup chopped almonds
¹/₄ cup coconut flakes
¹/₄ cup white chocolate
    shavings, loosely packed

1. Preheat the oven to 375° F. Lightly grease a 9-inch spring-form pan.

2. To prepare the crust: In a mixing bowl, cream together the butter and the sugars until smooth. Beat in the baking powder and vanilla. Beat in the eggs, one at a time. Beat in the flour. When the mixture is evenly blended, stir in the chocolate chips.

3. Spread the batter into the prepared pan and bake for 15 to 20 minutes. The dough will still be quite soft and lightly browned. Remove the pan and turn off the oven.

4. To assemble: Using a tablespoon, evenly distribute the peanut butter on top of the pizza crust. Scatter the mini-marshmallows and the butterscotch chips on top. Return the pan to the oven for 10 minutes. The heat should be off.

5. Scatter the remaining toppings on top of the pizza. Return the pan to the oven for 10 minutes longer.

6. Cool in the pan on a rack for 30 minutes. Remove the springform rim. Cut into wedges to serve.

THE COLUMBIA ICE FIELD

There have been at least seven ice ages during the earth's history. During each period the temperature dropped, snowfall increased, and ice covered large parts of the planet. During the last major ice age, which peaked about forty thousand years ago, most of Canada and the northern part of the United States lay under gigantic sheets of snow and ice. Some of the weather patterns that caused this ice to form are still operating.

Winds that are filled with moisture from their long passage across the Pacific Ocean come ashore along the coast of British Columbia. As they rise up to cross the Canadian Rockies the air cools, clouds are formed, and snow starts to fall.

At one point the snow clouds pass over some of the tallest mountains in the Canadian Rockies and across a high plateau. At this spot they release greater amounts of snow than at any time in their trip. More snow falls than melts and the weight of that snow mass is so great that it presses the air out of the snow and turns it to ice. It is similar to what happens on a city sidewalk when people constantly walk over new snow and press it into a sheet of ice. Only here the ice is hundreds of feet thick and it is called an ice field. When huge sheets of ice start flowing out of the field they are called glaciers.

You can get an excellent idea of what an ice age looked like by visiting the Athabasca Glacier. The glacier is part of the Columbia Ice Field that straddles the Canadian provinces of British Columbia and Alberta.

TANGERINE GRANITA

ITALY

MAKES 4 SERVINGS

¹/₄ cup water
¹/₂ cup sugar
3 cups tangerine juice
4 hollowed-out tangerine
    skins, frozen
Fresh mint for garnish

1. In a small saucepan, combine the water and sugar and bring to a boil. Cover and simmer for 3 minutes, until the sugar is dissolved into a syrup. Set aside to cool.

2. Mix the tangerine juice together with the syrup. Pour the mix into a pan, so that it is about an inch deep. Place the pan in the freezer. Let the mix freeze for 2 to 3 hours, or until it is almost completely set but not rock hard. Break the granita up and puree it in a food processor until it is uniformly combined and has a creamy look to it. Let the granita harden for at least 1 hour or overnight before serving. Alternatively, if you don't have a food processor, freeze it by the traditional method. Place the mix in the freezer, it will start to get slushy after about 30 minutes. Using a fork, "rake" the granita to form small ice crystals. Repeat this every 30 minutes for about 1¹/₂ to 2 hours, depending on your freezer, until the granita is uniformly frozen.

3. To serve, scoop the granita into the frozen tangerine halves and garnish with a sprig of mint.

Frozen Chocolate Soufflés

HYATT HOTEL, ARUBA

1. Take four ramekins, each with a 4-ounce volume, and line their bases with the pound cake. Layer the strawberry slices on top of the cake. Cut parchment paper into strips that are 6 inches wide and long enough to go around the circumference of the ramekins and overlap by 1 inch. Fold the parchment in half and wrap the strips around the ramekins. Tape them in place to form a collar that extends 2 inches above the rim of the ramekin.

2. In the top of a double boiler over simmering water, melt the chocolate and the butter, stirring until smooth. When the chocolate and the butter are fully incorporated, set the mixture aside to cool slightly.

3. Beat the cream, slowly adding in the 2 tablespoons confectioners' sugar, and continue beating until the cream stands in soft peaks. Refrigerate until ready to use.

4. In a bowl, beat the egg whites until foamy. Slowly add the granulated sugar and beat until soft peaks are formed. Fold one third of the egg whites into the melted chocolate, then fold the chocolate and egg white mixture into the remaining egg whites. Gently fold the whipped cream into the chocolate–egg white mixture. Spoon the mixture into the ramekins, using a spatula to level the top even with the rim of the parchment collar. Freeze for at least 3 hours.

5. Serve with a light dusting of confectioners' sugar.

MAKES 4 SERVINGS

4 slices pound cake,
  ¼ inch thick
4 strawberries, sliced
4 ounces semisweet
  chocolate, chopped
  into small pieces
2 tablespoons unsalted
  butter
1 cup heavy cream
2 tablespoons
  confectioners' sugar,
  plus extra for dusting
2 egg whites
¼ cup granulated sugar

Panna Cotta with Caramel Oranges

ITALY

MAKES 6 SERVINGS

FOR THE CREAM:
1 cup buttermilk
2¹/₂ teaspoons (1 envelope)
    powdered gelatin
3 cups heavy cream
²/₃ cup sugar
1 large piece orange zest,
    peeled off with a
    vegetable peeler
1 teaspoon vanilla extract

FOR THE CARAMEL
ORANGES:
³/₄ cup sugar
³/₄ cup water
2 oranges, peeled and
    cut into segments

1. To make the cream: Pour the buttermilk into a bowl and sprinkle the surface with the gelatin. Set aside to let the gelatin hydrate, about 5 minutes. In a medium saucepan, bring the cream and the sugar to a boil then remove from the heat. Whisk the heated cream into the buttermilk, and add the orange zest and vanilla extract. Set aside to let the orange flavor infuse while you make the caramel.

2. To make the caramel: In a heavy-bottomed saucepan, combine the sugar and ¹/₄ cup of the water. Cook over a medium-high heat until the sugar is a medium caramel color. Remove from the heat and carefully add 2 tablespoons of water, whisk if needed to ensure that the caramel is smooth. Pour 1 or 2 tablespoons of the caramel into the bottom of six ³/₄-cup ramekins. Add the rest of the water to the caramel and heat gently to dissolve; add the orange segments and set aside to use later to garnish the panna cotta.

3. Remove the orange zest from the cream and pour the cream into the prepared ramekins. Cover and refrigerate for 2 to 3 hours, or until completely set.

4. To serve, run a knife around the inside edge of each ramekin. Unmold the panna cotta onto individual plates and serve with the caramel oranges.

TIRAMISU

ITALY

1. To make the syrup: In a small saucepan, heat the water and sugar until thickened. Remove from the heat and add the espresso. Set aside.

2. To make the cream: In the bowl of a standing mixer or by hand, cream the mascarpone with the confectioners' sugar, Grand Marnier, and orange zest. In another bowl, whip the cream to soft peaks and then fold into the softened mascarpone.

3. To assemble the tiramisu: Break up 4 to 6 ladyfingers and soak them in a third of the syrup. Dip the remaining ladyfingers in the syrup and then rest them on the inside of 4 wineglasses. Dip the ladyfingers just enough to soak up the syrup but not to make them soggy. Pipe or spoon a third of the cream into the glasses, then add some of the soaked ladyfinger pieces, and a third of the chocolate. Repeat this until you have used all the cream.

4. Garnish the tiramisu with a dusting of cinnamon and the coffee. Chill for 1 to 2 hours and serve

MAKES 4 SERVINGS

FOR THE SYRUP:
1/4 cup water
1/4 cup granulated sugar
1/2 cup strong espresso

FOR THE CREAM:
12 ounces mascarpone
  cheese
3/4 cup confectioners' sugar
3 tablespoons Grand
  Marnier
1/2 teaspoon orange zest
1 1/2 cups heavy cream

16 to 18 ladyfingers
3 ounces chocolate, grated
  or chopped
Ground cinnamon for
  dusting
1 teaspoon ground coffee

Aruban Bread Pudding with Rum Sauce

PAPIAMENTO RESTAURANT, ARUBA

**MAKES 2 LOAVES,
10 TO 12 SERVINGS**

FOR THE BREAD
PUDDING:

4 cups small stale white
    bread pieces
2 cups milk
1 teaspoon vegetable oil
1/2 cup sugar
1/2 cup honey
6 eggs
2 tablespoons vanilla
    extract
1 cup raisins soaked in
    water or 1/2 cup rum for
    at least 30 minutes
1 cup small dried fruit
    pieces
2 tablespoons baking
    powder

FOR THE RUM SAUCE:

1 tablespoon cornstarch
1/2 cup sugar
1 3/4 cups milk
1/3 cup rum
4 tablespoons unsalted
    butter
1/2 teaspoon vanilla extract

The island of Aruba has a unique weather pattern. Being the most southerly of the islands that make up the Caribbean chain, it is well out of the way of the hurricane belt. It is consistently warm, sunny, breezy, and dry. Perfect for strolling beaches, bad for storing bread. The result is a nationally beloved pudding based on stale bread called *pan bollo.*

1. To make the bread pudding: In a mixing bowl, combine the bread and the milk, mash them together with the back of a fork, and let the mixture soak for at least 1 hour.

2. Preheat the oven to 350° F. Use the oil to coat the insides of 2 loaf pans that will hold all the pudding batter. The batter will have a total volume of about 9 cups.

3. Mix the remaining pudding ingredients into the bread and milk. Pour the mixture into the loaf pans.

4. Bake the puddings for 1 hour, or until fully cooked and brown on top. Let the pans cool on a wire rack.

5. To make the rum sauce: In a heavy saucepan over medium heat, mix the cornstarch and the sugar together and gradually add in the milk and rum. Stir constantly until the mixture almost boils. Reduce the heat and simmer uncovered for 3 minutes, stirring occasionally. Add the butter and vanilla. Pour some of the warm sauce onto a serving dish and place a slice of the pudding on top.

CHOCOLATE CRÈME BRÛLÉE

AMSTEL HOTEL, AMSTERDAM, HOLLAND

1. Preheat the oven to 325° F.

2. In a saucepan, over low heat, warm the chocolate and 1 cup of the cream, until the chocolate is melted. Pour the mixture into a medium bowl or a large liquid measuring cup and stir in the remaining cream.

3. In a bowl, whisk together the eggs and the granulated sugar. Whisk in the chocolate and cream mixture. Pour the mixture into six small crème brûlée dishes, or six 4-ounce ramekins.

4. Place the brûlée dishes or ramekins into a shallow baking pan. Pour hot water into the pan until it comes halfway up the outside of the brûlée pans or ramekins. Bake in the oven for 35 to 45 minutes, or until a knife inserted near the edge of the mixture comes out clean. The custard should be set at the edge and slightly soft in the center. Remove the dishes from the water bath and chill for at least 3 hours.

5. Preheat the broiler. Sprinkle the top of each brûlée with a teaspoon of brown sugar. Place the dishes under the broiler and heat until the brown sugar melts. Serve immediately.

MAKES 6 SERVINGS

2 ounces semisweet
  chocolate
2 cups heavy cream
5 eggs
½ cup granulated sugar
6 teaspoons brown sugar

CHOCOLATE FOR EATING

Fry & Sons had been producing drinking chocolate in their hometown of Bristol, England, since 1728. They were just one of a number of British chocolate companies with no particular claim to fame. However, that changed dramatically in 1847, for that was the year that Fry & Sons became the first company in the world to introduce "eating chocolate." Europeans who had spent the past three hundred years drinking their chocolate loved the new product. It was, you might say, a solid hit. And everyone in the chocolate business got into the act.

A charming British family named Cadbury started selling eating chocolate in their shop in Birmingham. Neuhaus opened the first eating chocolate shop in Belgium. Switzerland became a hotbed of activity. Henri Nestlé had started out as a maker of condensed milk for babies. Daniel Peter, who lived down the road, was a chocolate maker. When Nestlé's milk got mixed into Peter's chocolate, the two men decided to go into business and soon offered the public their new invention, milk chocolate.

Another Swiss, Rudolphe Lindt, came into the industry and invented the conching technology that gives eating chocolate its smooth texture.

Tobler, puttering around in his kitchen, mixed his milk chocolate with honey and almonds, inventing the Toblerone and added yet another Swiss company to the business. Their 15.4-pound Toblerone holds the record as the world's largest regularly produced chocolate bar.

In Italy the Buitonis were already a big deal in the pasta business when they decided to start making chocolate in a small town called Perugia. Giovanni Buitoni fell in love with a woman who was one of the company's leading recipe developers and therefore "off limits," and they found that the only way they could send their messages of love was by hiding them in the wrapping of the samples that they sent up and back between them as part of the business. Today, the company which is now called Perugina, finds its most successful product in the *Baci* which is the Italian word for kiss. And, if you look inside you will find that every Baci contains a message of love in the wrapping. Giovanni's tribute to the woman in his heart.

Domingo Ghirardelli was the son of a famous Italian chocolate maker. But the stories of gold that rushed around the world soon had him heading off to California. He failed to find gold in his claim, so he set up his conch, and did pretty well. Today, Ghirardelli is one of the outstanding names in American chocolate. The company's products are distributed nationally, and each year over a million people visit their shop at Ghirardelli Square in San Francisco. *(cont. on following page)*

In 1919, The Fanny Farmer Candy Shops were founded in Rochester, New York. The following year, the Fannie May candy company was founded in Chicago. When Fannie May purchased Fanny Farmer, the result was the largest chain of retail candy shops in the United States. They have over four hundred stores and they sell over 400 million pieces of candy each year. It actually calculates out to two pieces for each person in the United States. All those specific numbers are part of the Fanny Farmer tradition.

Fanny Farmer was a real person who lived at the end of the last century in Boston and ran the Boston Cooking School. She was very interested in standardizing recipes so they would always work. Before her influence, a recipe might call for "a handful" of flour or an oven "hot enough" to brown a piece of paper in a short time. After Fanny, those same recipes called for 6 ounces of sifted flour and a preheated oven at 350° F. Fanny Farmer was the mother of measuring and the shops were named in her memory. As a fitting tribute to Fanny's love of specificity, Fanny Farmer and Fannie May chocolates have a set of markings that tell you what's on the inside.

Milton Hershey was in the sugar-candy business until he saw a chocolate-making demonstration at the Chicago World's Fair of 1893, after which he rushed into the chocolate business.

In 1966, Godiva, a firm that was founded in Belgium, introduced their chocolates to North America, and almost single-handedly created the market for super-premium chocolate. At first, purchasers used Godiva primarily as gifts for other people. But when Godiva introduced packaging with only a few of their chocolates, most customers decided that if the old saying "Charity begins at home" was true, well maybe gift giving did too.

Today, Godiva makes its chocolate in Belgium and the United States and has shops all over the world, including over a hundred in the United States. During the fall of 1993, Godiva began offering a line of gourmet coffees, some flavored with vanilla and toasted almonds.

For me, the Godiva coffee brings the whole story full circle. Almost four hundred years ago, chocolate was first introduced to the general public in coffeehouses and often flavored with vanilla and almonds. Now chocolate houses are introducing coffee flavored with vanilla and almonds. As they say, "The more things change, the more they are the same."

FLAN

PAPIAMENTO RESTAURANT, ARUBA

MAKES 8 SERVINGS

FOR THE CARAMEL
SAUCE:
1 cup sugar
1 cup water

FOR THE FLAN:
One 14-ounce can
    sweetened condensed
    milk
14 ounces water
8 eggs
4 tablespoons vanilla
    extract

1. To prepare the sauce: Into a 3-quart heatproof bowl or mold (stainless steel is a good choice), put the sugar and the cup of water. Place the pan directly on the burner and heat over medium-high heat until the sugar and water caramelize to a dark brown color. This should take about 10 minutes. Much of the liquid will evaporate. Using potholders, carefully remove the pan from the burner and gently swirl the caramel sauce around the inside of the bowl until all the sides are coated lightly. Set the bowl inside a 9 × 13-inch baking pan and place it on a baking sheet.

2. Preheat the oven to 350° F.

3. To make the flan: In a blender, combine the sweetened condensed milk, water, and the eggs. Blend until smooth. Add the vanilla and blend briefly. Pour the flan mixture into the prepared bowl. Cover the bowl loosely with aluminum foil, gently crimping the edges to seal. The bowl will still be hot, so be sure to use a potholder when you touch it. Pour enough hot water around the bowl until it goes halfway up the outside of the bowl. Place the baking sheet, holding the water bath and the covered flan bowl, into the oven and bake for 1½ hours, until the custard is set.

4. After baking, carefully remove the flan from the oven and with potholders, lift the bowl out of the water bath and put the bowl onto a rack. Remove the foil cover. Let the flan cool at room temperature for 30 minutes, then refrigerate for 2 hours.

✳

5. To serve, run a knife between the flan and the edge of the bowl. Set a plate over the top of the bowl, turn the whole thing over and give it a shake. The flan will unmold onto the plate. Spoon out any of the caramel sauce that is left in the bowl. Slice the flan into wedges and spoon the caramel sauce on top.

Edward, Jaap, and Antoine Ellis, carrying on their father Eduardo's tradition at Papiamento Restaurant, Aruba.

PRALINE SAUCE FOR ICE CREAM

ROYAL VIKING SUN

MAKES 4 TO 5 SERVINGS

²/₃ cup pecan halves
¹/₂ cup firmly packed light
    brown sugar
¹/₂ cup dark corn syrup
1 tablespoon unsalted
    butter
Vanilla ice cream for
    serving

1. Into a pot with boiling water drop the pecans and boil for 5 minutes; drain and set aside.

2. Combine the sugar, corn syrup, and butter in the top of a double boiler. Place over boiling water. Heat and stir until the sugar has completely melted and the mixture is blended.

3. Stir in the pecans. Serve over the vanilla ice cream.

Keyholders at the hotel Le Sirenuse in Positano, Italy.

Cakes, Cupcakes, Cookies, and Confections

White Chocolate Grand Marnier Cheesecake

BANFF SPRINGS HOTEL, ALBERTA, CANADA

MAKES 8 SERVINGS

FOR THE CRUST:
3 tablespoons unsalted
    butter, melted
1 cup graham cracker
    crumbs
FOR THE FILLING:
14 ounces Philadelphia®
    cream cheese
1/4 cup confectioners' sugar
2 eggs
Juice of 1 orange and the
    zest, finely grated
2 tablespoons Grand
    Marnier liqueur
5 ounces white chocolate

FOR THE MERINGUE:
1/3 cup egg whites
    (2 large whites)
1/3 cup granulated sugar

FOR THE GARNISH:
16 mandarin orange
    sections
1 cup white chocolate
    shavings

Andreas Schwarzer is the pastry chef at the Banff Springs Hotel. Trained in his native Germany, he has become a skilled master of his craft. He operates from a special kitchen designed for the preparation of his own creations. The following recipe for a white chocolate cheesecake is one of the most popular desserts at the resort.

1. Preheat the oven to 350° F. Lightly butter an 8-inch springform pan.

2. To make the crust: In a mixing bowl, blend together the butter and the graham cracker crumbs and press that mixture into the bottom of the prepared pan.

3. To make the filling: In a mixing bowl, combine the cream cheese and confectioners' sugar. In another mixing bowl, blend together the eggs, orange juice, orange zest, and Grand Marnier. Add the Grand Marnier mixture to the cream cheese mixture and blend all of those ingredients together. In a bowl, over simmering water, melt the white chocolate and add it to the Grand Marnier and cream cheese mixture. The result is the basic batter.

4. To make the meringue: In a bowl, whip the egg whites until foamy, add the sugar, and continue whipping until the whites start to stand in peaks. Fold the meringue into the basic batter, and pour the result over the graham cracker crust.

5. Bake the cheesecake for 35 to 40 minutes.

6. When the cake comes out, let it cool completely in the pan on a rack. When it is fully cooled, remove it from the pan and slice into 8 pieces. The knife is dipped into hot water between each slice to keep the blade from sticking to the cake. Each slice of cake is decorated with two mandarin orange sections and garnished with white chocolate shavings.

ABOUT THE ICE IN YOUR KITCHEN

Any ice cubes that have been in your freezer for more than a week will have absorbed odors from the air in your freezer, and that can easily have a negative effect on the taste of the drink they are in. So, if you are serious about flavor, use fresh ice cubes. It's also a good idea to run a little water over your ice cubes before you use them. That will take off the top layer of ice and give you a very clean taste.

If you want to freeze food safely and properly, it is important to make sure that the temperature of your freezer is zero degrees Fahrenheit or lower. Foods that are held above zero will not store as well, or as long, as they will at zero or lower. The only way to check on that temperature is to use a freezer thermometer. Just because the food in your freezer feels frozen doesn't mean the temperature is low enough. Water freezes at 32 degrees; at that temperature you can reach into your freezer and everything will be hard, but the temperature may still be too high to properly hold many foods.

Finally, a note on freezing food and salt. Salt lowers the freezing point of water, so any food that has been salted will not freeze as well as food that is unsalted. If you are making a large batch of soup and plan to freeze some, set aside the soup that is going to be frozen before you salt it.

CHOCOLATE CHEESECAKE

HISTORIC HUDSON VALLEY, NEW YORK

1. Preheat the oven to 325° F.

2. **To make the crust:** In a bowl, mix together the ingredients until well combined. Press into a 9-inch springform pan or a 9-inch pie plate.

3. **To make the cheesecake:** In the top of a double boiler, melt 6 ounces of the chocolate over boiling water. In the container of a blender or food processor, blend together the eggs, corn syrup, cream, and vanilla until smooth. With the blender or food processor running, add the cream cheese, a few cubes at a time. Blend until smooth. Blend in the melted chocolate. Pour the mixture into the crust.

4. Bake the cake in the middle rack of the oven for 45 minutes, or until set. Cool on a rack.

5. In the top of a double boiler, melt the remaining chocolate over boiling water. Drizzle the melted chocolate over the cake.

MAKES 10 SERVINGS

FOR THE CRUMB CRUST:
1³/₄ cups chocolate cookies or graham cracker crumbs
2 tablespoons sugar
¹/₃ cup butter, melted

FOR THE CHEESECAKE:
8 ounces Baker's® German's® sweet chocolate
2 eggs
²/₃ cup light or dark corn syrup
¹/₃ cup heavy cream
1¹/₂ teaspoons vanilla extract
16 ounces cream cheese, cut into cubes

Ricotta Cheesecake

ITALY

MAKES 8 SERVINGS

FOR THE CRUST:
1½ cups amaretti cookie
   crumbs
5 tablespoons unsalted
   butter, melted

FOR THE FILLING:
¼ cup Amaretto
½ cup chopped dried
   apricots
3 cups whole-milk ricotta
   cheese
¼ cup all-purpose flour
⅔ cup sugar
⅛ teaspoon ground mace
1 teaspoon vanilla extract
4 large eggs, separated
Salt

1. To make the crust: Combine the cookie crumbs with 4 tablespoons of the butter. Brush a 10-inch springform pan with the remaining butter and then press in the crust. Refrigerate while you prepare the filling.

2. Preheat the oven to 350° F.

3. To make the filling: In a small pan, heat the Amaretto with the apricots to plump the fruit. Set aside. In a food processor, pulse the ricotta until it is creamy. Remove from the processor and mix it in a bowl together with the flour, sugar, mace, vanilla, egg yolks, and soaked apricots. In a stainless-steel bowl, whisk the egg whites with a pinch of salt to soft peaks. With a rubber spatula, fold a third of the beaten egg whites into the ricotta filling to lighten the batter. Fold in the remaining egg whites.

4. Pour the filling into the chilled crust and bake for 1 hour, or until the filling is golden brown and set. Remove from the oven and cool on a rack.

LEMON CHEESECAKE

CHILE

---

1. Preheat the oven to 350° F. Lightly butter or oil a 10-inch springform pan. Remove the bottom disk.

2. Roll and trim the dough so it fits the bottom of the springform pan. Place the dough on the bottom disk of the pan, then bake for 8 to 10 minutes, until lightly browned. Cool on a rack, then return the bottom to the springform pan with the dough on it to the springform collar and secure it in place. Lower the oven temperature to 325° F.

3. **To make the filling:** In a large bowl, beat the cream cheese until fluffy. Continue beating and pour in the sweetened condensed milk. Scrape the batter from the sides of the bowl, then beat in the egg yolks, one at a time. Mix in the lemon zest and raisins. In another bowl, beat the egg whites until stiff. Fold half of the beaten egg whites into the cream cheese mixture, then fold in the remaining half.

4. Spread the batter into the prepared crust and bake for 1 hour. Cool the cake on a rack, then chill.

5. **To serve:** Remove the cake from the springform, then dust with the confectioners' sugar.

MAKES 12 SERVINGS

Dough for a 9-inch
   piecrust

FOR THE FILLING:
2 pounds cream cheese,
   softened
One 14-ounce can
   sweetened condensed
   milk
4 eggs, separated
Grated zest of 1 lemon
1 cup raisins
Confectioners' sugar for
   dusting

✳

VALPARAISO, CHILE

In 1535, a Spanish expedition moved south from Peru hoping to find another civilization similar to the Incas. The Spanish conquistadors had just discovered the Incas, and that was thrilling. Thrilling for the conquistadors, that is. The Incas were into gold and so were the Spanish. Actually, the Spanish were into the Incas' gold. At any rate, the expedition had a rather bad time of it. Empty-handed, frustrated, and generally wasted, they headed for the coast to meet up with a fleet of Spanish ships. When the young, homesick lieutenant in charge of the march came out of the forest and saw the magnificent bay below him, he was reminded of his beloved Spain and named the area after his hometown, Valparaiso.

Valparaiso was the first Spanish coastal settlement in what was to become Chile. It also became the country's most important port. The original town was built around the central dock area and for many years was greatly influenced by big English corporations who settled into Valparaiso as Great Britain became Chile's largest trading partner. The old Grace shipping building and the Queen Victoria Hotel are reminders of the period, as is the downtown commercial area, which was built under the influence of British merchants to look like London. They even installed Turri Clock, their own version of Big Ben. As the town grew, it was forced to move up the surrounding hills. The result is a very unusual city with a population that moves up and down a series of very steep elevations. The residents make the trip many times throughout the day, and often in cable cars.

Because Valparaiso has such a long history, it holds the record for many Chilean firsts. It got the first telephone, the first gaslight, the first firehouse, and the first Spanish language newspaper in South America. The paper is called *El Mercurio*. First published in 1827, *El Mercurio* is still printed every day and it is as influential as ever.

CHOCOLATE LAYER CAKE WITH COCONUT PECAN FROSTING

HISTORIC HUDSON VALLEY, NEW YORK

1. Preheat the oven to 350° F. Lightly butter three 9-inch cake pans. Line the bottoms of the pans with waxed paper. Dust the pans with cocoa.

2. In a small saucepan, melt the chocolate in the boiling water. Stir until smooth. Let cool to room temperature.

3. In a mixing bowl, sift together the flour, baking soda, and salt.

4. In a large mixing bowl, with an electric mixer, cream the butter and sugar until light and fluffy. Beat in the egg yolks, one at a time, beating after each addition. Blend in the melted chocolate and the vanilla. Blend in 1/2 cup of the flour mixture and 1/4 cup of the buttermilk. Mix until smooth. Repeat until all the flour and buttermilk are used.

5. In a mixing bowl, with an electric mixer or a whisk, beat the egg whites until they form stiff peaks. Using one of the beaters or a whisk, fold the egg whites into the batter. Pour the batter into the prepared cake pans.

6. Bake the layers on the middle rack of the oven for 30 to 35 minutes, or until the layers spring back when lightly pressed in the centers.

7. Remove the layers from the oven. Run the edge of a knife between the cake and the sides of the pans. Let the cake cool in the pans for 15 minutes. Remove the layers from the pans and place on a rack. Let them cool to room temperature.

8. Fill and frost the cake with Coconut Pecan Frosting, using 2 tablespoons of frosting between each layer.

MAKES 12 SERVINGS

Unsweetened cocoa
  powder
One 4-ounce package
  Baker's® German's®
  sweet chocolate
1/2 cup boiling water
2 cups all-purpose flour
1 teaspoon baking soda
1/2 teaspoon salt
1 cup unsalted butter,
  softened
2 cups sugar
4 eggs, separated
1 teaspoon vanilla extract
1 cup buttermilk
Coconut Pecan Frosting
  (recipe follows)

Coconut Pecan Frosting

MAKES 2½ CUPS

1 cup evaporated milk or
　heavy cream
1 cup sugar
3 egg yolks, slightly beaten
½ cup unsalted butter
1 teaspoon vanilla extract
1⅓ cups shredded coconut
1 cup chopped pecans

1. In a 3-quart saucepan, combine the milk or cream, sugar, egg yolks, butter, and vanilla. Cook the mixture over medium heat, stirring often, until it thickens to the consistency of custard, about 12 minutes.

2. Remove the pan from the heat. Stir in the coconut and pecans. Let cool to room temperature, stirring occasionally.

THE HISTORY OF BAKER'S CHOCOLATE

The power behind the growth of manufacturing during the American colonial period came from the water that flowed through the rivers of New England and powered the mills. The most famous colonial mill site was probably the falls of the Neposet River at Dorchester, Massachusetts, about seven miles outside the city of Boston. In the 1630s, settlers built a mill on the Neposet and used the power of the water coming down the falls to grind corn. The neighborhood eventually became home for New England's first gunpowder mill, paper mill, flour mill, iron mill, and most importantly from my point of view, chocolate mill.

　　The Dorchester area is now a suburb of Boston and the mills are gone, but you can still see what a colonial mill of the period looked like by visiting Philipsburg Manor in North Tarrytown, New York. It is a restored mill that operates just as it would have during the middle of the 1700s. Philipsburg was used to grind grain into flour, but it just as easily could have been used to grind cocoa beans for the making of chocolate.

　　The first cocoa beans to come into the American colonies arrived in 1755. Fishermen from Gloucester, Massachusetts, made a deal with growers in the Caribbean to trade fish for cocoa. Ten years later, Dr. James Baker, a physician of Dorchester, Massachusetts, put up the money for an Irish immigrant named John Hannon to start a *(cont.)*

chocolate-making business. It was set up in an old gristmill and became the first chocolate factory in the American colonies.

While I was going through the old papers at the Baker's company I came across a piece of business advice from one of Dr. Baker's neighbors:

> Since man to man is so unjust
> Tis hard to say whom I can trust
> I've trusted many to my sorrow
> Pay me to-day. I'll trust you
> to-morrow.

Baker and his chocolates, however, were trusted. The company documents show that when honest Abe Lincoln ran a store in Illinois before he became President, the only branded food that he offered for sale in the shop was Baker's chocolate. How about that for a product endorsement? Actually, Baker and Lincoln agreed on a number of things. There is a letter in the company files that was written by Dr. Baker's son Walter on May 23, 1848. In the letter, Baker states the company policy of only buying cocoa from countries where slavery did not exist.

When you look at the products that Baker's makes today, you realize that they are to be used primarily as ingredients. There are unsweetened baking chocolate squares, semisweet baking chocolate squares, chocolate chips, and something called German's sweet chocolate bars.

For years I have seen German's sweet chocolate and I always thought it must be some special manufacturing recipe like Dutched chocolate. But while I was looking through the historical documents at Baker's I discovered that the German in Baker's German's chocolate was an Englishman named Samuel German. Sam was Walter Baker's coachman during the 1840s, and along with having a talent for horses, he had a talent for chocolate. He perfected the recipe for the company's sweetest product and had his name placed upon it as part of Baker's expression of appreciation.

Baker's is not only the oldest chocolate manufacturer in the United States but it also holds one of the oldest trademarks. In 1745, an Austrian Prince named Dietrichstein was visiting a chocolate shop in Vienna. The waitress, Anna Baltauf, who was serving him, was so beautiful and so charming that along with his tip he left her his heart. Soon after, Anna and the Prince were married.

To celebrate their marriage the Prince had her portrait painted by one of the leading artists of the time. Instead of posing Anna in the usual formal dress, he painted her as the Prince had first seen her, in the costume of a chocolate server. In the 1860s, a Baker's executive was traveling in Germany and saw the painting in the Dresden Art Gallery. He realized that the picture would make a perfect trademark for his company. The work, which is called *La Belle Chocolatière,* began to appear in Baker's advertising in 1872. And, she still shows up on Baker's packages.

Flourless Chocolate Cake

HYATT HOTEL, ARUBA

MAKES 10 SERVINGS

13 tablespoons unsalted
  butter
10 ounces semisweet
  chocolate, chopped
2 tablespoons Grand
  Marnier liqueur
6 large eggs, separated
1 cup granulated sugar
¼ cup confectioners' sugar
Strawberries for garnishing

1. Preheat the oven to 350° F. Lightly butter a 10-inch springform pan and line the bottom with a circle of parchment paper that has been cut to match the base.

2. In a heatproof bowl over simmering water, melt together the butter and the chocolate, then mix in the Grand Marnier. Set the mixture aside to cool to room temperature.

3. Separate the eggs. Place the yolks into a bowl. Add ½ cup of the granulated sugar and beat the mixture together until it is about triple in volume.

4. Place the egg whites into a bowl and whisk them until they begin to stiffen, then slowly add in the remaining ½ cup of granulated sugar and continue whisking until they stand in peaks.

5. Fold the butter-chocolate mixture into the egg yolks. Fold in the egg whites, one third at a time. Pour the batter into the prepared baking pan.

6. Place the pan onto a baking sheet and into the oven. Bake for 20 minutes, then turn down the heat to 300° F. and bake for an additional 20 minutes. Finally, reduce the heat to 250° F. and bake for 1 hour. Test for doneness by inserting the tip of a knife or a toothpick into the center of the cake. If the knife or toothpick comes out free of any moist batter, the cake is ready. If the cake is not done, continue baking for an additional 5 to 10 minutes.

7. Remove the cake from the oven, release from the springform pan, and carefully flip the cake over onto a flat plate so the parchment paper can be peeled off, then carefully flip back and cool to room temperature.

8. Lightly dust the cooled cake with the confectioners' sugar. Individual servings are garnished with slices of strawberries.

NOTE: The baking sheet is placed under the baking pan to catch any spills that might come up when the cake rises in the oven. The baking sheet will also even out the heat of the oven as it comes in contact with the bottom of the pan and thereby help prevent any burned areas on the base.

The Alan Lavine family, who moved from New Jersey to set up Aruba's first bagel bakery—a gastronomic landmark in the island's history.

CHOCOLATE SACHER CAKE

ENTRE LAGOS, VALDIVIA, CHILE

MAKES 10 SERVINGS

FOR THE CAKE:
1¼ cups cake flour
2 teaspoons baking
    powder
8 tablespoons unsalted
    butter, softened
¾ cup sugar
4 eggs, separated, plus
    1 egg white
6 ounces semisweet
    chocolate, melted
½ cup ground hazelnuts
1 teaspoon vanilla extract

FOR THE ICING AND
FILLING:
8 ounces semisweet
    chocolate, chopped
1 cup heavy cream
¼ cup
    cherry-flavored liqueur
⅔ cup cherry preserves

1. Preheat the oven to 350° F. Lightly butter a 9-inch spring-form pan then set it aside.

2. **To make the cake:** In a bowl, combine the flour and baking powder, then set aside. In another bowl, using an electric mixer, beat together the butter and sugar until smooth. Beat in the egg yolks, one at a time, then beat in the chocolate. Stir in the hazelnuts and vanilla. In a clean bowl, beat the egg whites until stiff. Alternately fold the beaten whites and the flour into the batter.

3. Spread the batter evenly in the prepared springform pan. Bake for 1 hour, or until a toothpick comes out clean. Cool the cake on a rack.

4. **To prepare the icing:** In the top of a double boiler, over simmering water, melt the chocolate. In a small saucepan, heat the cream. Remove the bowl from the heat and stir the cream into the chocolate, then set aside.

5. When the cake is cool, using a long serrated knife, slice it horizontally into 3 layers. Remove the top 2 layers. Brush the bottom layer with some of the cherry-flavored liqueur, then spread with a third of the chocolate filling on the first layer and finally half of the cherry preserves. Place the second layer and repeat the process with the liqueur, chocolate, and preserves. Put the remaining layer of cake on top and pour the remaining chocolate over the top. Place the cake in the refrigerator to set for 1 hour.

NOTE: To serve the cake, slice with a serrated knife that has been dipped in warm water. Wipe the blade clean between each cut.

THE LAKE DISTRICT OF CHILE

Chile's Lake District is set in the lower third of the country, the south. Though I should point out that we think of the southern part of the world as "lower" only because the first guys to draw the maps that we use were from the north, and they liked the idea of being on top of the world. Nevertheless, I think it would be quite clear to any visitor to Chile that things are definitely "up" around here.

During the 1600s, the Bío-bío River was marked as the boundary between the Spanish colonists and the native Mapuches. Since the Lake District is considerably below this line, the land was under the control of the tribes and not a very safe place for European settlers.

It wasn't until well into the second half of the 1800s that the Lake District was fully colonized. Today the district is a symbol to all Chileans of the honest life. Clean, healthy, unspoiled, down-home, real people. There are also a number of geographic features that make this district popular.

First of all it has the lakes, which are the largest in South America. The lakes were originally formed by glaciers passing through during the last ice age. As the ice advanced north from the South Pole it dug out huge basins in the earth. Then when things got too hot for the glaciers and they headed south again, their melting ice filled the basins and pure, clear lakes were formed. The lakes are now fed by rivers that pour down from the snowmelt in the Andes mountains, and drained by rivers that run from the lakes into the Pacific Ocean.

The eastern edge of the Lake District runs along what is called the Pacific Rim of Fire. It starts out in Alaska, runs down the west coast of North America, Central America, and South America. Then it slides down into the Pacific Ocean and pops up again in New Zealand. From there on it island-hops in a sweeping curve up through and past Japan. The entire rim is dotted with volcanoes. It is this unique combination of volcanoes and lakes that gives the Lake District its signature landscape.

There are also the araucaria trees. Found in this part of the world, they take about five hundred years to reach maturity. Then they live for over two thousand. They are considered a national treasure and are protected against cutting by the federal government. And finally, there are the rolling green hills covered with farms that remind people of southern Germany, Austria, and Switzerland.

Angel Food Cake with Mixed Berry Compote

CALIFORNIA

MAKES 12 SERVINGS

FOR THE CAKE:
1 cup cake flour
1½ cups granulated sugar
1¼ cups egg whites
    (10 to 12 whites)
1¼ teaspoons cream of
    tartar
¼ teaspoon salt
1 teaspoon vanilla extract

FOR THE COMPOTE:
3 cups strawberries, hulled
    and sliced
3 cups raspberries,
    blackberries, or
    blueberries, or any
    combination of them
3 tablespoons orange juice
    or orange-flavored
    liqueur
½ cup sugar

1. Preheat the oven to 325° F. Rinse a 10-inch angel food cake or tube cake pan with cold water and drain.

2. To make the cake: Sift together the cake flour and 1 cup of the sugar. Repeat the sifting 3 times, then set aside. In a large bowl, beat the egg whites until foamy. Add the cream of tartar and salt. Continue beating until soft peaks form. Add the remaining ½ cup of sugar, 2 tablespoons at a time, beating after each addition. Beat in the vanilla extract. Sift a third of the flour-sugar mixture into the beaten egg whites, folding quickly with a rubber spatula until no flour shows. Repeat the process twice again with a third of the flour-sugar mixture.

3. Transfer the batter into the prepared pan and bake for 45 to 50 minutes, until the cake is springy to the touch and a toothpick inserted in the center comes out clean.

4. Immediately invert the pan onto a cooling rack. Let the cake cool completely in the pan. Run a thin knife around the edge to loosen before unmolding.

5. To make the compote: In a medium bowl, combine all the berries, orange juice or liqueur, and sugar. Cover the bowl and refrigerate. Stir the mixture just before serving.

6. To serve, place a slice of the cake onto a dessert plate and surround it with some of the compote.

APPLE CAKE

CHILE

1. Preheat the oven to 350° F. Lightly butter or oil an 8-inch square baking pan.

2. **To make the cake:** In a large bowl, combine the apples, walnuts, and raisins. Stir in the oil, sugar, eggs, and vanilla. In another bowl, combine the remaining ingredients. Stir the dry ingredients into the wet ingredients.

3. Pour the batter into the prepared pan. Tap the pan on the countertop to remove any air bubbles. Bake for 30 to 35 minutes, until the cake is golden and feels springy to the touch. Cool the cake on a rack.

4. **To prepare the icing:** In a bowl, beat together the ingredients until smooth.

5. Spread the icing on the cooled cake.

MAKES 8 SERVINGS

FOR THE CAKE:
1 cup chopped, peeled
    apples
1/2 cup chopped walnuts
1/2 cup golden raisins
1/2 cup vegetable oil
1 cup granulated sugar
2 eggs
1 tablespoon vanilla extract
2 cups all-purpose flour
1 tablespoon baking
    powder
1 1/2 teaspoons baking soda
1/4 teaspoon salt
1/8 teaspoon ground
    nutmeg

FOR THE ICING:
1/3 cup nonfat sour cream
1/2 cup confectioners' sugar
1/8 teaspoon ground
    cinnamon

THE GERMAN TRADITION
IN CHILE'S LAKE DISTRICT

The fact that the Lake District of Chile looks and feels very much like Germany has played an important part in Chile's history. During the middle of the 1800s, an adviser to the President of Chile by the name of Vicente Perez Rosales decided that the Lake District had to be colonized. Perez Rosales had two things spurring him on: He felt that it was time to pacify the local tribes, and to send a signal to Argentina that the land in the area was clearly part of Chile. He felt that these objectives could only be met by new European colonists who were strong and motivated enough to do the job.

Perez Rosales went around telling everyone that the word for "foreigner" had been eliminated in the Chilean language. Colonization offices were set up in Germany with the objective of convincing people to immigrate to Chile.

The government offered land at very reduced prices, there was a long period without taxes, and a clear promise of freedom of religion—three very important selling points for his German audience. In no uncertain terms Rosales was saying "Come on down."

By 1860, over three thousand Germans had settled into this area. By 1900, there were over thirty thousand. Some had come from the German countryside and immediately set up farms. Today you can drive along the roads in the Lake District and easily think you are driving through the German countryside. The farm buildings are built to look as European as possible. And the local names make the place sound German.

But many of the Germans who came into the district had come not from farms but from light industry. They moved in and set up small towns. They practiced their old skills. The Lake District got Chile's first beer brewery. Woodworkers arrived and quickly reproduced the same furniture that they had been making in Germany. The roots were in Europe, but the tree blossomed in Chile.

GLAZED APPLESAUCE CAKE

CHILE

1. Preheat the oven to 350° F. Butter and flour a 9-inch springform pan.

2. **To make the cake:** In a mixing bowl, cream the butter and gradually add the sugar. Beat until light and fluffy. Beat in the egg and blend in the applesauce. In another bowl, sift together the dry ingredients. Fold the mixture into the cake batter. Add the pecans and diced apple.

3. Pour the mixture into the prepared pan and arrange the apple slices decoratively on top. Bake for 1¼ hours, until the cake is springy to the touch and a toothpick inserted in the center comes out clean. Remove to a rack and allow to cool. Release the sides of the pan.

4. **To prepare the glaze:** In a small saucepan over low heat, combine the ingredients and stir until melted and smooth.

5. Brush the top of the cooled cake with the glaze.

MAKES 8 SERVINGS

FOR THE CAKE:
½ cup unsalted butter
1½ cups sugar
1 egg
2 cups sweetened or
    unsweetened applesauce
2¼ cups all-purpose flour
1 teaspoon ground
    cinnamon
½ teaspoon ground
    nutmeg
⅛ teaspoon ground cloves
¼ teaspoon salt
2 teaspoons baking soda
½ cup pecan halves
1 apple, peeled, cored,
    and finely diced, plus
    1 apple, thinly sliced

FOR THE GLAZE:
1 cup apricot jam
¼ cup honey
1 tablespoon water

CRUMB CAKE

CHILE

MAKES 8 SERVINGS

Dough for a 9-inch
    piecrust
1/4 cup apricot jam

FOR THE TOPPING:
6 tablespoons unsalted
    butter
1/2 cup sugar
3/4 cup all-purpose flour

FOR THE APPLE
FILLING:
3 1/2 cups peeled, chopped
    apples
1/4 cup sugar
1/4 cup raisins or currants
1/2 cup ground almonds
Zest of 1 lemon
1 tablespoon ground
    cinnamon

FOR THE BATTER:
1 cup all-purpose flour
1/4 cup sugar
1/4 teaspoon salt
1 egg
1 cup milk

1. Preheat the oven to 350° F.

2. Line the bottom and sides of a 9-inch springform pan with the pie dough. In a saucepan, over low heat, heat the apricot jam. Brush the dough with the jam.

3. **To prepare the topping:** In a saucepan over low heat, melt the butter and mix in the sugar. Remove the pan from the heat, stir in the flour, then set the topping aside.

4. **To prepare the apple filling:** In a bowl, combine the apples, sugar, raisins, ground almonds, lemon zest, and cinnamon. Place the mixture in the prepared crust.

5. **To prepare the batter:** In another bowl, combine the ingredients.

6. **To assemble:** Pour the batter over the apple filling. Break the topping into small pieces with a spoon and sprinkle it on top. Bake for 1 hour and 10 minutes or until the topping is golden brown.

7. Cool the cake on a rack. Loosen the crust by running a spatula around the pan, then release the springform pan.

✳

HOTSHOTS AT FORT VALDIVIA

For years Valdivia was one of the most important settlements in Spain's New World. The only problem with Valdivia was that the native Mapuches believed that the land here was part of the Mapuches' Old World. And in 1599, they destroyed all the Spanish settlements in the area.

For the next two hundred years everyone was pretty much forced to agree that this was Mapuches territory. Then in the second half of the 1700s, the Spanish decided to try and fortify their west coast settlements in South America, and they built a series of forts.

The most important fort is called the Castle of the Pure and Clean Conception. It was built at the point where the Pacific Ocean meets the river that comes down from Valdivia. It was actually started in the 1600s, but the real work took place in the late 1700s, when the Spanish were getting nervous about the possibility of a war with England. They also built a fort on the other side of the river so they would have a concentration of firepower in the center of the channel.

The Germans who immigrated to Valdivia during the 1800s were not farmers. For the most part they were professionals, craftsmen, and scholars, with enough money to set up their own businesses. The Hispanic community that was here when the Germans arrived were pleased to have the Germans in their population, and the two groups progressively fused together. Today Valdivia is still a town of readers, thinkers, and artists.

During the 1950s, Valdivia built its own university. The work was done by the students and the faculty. It was the idea of a local doctor who wanted to have a university in town and just made it happen. In the early days, the students and the faculty actually put the place together building by building. Now it has ten thousand students and a thousand teachers. There is a general liberal arts program, a science department, and an agricultural college, with a special division that just deals with milk and milk products. Imagine going to school to study ice cream—I love it. Ice cream as a major, hot fudge as a minor. *(cont. on following page)*

Just across the river from the university is the city center. Like all Chilean towns, there is a central plaza with a band that plays there on Sundays during the summer. As you walk around town you get a good feeling of what urban life is like in the south of Chile. There are strong family ties here, and they are constantly expressed in the pattern of daily life. There's a street market that's been at this location for hundreds and hundreds of years. Farmers come in from their fields and display their produce on the land side of the street. Fishermen tie up their boats and display their catch on the sea side of the street. At the end of the fish and produce stalls is a small area for local crafts. Where the market ends, a promenade begins and runs along the riverfront for about a mile and a half. It's the place where people come to walk and talk.

José Luis Birke, owner of the EntreLagos Sweet Shop. Valdivia, Chile.

Banana Cake with Fudge Frosting

CALIFORNIA

1. Preheat the oven to 350° F. Lightly grease an 8-inch square baking pan.

2. **To make the cake:** In a bowl, mix the bananas with the sugar and let stand for 10 minutes. In a second bowl, combine the dry ingredients. In a third bowl, whisk together the oil, milk, eggs, and vanilla. Stir in the bananas. Then stir the dry ingredients into the wet ingredients to make the batter. Quickly stir in the nuts.

3. Spread the batter evenly in the prepared baking pan. Bake for 45 to 50 minutes, or until a wooden toothpick comes out clean. On a rack, cool the cake for 10 minutes, then remove it from the baking pan. Let the cake cool completely before frosting.

4. **To prepare the frosting:** In the top of a double boiler, over gently simmering water, melt the chocolate, stirring occasionally. Put the nonfat sour cream into a bowl, then quickly stir the melted chocolate into it.

5. Frost the cake immediately. Cut the cake into squares to serve.

MAKES 12 SERVINGS

FOR THE CAKE:
1 cup mashed ripe bananas
    (2 to 3 medium bananas)
3/4 cup sugar
1 3/4 cups all-purpose flour
1/2 teaspoon baking soda
1/4 teaspoon salt
Pinch of ground nutmeg
1/3 cup vegetable oil
1/2 cup milk
2 eggs
1 teaspoon vanilla extract
1/2 cup chopped hazelnuts
    (optional)

FOR THE FUDGE
FROSTING:
6 ounces semisweet
    chocolate, chopped
    coarsely
1/3 cup nonfat sour cream

Carrot Cake

BANFF SPRINGS HOTEL, ALBERTA, CANADA

MAKES 10 SERVINGS

FOR THE CAKE:
5 medium carrots, peeled
    and grated (3½ cups)
1 cup firmly packed brown
    sugar
1 cup vegetable oil
3 eggs
1 teaspoon vanilla extract
2½ cups all-purpose flour
¼ teaspoon ground
    cinnamon
¼ teaspoon baking soda
½ teaspoon baking
    powder
⅓ cup chopped pecans
    or walnuts or a
    combination of
    the two

FOR THE ICING:
8 ounces Philadelphia®
    cream cheese, softened
1¾ cups confectioners'
    sugar, sifted
½ cup unsalted butter,
    softened
1 tablespoon vanilla extract
1 cup lightly toasted sliced
    almonds for garnish

The carrot contains more sugar than any other vegetable except the beet. As a result, carrots have been used as a "sweet" ingredient for hundreds of years. There are Irish recipes that describe carrots as "underground honey," and middle eastern cooks have used carrots in desserts since the time of the ancient Greeks. During the 1960s, carrot cake became popular in North America and has remained on the dessert menu of many restaurants. The following version is particularly moist and tasty.

1. Preheat the oven to 350° F. Lightly oil a 9-inch spring-form pan.

2. To make the cake: In a bowl, mix together the grated carrots and the brown sugar and let that mixture stand for 30 minutes. At the end of that time a considerable amount of juice will have been drawn out of the carrots. This liquid keeps the cake extremely moist. To the carrots and sugar add the oil and the eggs. Incorporate the eggs one at a time. Add the vanilla extract. In a second bowl, combine the dry ingredients and nuts. Add this mixture of dry ingredients to the moist ingredients. Add the dry ingredients in 4 equal amounts and mix well after each addition. This technique will help avoid lumps in the batter. Pour this batter into the prepared pan.

3. Place the pan on a baking sheet and bake the cake for 40 minutes, until the top feels springy to the touch and a toothpick inserted in the center comes out clean.

4. While the cake is baking prepare the icing: In a bowl, combine the cream cheese with half of the confectioners' sugar. Blend in the butter and the vanilla extract. Blend in the remaining half of the confectioners' sugar.

5. When the cake comes out of the oven, allow it to cool. Then remove it from the springform pan and slice it in half into 2 disks. Place a third of the icing mixture on the top of the bottom disk and spread it evenly. Place the top half of the cake on top of the icing. Use the remaining icing to cover the top and sides of the cake. Press the almond slices into the side of the cake.

Old postcard of Canada.

HAZELNUT CAKE

TORNAVENTO RISTORANTE, TREISO, ITALY

MAKES 10 SERVINGS

1½ cups chopped
    hazelnuts
1 cup granulated sugar
8 tablespoons unsalted
    butter
1 cup cake flour
1 teaspoon baking powder
½ teaspoon salt
7 egg yolks
Confectioners' sugar for
    dusting

The hazelnut is one of the traditional agricultural products of the Piedmont region of Italy and the following is a very traditional Piedmontese cake based on the nut. I first tasted the cake at the Restaurant Tornavento in the Piedmont town of Treiso. The chef was Marco Serra.

1. Preheat the oven to 350° F. Lightly butter a 9-inch round cake pan that has been lined with waxed or parchment paper. Dust lightly with flour.

2. In a food processor, process together the hazelnuts and granulated sugar until the nuts are finely ground. Add the butter and process again. Add the cake flour, baking powder, and salt and process until blended. With the food processor running, add the egg yolks one at a time, making sure that each one is blended before the next one is added. The batter will be very thick.

3. Spread the batter evenly in the prepared cake pan. Tap the pan lightly to remove any air bubbles. Bake for 30 to 35 minutes, or until a wooden toothpick inserted in the cake comes out clean.

4. Cool the cake on a rack for 10 minutes. Loosen the cake by running a knife around the rim of the pan. Invert the cake, remove the pan and the waxed paper. Invert the cake again onto the rack and cool completely.

5. Dust the top with confectioners' sugar before serving.

LEMON GINGER CAKE

CANADA

1. Preheat the oven to 350° F. Lightly butter an 8-inch springform pan.

2. **To make the cake:** In a bowl, combine the flour, baking powder, baking soda, salt, and ground ginger, then set it aside. In a second bowl, using an electric mixer, cream together the sugar and the butter. When the sugar and butter are light and fluffy, beat in the eggs. With the mixer on low speed, add half of the dry ingredients into the wet ingredients until just blended. Then add half of the sour cream. Blend in the remaining dry ingredients and sour cream.

3. Pour the batter into the prepared cake pan. Bake in the preheated oven for 30 to 35 minutes, or until a wooden toothpick inserted in the cake comes out clean. Cool the cake on a rack for 10 minutes, then remove the springform pan. Cool the cake completely before glazing.

4. **To prepare the glaze:** In a bowl, stir together the confectioners' sugar and ginger. Add the lemon juice and stir together until smooth.

5. Pour the glaze over the cake and serve.

MAKES 8 SERVINGS

FOR THE CAKE:
1¼ cups all-purpose flour
½ teaspoon baking powder
½ teaspoon baking soda
½ teaspoon salt
2 teaspoons ground ginger
¾ cup sugar
4 tablespoons unsalted butter
2 eggs
½ cup nonfat sour cream

FOR THE GLAZE:
⅔ cup confectioners' sugar, sifted
½ teaspoon ground ginger
2 tablespoons fresh lemon juice

Orange-Glazed Pumpkin Cake

CHILE

MAKES 8 SERVINGS

FOR THE CAKE:
1½ cups all-purpose flour
1 teaspoon baking powder
1 teaspoon baking soda
1 teaspoon ground
    cinnamon
½ teaspoon ground ginger
½ teaspoon salt
8 tablespoons unsalted
    butter or margarine
1 cup granulated sugar
2 eggs
1 cup canned pumpkin
    puree

FOR THE ORANGE
GLAZE:
1 cup confectioners' sugar,
    sifted
2 tablespoons orange juice
Grated zest of 1 orange

1. Preheat the oven to 350° F. Lightly butter or oil a 6-cup Bundt pan, then dust the pan lightly with flour.

2. To make the cake: In a bowl, combine the flour, baking powder, baking soda, cinnamon, ginger, and salt, then set aside. In another bowl, using an electric mixer, beat together the butter or margarine and sugar. Add the eggs, one at a time, beating to blend. Add the pumpkin and beat until combined. Stir the dry ingredients into the wet ingredients.

3. Pour the batter into the prepared pan and bake for 30 to 35 minutes, or until a wooden toothpick comes out clean. Cool the cake on a rack.

4. To prepare the glaze: In a bowl, stir together the ingredients until smooth.

5. Pour the glaze over the cooled cake.

Rum Cake

ARUBA

---

1. Preheat the oven to 350° F. Lightly butter and flour a 6-cup Bundt pan.

2. In a bowl, combine the flour, baking powder, and salt, then set aside.

3. In another bowl, beat together the butter and sugar. Add the eggs, one at a time, beating until blended. Stir in the rum and pineapple.

4. Add half of the dry ingredients to the wet ingredients, beating until blended, then beat in the remaining dry ingredients. Pour the batter into the prepared Bundt pan.

5. Bake for 30 to 35 minutes, or until a wooden toothpick inserted in the cake comes out clean. Cool the cake in the pan on a rack for 10 minutes, then remove it from the pan and cool completely.

6. Dust with confectioners' sugar before serving.

MAKES 8 SERVINGS

$1\frac{1}{2}$ cups cake flour
2 teaspoons baking powder
$\frac{1}{2}$ teaspoon salt
4 tablespoons unsalted butter, softened
$\frac{2}{3}$ cup granulated sugar
4 eggs
4 to 6 tablespoons dark rum or orange juice, or 3 tablespoons rum extract
One 8-ounce can crushed pineapple, drained of juice
Confectioners' sugar for dusting

CHOCOLATE BISCOTTI

ITALY

**MAKES
APPROXIMATELY
4 DOZEN COOKIES**

2 cups all-purpose flour
1/2 cup unsweetened cocoa
1/2 cup sugar
1 1/2 teaspoons ground
    cinnamon
1 teaspoon baking
    powder
1 cup chopped hazelnuts
6 tablespoons unsalted
    butter, room
    temperature
2 eggs
2/3 cup honey

1. Heat the oven to 350° F. Line a cookie sheet with parchment.

2. Sift into the bowl of a standing mixer or a large bowl, the dry ingredients. Add the nuts. Using low speed, mix thoroughly with the paddle attachment. Or mix by hand.

3. Add the butter and continue mixing until the dough has the consistency of wet sand.

4. Mix the eggs and honey together and add to the dough. Mix until a soft dough is formed.

5. Remove the dough to a clean work space and divide in half. Form the dough into 2 flattish logs, about 14 inches long.

6. Place the logs on the prepared cookie sheet and bake for 30 minutes. The logs should be firm but still pliable. Cool for 10 minutes.

7. When the logs are cool, cut them on an angle into 1/2-inch slices.

8. Lay the cookies out on the cookie sheet. Lower the oven to 300° F. and bake for 35 minutes. To check that the biscotti are dry enough, remove one from the oven and let cool. The cookies should be dry and crisp. Cool and store, well covered.

Peanut Butter Cookies

ROYAL VIKING SUN

---

1. Preheat the oven to 350° F. Line 2 baking sheets with parchment paper.

2. In a large mixing bowl, cream the butter with the sugar.

3. Beat in the peanut butter, egg, and vanilla.

4. Sift together the flour and baking soda. Add to the cookie dough and mix well.

5. Roll the dough into golf ball–sized balls. Place them about 2 inches apart on the prepared baking sheets. Place another sheet of parchment paper on top and press lightly to flatten the cookies. Remove the top sheet of parchment paper.

6. Bake the cookies for 10 to 15 minutes, or until the edges begin to brown. Carefully remove and let cool on a wire rack.

MAKES ABOUT 3 DOZEN COOKIES

12 tablespoons unsalted butter, at room temperature
1 cup sugar
1¼ cups peanut butter (smooth or chunky)
1 egg
½ teaspoon vanilla extract
1½ cups all-purpose flour
½ teaspoon baking soda

CHOCOLATE BROWNIE CUPCAKES

DOWNTOWN BAKERY & CREAMERY, HEALDSBURG, CALIFORNIA

MAKES 24 CUPCAKES

1½ cups water
5 ounces bittersweet
    chocolate
4 ounces unsweetened
    chocolate
10 ounces (20 tablespoons)
    unsalted butter
1¾ cups all-purpose flour
2¼ cups granulated sugar
6 eggs
Confectioners' sugar for
    garnish

1. In a saucepan, heat the water to a simmer. Put both of the chocolates and the butter into a heatproof bowl. Place the bowl over the saucepan of simmering water, making sure that the bottom of the bowl does not touch the water. You can also use a double boiler for this process. Stir occasionally until the chocolate is melted. Remove the bowl from the saucepan and set the melted chocolate aside.

2. In a mixing bowl or the bowl of an electric mixer, combine the flour and granulated sugar until blended. Using an electric mixer on low speed, beat in the eggs, one at a time, until blended, making sure that the batter is smooth. Slowly add the chocolate-butter mixture, and beat until all the ingredients are fully incorporated. Then beat for 1 minute more.

3. Pour the batter into an airtight container and refrigerate for at least 1 hour, the batter can be held in an airtight container in the refrigerator for up to 2 weeks and baked in small batches.

4. Preheat the oven to 350° F. Line a muffin pan with paper liners. Using an ice cream scoop, scoop the batter into the muffin liners. Dip the ice cream scoop into a container of warm water to keep the surface of the scoop from sticking to the batter.

5. Bake for 20 to 25 minutes, until a toothpick inserted in the center comes out clean. Cool on a rack. Remove the cupcakes from the pan.

6. Dust the top of the cupcakes with confectioners' sugar before serving.

CHOCOLATE-COATED ALMONDS

LE CIRQUE RESTAURANT, NEW YORK CITY

1. Place a sheet of parchment paper on top of a baking sheet or jelly-roll pan.

2. In a heavy saucepan or a bowl that can withstand the direct heat of the range, combine the almonds, granulated sugar, and the water. Over medium-high heat, heat the contents, stirring occasionally with a wooden spatula or spoon. At first, the sugar will begin to give up liquid, appearing to melt. After about 5 minutes, the sugar will start to turn sandy and coat the almonds.

3. When the almonds are all coated, turn them out onto the parchment paper, spread out, and place into the freezer for 15 minutes.

4. Chop the chocolate into small pieces. Place the pieces into a heatproof bowl and place the bowl over a saucepan of simmering water. Melt the chocolate and continue heating it until it reaches a temperature between 88° and 91° F.

5. Remove the nuts from the freezer and place them into a mixing bowl. Add half the melted chocolate to the nuts and stir to coat the nuts. Add the remaining half of the chocolate and stir again to coat the nuts. When all the nuts have been coated with chocolate, place them on a paper-lined baking sheet and chill in the refrigerator for 15 minutes.

6. When chilled, toss the almonds in small batches in a bowl of the confectioners' sugar. Remove the coated nuts to a container and repeat with another batch until all of the almonds are coated. If any nuts are sticking together, break them apart. Store the coated nuts in an airtight container outside the refrigerator.

MAKES 3¾ CUPS

3¾ cups (about 1¼ pounds) shelled almonds, skins on
2 cups granulated sugar
1 cup water
28 ounces semisweet chocolate
1 cup confectioners' sugar, sifted

PRE-COLUMBIAN CHOCOLATE

Mayan culture began in Central America about 3,500 years ago. Their leaders appear to have been able administrators, talented scholars, and gifted architects. Mathematics and astronomy were two of their most valued skills and eventually led to the development of the first calendar that calculated a solar year into 365 days.

The word *Mayan* actually means "men of corn," and the Mayans believed that they had originally been made of corn and put on earth for the express purpose of preparing great foods for the gods. Their sacred texts also told them that if the food was not up to the standards of the gods, the universe would come to an end. Obviously, the Mayans became great cooks and great eaters.

The Mayans appeared to have been the first people to have noticed the cacao tree. It was growing in the river valleys of South America and the Mayans brought it to Mexico. They began cultivating it and spread the word of its value.

The first Europeans to see the cacao tree were the sailors who took part in Columbus's fourth voyage in 1502. They brought a few beans back to Spain, but nobody was very interested in the stuff. Chocolate's first big break came when the Spanish conquistador Cortez arrived at the court of Montezuma, ruler of the Aztec Empire.

The year was 1519, and things had not been all that great for Montezuma. Sure he was king, and sure his empire was at the height of its power, but there had been some bad signs. Flaming ears of corn shooting across the sky, probably a comet, but Montezuma did not know that. Floods sweeping through the main city on what was otherwise a perfectly nice day. Birds with mirrors on their heads in which you could see the future. "Weird stuff, man."

Most unnerving of all, there was word that the ancient god Quetzalcoatl was coming back to earth to take over. He was the god of the arts and sciences and was in charge of gold. He had given people the gift of chocolate. He also was a deity with light skin and a dark beard.

When Cortez showed up with his Spanish troops, Montezuma thought he had come directly from the gods, and he was given a great welcome and a cup of his traditional drink, chocolate.

Montezuma's chocolate might have been mixed with an alcohol-based corn mash, which might be the reason that people felt high after drinking Aztec chocolate. The chocolate was served in a gold cup. It was on the bitter side and not a great gastronomic pleasure for Cortez, but Cortez loved the gold cup and the chocolate was different enough to send some back to Spain along with the special instructions and utensils that accompanied its preparation.

CHOCOLATE FUDGE

LE CIRQUE RESTAURANT, NEW YORK CITY

1. In a heatproof mixing bowl or a heavy saucepan, combine the cream, sugar, and corn syrup. Place the bowl over the saucepan on the range, over a medium-high heat. Heat the mixture, stirring occasionally, until a sugar thermometer reads 222° to 224° F.

2. Add the butter and the two chocolates to the cream and sugar mixture, and continue stirring until the chocolate is melted and all of the ingredients are combined.

3. Line an 8-inch square pan with plastic wrap, covering the entire surface. Pour in the fudge mixture and smooth it out until it forms a flat sheet. Place the pan in the refrigerator for 1 hour.

4. Remove the pan from the refrigerator and turn it upside down on a clean cutting surface. Peel the plastic wrap away from the fudge. Slice the fudge into 1-inch squares.

NOTE: The chef heats the ingredients in a restaurant-quality copper bowl because copper is an excellent conductor of heat. The bowl shape is valuable because it has no corners to catch and overheat the mixture. If you use a heavy pot instead of a bowl, make sure to keep stirring in the corners and against the sides to avoid any burning.

MAKES 40 PIECES

1 cup heavy cream
1 cup sugar
$1/3$ cup light corn syrup
1 tablespoon unsalted butter
3 ounces bittersweet chocolate, finely chopped
2 ounces unsweetened chocolate, finely chopped

✴

CHOCOLATE COMES TO EUROPE

The words *chocolate* and *cocoa* come from Aztec words. One was the name of the cacao tree on which the beans grew, the other meant "bitter water." Bitter was not a happy thing for a king, so when Charles V of Spain got his first taste of chocolate he called for his royal sweetener to improve the taste. His Sucroseness had some sugar added and some vanilla, cinnamon, and cloves, plus a few ground almonds, and hazelnuts. Sounds like they were well on their way to making a Snickers, but that was not the case. At this point, chocolate was always something to drink. The candy bar was centuries away.

The first chocolate-making facilities were set up by Spanish monks who not only made the chocolate but drank quite a bit on their own and sold substantial quantities to the Spanish.

In the city of San Cristóbal the local ladies started a custom of having a cup of chocolate brought to them whenever they came to church. The bishop did not approve and threatened to excommunicate the ladies if they did not put an end to their chocolate drinking during mass. When he tried to physically take away the chocolate cups the ladies were defended by their swordsmen. Shortly thereafter the ladies had the bishop poisoned. Rumor had it that he was given the poison in a cup of chocolate.

The Spanish controlled the cacao tree–growing areas in the New World and wanted to keep the whole operation a secret. For almost one hundred years the rest of Europe had very little information about chocolate. The monks, however, were so proud of their chocolate-making skills that they couldn't resist showing off to visiting monks from other countries and eventually the word got out.

In 1615, Louis, the King of France, got married to Anna, the daughter of the King of Spain. She brought a splendid gift of Spanish chocolate to the wedding. Chocolate had a reputation as an aphrodisiac from its days with Montezuma, but it almost lost it with Anna and Louis. They were not very interested in each other as lovers. After twenty-three years, however, they did get around to producing an heir to the throne, who turned out to be the French King of Kings. The one, the only, the Sunniest king of them all . . . Louis XIV. Louis XIV was the last word in "rich and famous." "Lifestyles" could have done ten years worth of shows and never left Louis's drawing room. The king loved chocolate. The king's wife, Maria Theresa, who came to him from Spain, loved chocolate. So everyone in Europe loved chocolate.

While Louis and Maria Theresa were giving chocolate an image as something of good taste, doctors all over Europe were giving chocolate an image of something for good health. *(cont. on following page)*

When chocolate crossed the channel to England, it also managed to escape from the royal palaces of Paris and Madrid and take up residence in the public houses of London. London had coffeehouses since the mid-1600s. But with the arrival of chocolate at the end of the century, London saw the introduction of the chocolate house. They were really more or less open-membership men's clubs. The artist William Hogarth in his series called *The Rake's Progress* used a chocolate house called White's as the setting for some of his seamier scenes. During the mid-1700s, many of these chocolate houses introduced a closed membership and eventually became the elegant private men's clubs of London.

Peter Curtis, the Master Miller at Philipsburg.

The mill at Philipsburg Manor, North Tarrytown, New York. It's similar to the kind of mills used in the grinding of cocoa for chocolate.

PIES AND TARTS

CHOCOLATE SILK PIE

THE CLIFT, SAN FRANCISCO, CALIFORNIA

MAKES 10 SERVINGS

FOR THE CRUST:
8 tablespoons unsalted
    butter
³/4 cup walnuts
1 cup pecans
1 cup brown sugar
1 tablespoon ground
    cinnamon

FOR THE FILLING:
1 cup heavy cream
1 tablespoon vanilla extract
6 tablespoons unsalted
    butter
½ cup granulated sugar
10 ounces semisweet
    chocolate
3 eggs

FOR THE COATING
AND GARNISH:
1½ cups heavy cream
1 ounce semisweet
    chocolate
Chocolate sauce
1 pint strawberries
1 cup fresh mint leaves

At the Four Seasons Clift Hotel in San Francisco, Alan Gontowski is the pastry chef. His recipe for Chocolate Silk Pie is yet another example of the truth of the old adage that the new is really the old, repackaged.

1. To make the crust: Melt the butter and allow it to cool to room temperature. *Note:* The butter is brought to room temperature in order to avoid melting the brown sugar and creating clumps. In the bowl of a food processor, combine the nuts, brown sugar, and cinnamon and process until finely ground. Add the cooled, melted butter and process until the butter is incorporated with the nut mixture. Press the mixture into the bottom of a 9-inch springform pan to form a bottom crust. Place the pan into the refrigerator for 1 hour.

2. To make the filling: In a mixing bowl, whip the cream and the vanilla until the cream stands in peaks. Place the mixture and the bowl into the refrigerator. In another bowl, cream together the butter and the granulated sugar. In a heatproof bowl over a saucepan of simmering water, or in a microwave oven, melt the chocolate. Place the eggs into a mixing bowl. Place the bowl over a saucepan of simmering water, and whisk the mixture together continuously until it begins to warm, about 3 minutes. Be careful not to cook the eggs. Add the melted chocolate to the butter and granulated sugar mixture. Add the eggs. Fold in the whipped cream. Pour this batter over the crust in the springform pan, and place the pan into the refrigerator for a minimum of 3 hours.

3. When the pan is removed from the refrigerator, run a thin knife between the cake and the pan; open and remove the springform. Whip the cream for the garnish until it stands in peaks and use it to coat the top of the cake as if it were an icing.

4. Place the garnishing chocolate in a Ziploc bag and melt the chocolate in a microwave oven. Use a high setting for a minute to a minute and a half. Press the melted chocolate to a corner of the bag as if it were a pastry bag. Cut a tiny edge off the tip of the bag. Press out the chocolate in a series of lines on the top of the whipped cream. Refrigerate the cake for 10 minutes.

5. Individual slices are served with a garnish of chocolate sauce, a few berries, and a few mint leaves.

Tropical Fruit Pie with Coconut Streusel

ARUBA

MAKES 8 SERVINGS

One prepared crust for a
9-inch pie

FOR THE FILLING:
3½ cups pineapple chunks,
or 2½ cups pineapple
chunks plus 1 cup
mango chunks
¼ cup granulated sugar
1 teaspoon ground
cinnamon
1 teaspoon ground ginger
1 teaspoon vanilla extract
2 tablespoons cornstarch
mixed with
3 tablespoons water

FOR THE COCONUT
STREUSEL:
⅓ cup light brown sugar
5 tablespoons unsalted
butter, softened
⅔ cup all-purpose flour
½ cup shredded or flaked
sweetened coconut

1. Preheat the oven to 375° F. Line a 9-inch pie plate with the prepared crust. Place a piece of aluminum foil in the crust and fill with rice or dried beans.

2. To prepare the filling: In a saucepan over low heat, combine the fruit, sugar, cinnamon, ginger, and vanilla. Cook for 10 minutes. Stir in the cornstarch mixture and cook for 1 minute. The mixture will thicken. Cool the filling.

3. While the filling cools, bake the piecrust for 6 minutes, remove the aluminum foil and rice, and bake for 4 minutes longer.

4. To prepare the coconut streusel: In a bowl, combine the ingredients and set aside.

5. Place the cooked fruit in the prebaked crust, then cover the top with the coconut streusel. Bake for 25 to 30 minutes, or until the top is lightly browned. Cool the pie on a rack until ready to serve.

6. Serve warm or at room temperature.

Lemon Tart

ARUBA

1. Preheat the oven to 350° F.

2. **To make the crust:** In a bowl, combine the ingredients. Line a 9-inch pie or loose-bottom tart pan with the crumb crust. Bake the crust for 7 minutes. Cool on a rack.

3. **To make the filling:** In another bowl, combine the filling ingredients. Pour the filling into the prepared crust.

4. Bake the tart for 15 minutes, or until the filling is set. Let the pie cool on a rack, then chill in the refrigerator for 1½ hours before serving.

MAKES 8 SERVINGS

FOR THE CRUST:
1½ cups vanilla cookie
    crumbs
¼ cup sugar
6 tablespoons unsalted
    butter or margarine,
    melted

FOR THE FILLING:
2 eggs
One 14-ounce can
    sweetened condensed
    milk
½ cup fresh lemon juice
2 teaspoons grated lemon
    zest
1 teaspoon vanilla extract

Sand dunes, Aruba.

Honey Nut Tart

DOWNTOWN BAKERY & CREAMERY, HEALDSBURG, CALIFORNIA

MAKES 8 SERVINGS

FOR THE CRUST:
1 cup all-purpose flour
1 tablespoon plus 1½
    teaspoons granulated
    sugar
4 tablespoons unsalted
    butter, sliced into
    ½-inch pieces
4 tablespoons salted butter,
    sliced into ½-inch pieces
1 tablespoon plus 1½
    teaspoons cold water

FOR THE FILLING:
8 tablespoons unsalted
    butter
4 tablespoons honey
2 tablespoons granulated
    sugar
½ cup firmly packed
    brown sugar
2 tablespoons heavy cream
1½ cups chopped nuts
    (hazelnuts, walnuts, or
    pecans)

Kathleen Stewart was born in Los Angeles and went to school at the California College of Arts and Crafts at Berkeley. There she was introduced to the cooking at the famous Chez Panisse restaurant. Eventually Kathleen and the pastry chef at Chez Panisse opened their own bakery in Healdsburg—a bakery that specializes in using ingredients from the area and catering to the real needs of the neighbors. They even make old-fashioned hot dog and hamburger buns.

1. **To make the crust:** In a medium bowl, combine the flour and the sugar. With 2 knives or a pastry blender, cut in the butter until it resembles coarse cornmeal. Add just enough water until the dough holds together if pressed. Form the dough into a ball, then wrap it in plastic. Refrigerate for 30 minutes to allow the dough to rest. Then press the pastry into an 8-inch loose-bottom tart pan. Wrap the tart pan in foil and freeze for 30 minutes.

2. Preheat the oven to 350° F. Place the tart pan on a baking sheet, then line the pastry shell with aluminum foil. Prick the surface with the tines of a fork, making a series of small holes in the dough every few inches. These will allow the steam to escape and help prevent bubbling up of the crust. Cover the aluminum foil with a light coating of rice or beans. The rice or beans are there to hold down the aluminum foil. Bake for 25 minutes. Remove the foil and rice. Cool the shell briefly on a rack.

3. While the pastry shell is baking, prepare the filling: In a large deep saucepan, melt together the butter, honey, and sugars. Heat to a rolling boil for 2 minutes. Remove from the heat and carefully stir in the cream, then the nuts. Let the mixture stand for 15 minutes.

4. Fill the prebaked shell with the warm filling, making sure the nuts float evenly in the filling, not just on top. Place the tart pan on a baking sheet and bake for 30 minutes.

5. Cool on a rack until set, about 15 minutes. Carefully remove the rim of the tart pan and place the tart on a serving plate. Serve warm or at room temperature.

Kathleen Stewart, CEO (Chief Eating Operative) of the Downtown Bakery & Creamery, Healdsburg, California.

Fresh Fruit Tart in a Cornmeal Crust

DOWNTOWN BAKERY & CREAMERY, HEALDSBURG, CALIFORNIA

MAKES 8 SERVINGS

FOR THE CRUST:
1 cup all-purpose flour
$1/3$ cup finely ground
   cornmeal
$1/2$ teaspoon salt
$1/2$ cup sugar
6 tablespoons unsalted
   butter
2 egg yolks

FOR THE FILLING:
3 tablespoons all-purpose
   flour
1 tablespoon finely ground
   cornmeal
$1/2$ teaspoon ground
   cinnamon
2 tablespoons sugar
2 cups peeled, cored, and
   sliced baking apples,
   nectarine sections,
   peeled peaches, or
   peeled pears (about
   1 pound)

1 tablespoon heavy cream
1 tablespoon sugar

Healdsburg is about as picturesque a northern California town as you can find. The physical center of Healdsburg is the town square; the gastronomic center is the Downtown Bakery & Creamery. Opened in 1987, it is exactly what a real down-home bakery should be—good bread, sticky buns, great coffee in the morning, pies, cakes, desserts, and ice creams made fresh every few hours throughout the day.

Kathleen Stewart is the CEO of the company, which stands for Chief Eating Operative. She is also the boss baker. The following is her recipe for fresh fruit pie in a cornmeal or polenta pastry.

1. To make the crust: In a small bowl, combine the flour, cornmeal, and salt and set aside. In a medium bowl, using an electric mixer, cream together the sugar and the butter. Beat in the egg yolks. Blend in the dry ingredients until the dough holds together. Divide the dough into 2 balls, one slightly larger than the other. Wrap each in plastic wrap and refrigerate for 1 hour. Remove the larger ball of dough from the refrigerator. On a floured board, roll the dough into $1/4$-inch-thick circles to fit an 8-inch loose-bottom tart pan. Fit the dough into the pans and freeze for 20 minutes.

2. Preheat the oven to 350° F. Place the tart pans on a baking sheet, then cover the dough with aluminum foil, fitting it to the shape of the dough, and then cover the foil with rice or beans. Bake for 15 minutes. Remove the foil and rice. Cool the shell briefly on a rack.

3. To make the filling: In a small bowl, combine the flour and the cornmeal. Sprinkle this mixture evenly on the bottom of the tart shell. In a medium bowl, combine the cinnamon with the sugar, then toss the sliced apples (or other fruit) in the cinnamon sugar and coat evenly. Arrange the apples in the shell.

4. On a floured board, roll out the remaining pieces of dough into an 8-inch round and fit it on top of the tart. Lightly press the edges to seal and trim off any excess. With a pastry brush, gently brush the cream on the top crust, then dust it with the sugar.

5. Bake for 1 hour, or until the crust is golden brown. Cool on a rack. Remove the rim of the tart pan and place the tart on a serving plate.

✳

Pear Tart

HOTEL CERTOSA DI MAGGIANO, SIENA, ITALY

MAKES 8 SERVINGS

Two unbaked prepared
   piecrusts for an 8-inch
   tart pan
2 tablespoons unsalted
   butter
3 pears, peeled, cored,
   and sliced
2 tablespoons granulated
   sugar
$1/4$ cup red wine
$1/2$ cup ricotta cheese
1 egg, separated, white
   lightly beaten
3 tablespoons
   confectioners' sugar
$1/4$ teaspoon vanilla extract
5 slices pound cake,
   $1/2$ inch thick

1. Preheat the oven to 350° F. Line an 8-inch loose-bottom tart pan with one prepared crust. Trim the pastry so it overhangs by $1/2$ inch.

2. In a sauté pan over medium heat, melt the butter. Add the pears and sugar and cook until the edges start to turn brown, about 4 minutes. Pour in the red wine and cook for 2 minutes more, or until the liquid is absorbed. Set the pears aside to cool.

3. In a small bowl, combine the ricotta cheese, egg yolk, confectioners' sugar, and vanilla. Spread the mixture evenly in the bottom of the prepared tart shell.

4. Place the pound cake slices on top of the ricotta mixture in the tart shell. Then place the pears on top of the pound cake.

5. Cover the tart with the second piecrust. Pinch the bottom and top crusts together to seal, making a slightly raised rim. Brush the top with the egg white.

6. Bake the tart in the lower third of the oven for 50 minutes, or until the crust is lightly browned. Cool the pie on a wire rack. Serve warm.

INDEX